Effective Communication for Criminal Justice Professionals

Robert E. Grubb, Jr. Ph.D.

K. Virginia Hemby Ph.D.

CENGAGE
Learning™

Australia • Brazil • Japan • Korea • Mexico • Singapore • Spain • United Kingdom • United States

CENGAGE
Learning™

**Effective Communication for
Criminal Justice Professionals**

Robert E. Grubb Jr. Ph.D.
K. Virginia Hemby Ph.D.

Executive Editors:
Michele Baird

Maureen Staudt

Michael Stranz

Project Development Manager:
Linda deStefano

Senior Marketing Coordinators:
Sara Mercurio

Lindsay Shapiro

Production/Manufacturing Manager:
Donna M. Brown

PreMedia Services Supervisor:
Rebecca A. Walker

Rights & Permissions Specialist:
Kalina Hintz

Cover Image:
Getty Images*

For product information and technology assistance, contact us at
Cengage Learning Customer & Sales Support, 1-800-354-9706

For permission to use material from this text or product,
submit all requests online at **cengage.com/permissions**
Further permissions questions can be emailed to
permissionrequest@cengage.com

ISBN-13: 978-0-534-14993-2

ISBN-10: 0-534-14993-6

Cengage Learning
5191 Natorp Boulevard
Mason, Ohio 45040
USA

Cengage Learning is a leading provider of customized learning solutions with
office locations around the globe, including Singapore, the United Kingdom,
Australia, Mexico, Brazil, and Japan. Locate your local office at:
international.cengage.com/region

Cengage Learning products are represented in Canada by Nelson Education, Ltd.

For your lifelong learning solutions, visit **custom.cengage.com**

Visit our corporate website at **cengage.com**

Printed in the United States of America

TABLE OF CONTENTS

Dr. Robert E. "Skip" Grubb, Jr., retired from the Roanoke, VA, Police Department. He earned his Ph.D. from The University of Southern Mississippi and is currently an Associate Professor in the Department of Criminal Justice at Marshall University, Huntingdon, WV.

Dr. K. Virginia Hemby earned her Ph.D. in Adult Education from The University of Southern Mississippi. She has taught Business Communication for the past eight years at Indiana University of Pennsylvania. Dr. Grubb and she have recently formed TBI Group, Inc., a training and consulting firm specializing in the development of effective communication skills.

CHAPTER 1

COMMUNICATION: WORDS ARE NOT ENOUGH

Learning Objectives:

1. To understand the importance of communication skills in criminal justice professions.

2. To describe the process of communication.

3. To define communication and its components.

4. To understand the verbal and nonverbal components of communication.

5. To identify the aspects of verbal communication.

6. To identify the aspects of nonverbal communication.

7. To describe the flow of communication in organizations.

8. To discuss barriers to communication.

9. To identify methods of overcoming barriers to communication.

The People of the State of California versus Orenthal James Simpson—the complex and never ending trial. Enter Mark Fuhrman, a detective with the Los Angeles Police Department. Fuhrman never imagined how his use of a racial slur would come to play a major role in the trial of the century.

Going from the Marines to the 77th Street station, Fuhrman tackled the insanity and chaos of the street much as he had basic training—the more brutal it was, the more he seemed to enjoy it. The area around the 77th Street Station was impoverished, and some of the officers seemed to enjoy goading suspects by calling them racially motivated names.

As Fuhrman moved through the ranks of the department, he was alternately labeled exemplary and nonproductive. He spent time on temporary disability due to stress, and subsequently filed for a disability pension, which was ultimately denied. Fuhrman developed a somewhat checkered reputation in the department because of his attitude and outspokenness. He had friends who were like him—those who were proactive on the job. Fuhrman was very outspoken. He said what was on his mind. In the end, what he said overshadowed the meticulous work of the detective he was.

The People of the State of California versus Mark Fuhrman, October 2, 1996.
    Deputy Attorney General John Gordnier*: Do you realize, sir, that by entering the plea of no contest to this charge that you are incriminating yourself with respect to the charge?*
    Fuhrman*: Yes.*[1]

Following the September 11, 2001 act of terrorism in New York City, law enforcement became more visible to Americans. Baseball caps sporting the logo "NYPD" turned up all across the United States, everywhere from local malls to government offices. People wanted to show their support for the law enforcement community, to encourage them in their search and recovery efforts, and to genuinely display their faith and belief in the legal system. Because of this 9/11 tragedy, law enforcement personnel became more visible to the public eye: responding to questions asked by reporters for the local, state, and national news affiliates, appearing on talk shows to discuss the search and recovery efforts at Ground Zero, and speaking to philanthropical groups in an effort to raise money for people who lost family members in the destruction of the Twin Towers. Through this visibility, the criminal justice community had to display its communication skills to the entire world. People wanted answers to questions that sometimes had no answers, and even though many law enforcement officers had been lost in this mass destruction, the criminal justice community still had to move forward.

The Role of Communication in Law Enforcement

The dangers of law enforcement are well documented. The threat of bodily harm is a daily occurrence. However, navigating the obstacles on the path to effective communication can also be particularly hazardous for unprepared or ill-prepared criminal justice professionals. In an era when the law enforcement profession has become identified with racism and racist statements of officers as well as a lack of communication skills—as witnessed by the malapropisms of personnel—an effort to train law enforcement personnel to use communication skills effectively to enhance the image created by speech is essential.

Turn on the television, pick up any newspaper, access any radio station or news network and you hear about the latest problems in the law enforcement community. A police officer accepts a bribe, a state trooper assaults a speeding motorist, a federal agent supplies sensitive information to a foreign power, mishandled evidence, perjury on the witness stand, the accounts go on and on. Review the fiascos of Waco, Ruby Ridge, O.J. Simpson, and Richard Jewell—all cases in which law enforcement failed in its attempt to serve the ends of justice. Not only did law enforcement fail, but its image was severely tarnished as a result of these abysmal events. Is there a single cause or series of causes that resulted in these less than successful outcomes? While poor planning and execution might be an explanation offered by law enforcement, more likely than not the proximal cause may be a lack of adequate communication skills on the part of officers, agents, and other personnel.

What is Communication?

Communication has been defined in numerous fashions. Notwithstanding the varying definitions, however, the common element in any communication process is the exchange of information through a shared system of symbols between two or more persons. The essence of communication is the conveyance of a message—a common understanding between the sender and the receiver. A concept which is not particularly difficult or abstract when viewed superficially, but one for which the true key to grasping the essence of communication is appreciating all of the nuances involved in this process. When people communicate optimally, both the sender and the receiver are able to transmit, receive, and process information.

In the communication process, the parties involved engage in certain unconscious behaviors that direct the flow of communication. When we break this process down, we see that it involves a **sender**, a **receiver**, a **message**, a **communication channel**, **encoding**, **decoding**, and **feedback**[2].

The **sender** of the message is the party with whom the idea originated. Think of a light bulb being turned on when the switch is flipped, and you have the concept of what the sender experiences when he or she has an idea and wishes to communicate that information to another party or parties. The sender then **encodes** the message by converting his or her idea into words or gestures that will convey meaning to the receiver. In essence, encoding involves putting the idea into a shared system of language that both parties understand. A major problem can occur at this stage of the communication cycle since words have different meanings for different persons. To avoid this mishap of **bypassing** (a barrier to communication which will be discussed later in the chapter), the sender must choose his or her words carefully, selecting those with concrete meanings that are sure to elicit the same meanings from both sender and receiver. An important point to remember is that since the sender is the person who initiated the communication process, he or she has primary responsibility for its success. Taking care to ensure the selection of the appropriate words or symbols is the first step in successful communication.

The **communication channel** is the medium by which the message is physically transmitted. Messages may be transmitted by telephone, fax, computer (e-mail or chat room), letter, memorandum, report, announcement, picture, face-to-face delivery, or through some other medium. Senders must choose the communication channel very carefully since situations dictate which method of delivery is most appropriate. Both verbal and nonverbal messages are conveyed through communication channels, and the sender must ensure that both verbal and nonverbal signals are in harmony with each other as well.

Noise is anything that interrupts the communication process. While most people think of noise as physical sounds that are disruptive and prohibit the communication from being heard, things such as typographical or spelling errors in reports, letters, or memoranda may also be damaging to the transmission of a message. Channel noise might also include the annoyance of a receiver at the sender's inappropriate selection of a medium for transmitting the message, such as when a person is fired via a memorandum. The issue of selecting the appropriate medium for sending a message will be discussed later in this chapter.

The individual to whom the message is sent or transmitted is the **receiver**. The receiver has to translate the message from the sender into words or symbols that he or she can understand. This process is called **decoding**. Communication can only take place when the receiver decodes the message and understands the meaning intended by the sender. Decoding is not a simple process, however. As mentioned previously, many problems exist in communicating between individuals. Since no two people share the same life experiences and no communication process is free from barriers—physical, cultural, semantic, etc.—coding a message to derive the meaning intended by the sender is very difficult.

The response a receiver makes to the message communicated by the sender is called **feedback**. In an optimum communication situation, the receiver will provide the sender with comments that let the sender know the message was received and processed as it was intended. The sender and receiver can engage in questioning or paraphrasing techniques to ensure a clear understanding of the ensuing messages. In any event, feedback is the final step in the initial communication process. Once the receiver provides feedback to the sender, communication may continue in a to and fro rotation between the parties, again encompassing the communication process.

Communication Styles[3]

In most instances, interpersonal communication means being able to talk with our friends, family, business acquaintances, colleagues, and others. In the criminal justice profession, however, optimal communication can mean the difference between life and death, success and failure, guilty and not guilty. Merely knowing how to speak is not sufficient in these situations; law enforcement officials must have the ability to overcome many barriers to the communication process as well.

Effective communication occurs between a law enforcement officer and a citizen if, and only if, each person involved in the process assumes the appropriate communication style for the

Selecting the Appropriate Communication Channel

Ask yourself these questions:

✓ Does this message require a written record? ☞ **YES** ☞ Use email /memo
                                                        OR
                                                        Letters
                                                        OR
                                                        Reports

✓ Does this message require a written record? ☞ **NO** ✐

    ✓ Do I need immediate feedback? ☞ **YES** ☞   Telephone Call
                                                                OR
                                                                Personal Visit
                                                                OR
                                                                Email

    ✓ Do I need immediate feedback? ☞ **NO** ✐

    ✓ Does this message require careful ☞ **YES** ☞   Long
       organization and supporting   Memorandum
       documentation?   OR
                                      Reports with
                                      Visual Aids

    ✓ Does this message require careful ☞ **NO** ✐
       organization and supporting
       documentation?

       ✓ How urgent is the message? ☞ URGENT   Personal Visit
                                           OR
                                           Telephone Call

                                  ☞ ROUTINE   Memorandum
                                               OR
                                               Letter

occasion. Traditionally the style among law enforcement personnel has been authoritative as in "I am the police officer here, and I will act in your best interests." The typical police officer really did not solicit any input or information with regard to making a decision concerning the enforcement of law. This concept worked in its infancy because of the time frame and society's expectations concerning law enforcement. However, as the song says, "the times they are a-changing," and law enforcement officers have been mandated to change the manner in which they relate to the public.

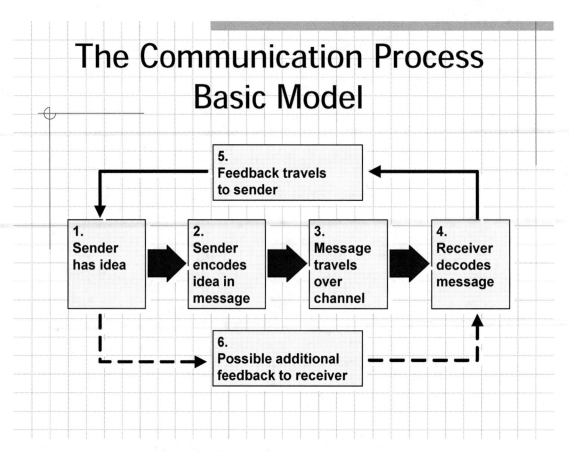

Figure 3-1. <u>The Communication Process Basic Model</u>

The turbulence of the 1960s and 1970s made police officers re-evaluate not only their training regimen but also the manner in which they dealt with the public. The 1968 Chicago Democratic National Convention in which Mayor Daley advised his police officers that public order would be maintained is a prime example of a clash between the old traditional concept of communication and the change to a more adaptive communication style. Even as late as 1996, the Pittsburgh Police Department became embroiled in an investigation conducted by the U.S. Department of Justice as the result of a lawsuit filed by the American Civil Liberties Union concerning the accusation of an institutionalized pattern of brutality over the last decade against minority citizens. The Department of Justice (DOJ) recommendations were not readily accepted by the Mayor and Chief of Police in Pittsburgh. Rather than accept them in a constructive manner, Mayor Murphy, in a press conference which followed on the heels of the DOJ's announcement concerning its investigation, made the statement that "If they [think they] understand what it means to run a police department in a city today, then my son knows more than they do. And he is 6 years old"[4] (*Pittsburgh Post-Gazette,* February 13, 1997). This defensive posture is typical of the position taken by traditional law enforcement and this stance further exemplifies the difficulty in transition from the traditional policing approach to the popular concept of community policing.

Communication styles come in various forms. Researchers are unable to reach a consensus on the exact number of styles; however, most are willing to concede that they cluster around four dimensions: blaming, directing, persuading, and problem solving. The old style in law enforcement would be most comfortable with the blaming and directing dimensions; but with the advent of community policing, persuading and problem solving are rising to the forefront.

An officer who uses the blaming style basically attempts to find fault or to ascribe blame for a problem. For instance, "If these people would stay in school, stop having babies, and get a job, I wouldn't have to be here at 3 a.m. babysitting them." Clearly this is an example of a frustrated officer. The use of the negative tone in this communication style evokes hostile feelings in the receiver, which could lead to the escalation of hostilities in an already tense situation. Since officers may find themselves in situations that are hostile by their very nature (domestic disturbances, neighborhood disorders, assaults), one of the parties present may already be in a combative state or in an emotionally charged state. This style of communication should be avoided unless and until all other avenues of communication have been pursued and all of the facts of the case are absolutely clear.

The directing style of communication is just another name for the authoritative style of management. "It's my way or the highway!" No feedback is solicited; communication flows unidirectional (from the top) and often creates an insurmountable barrier for communication. In limited situations, however, the directing style may be essential (SWAT teams or special operations) to ensure the safety of an individual or the successful conclusion of an operation such as, "Halt! Put the gun down or I will fire." Another example would be, "Put your hands on your head and drop to your knees, crossing your ankles." Clearly, these examples of unidirectional communication are confrontational by definition and designed for prompt compliance, leaving no room for discussion. Due to the very nature of the aforementioned strategic teams, the directing style of communication is required so as to reduce or eliminate any ambiguities or confusion. Each member of special operations teams is not only familiar with but also comfortable with this style of communication because it provides them with a sense of security and operational effectiveness.

The persuading style of communication involves information-sharing and acceptance techniques. Interviewing and interrogating suspects requires criminal justice personnel to utilize this method of communicating. It is really a matter of tact wherein a police officer is attempting to persuade someone to reveal information that may be against his or her best interests in a court of law or an institutional hearing. Professionals realize that a great deal of psychological comfort may be attained by a suspect when the barrier of concealment is finally broken. Therefore, the officer will work to lower this barrier by being as persuasive as possible. Hostage negotiation is another example where the persuading style would be effective and essential. The ultimate goal in this situation is to have the suspect surrender and neither the suspect nor the hostage(s) be injured or killed. An officer utilizing a truly persuasive communication style will be able to have the suspect realize that it is in his or her best interest to resolve this stand-off as peacefully as possible. In order to engender a peaceful resolution, however, mutual concessions are necessary.

Utilizing a blaming or directing communication style in these types of situations may only serve to enflame the situation or to make the suspect more resolute in his or her efforts to carry out the original plan of action.

One problem with the persuasive style of communication is that it is not always productive. While an individual may be able to persuade others to follow his or her course of action, merely accepting or following does not insure an identification or resolution of the original problem. If the problem can be identified and resolved, no need exists to re-visit persuasion.

The problem-solving style of communication may prove to be a beneficial and productive method. Community policing is predicated upon discussions between citizens and the police. This return to the "cop on the beat" style of policing incorporates local law enforcement officers knowing inhabitants of their district and the inherent problems within that community. Police officers attend crime watch meetings and community awareness meetings in an effort to resolve not only the problems with crime but also with situations that foster an atmosphere for criminal acts to occur. This proactive approach to law enforcement attempts to eliminate situations that hamper a community's growth, prosperity, and well-being.

Two recent innovations in criminal justice are problem-oriented policing (POP) and community-oriented policing (COP). Problem-oriented policing deals primarily with correcting or eliminating those physical or environmental matters that facilitate the commission of a crime. An example of POP would be additional lighting in a shopping mall parking lot or the removal of condemned buildings utilized as crack houses or havens for drug addicts.

Community-oriented policing (COP) involves a team approach to removing the sociological barriers that cause crime. An example of COP would be the creation and funding of rehabilitation programs in an effort to reduce or eliminate substance abuse. The current emphasis on programs designed to reduce teen pregnancy and to lower the high school dropout rate are two more examples of community-oriented policing. Community-based corrections programs also serve as a means to involve citizens and correctional personnel in reducing prison costs and in lowering inmate populations. COP is discussed in great detail in later chapters of this textbook.

In discussing the four dimensions of communication styles, the evidence presented demonstrates that no single style is perfect for every occasion. The ability to select the appropriate style and to adapt your inherent communication style to fit that situation is the key to successful interaction with other individuals through verbal communication.

To find out what your individual communication style may be, complete the Self-Assessment of Communication Style, which follows. This instrument measures the dominant technique that you use to communicate based on the two extremes of blaming and problem solving. Realize that most individuals fall somewhere in between these two styles.

Self-Assessment of Communication Style©

Indicate the degree to which you do the following:

	Very Little	Little	Some	Great	Very Great
1. Make judgments early in the conversation.	____	____	____	____	____
2. Share my feelings with others.	____	____	____	____	____
3. Talk about the issues.	____	____	____	____	____
4. Have analyzed others' motives.	____	____	____	____	____
5. Talk about the person.	____	____	____	____	____
6. Use clear and precise language.	____	____	____	____	____
7. Decide on the action before the conversation.	____	____	____	____	____
8. Encourage the other person to discuss feelings.	____	____	____	____	____
9. Am open for new information.	____	____	____	____	____
10. Ask questions that seek agreement with me.	____	____	____	____	____
11. Talk the majority of the time.	____	____	____	____	____
12. Ask questions that get others to describe events.	____	____	____	____	____
13. Talk half the time or less.	____	____	____	____	____
14. Allow others to defend their position to me.	____	____	____	____	____

Scoring Sheet

Item No.		Score
1.	_____	
2.		_____
3.		_____
4.	_____	
5.	_____	
6.		_____
7.	_____	
8.		_____
9.		_____
10.	_____	
11.	_____	
12.		_____
13.		_____
14.	_____	

TOTALS _____   _____

Total column 1_____
Total column 2_____

Interpretation of scores:
Very little = 1 point
Little = 2 points
Some = 3 points
Great = 4 points
Very great = 5 points

Explanation of Self-Assessment of Communication Style

This instrument measures the tendency to use blaming and problem-solving styles. Having evaluated these, you should be able to determine your abilities on the styles between these extremes.

If your score for the LEFT COLUMN is between 21 and 28 you are probably a MODERATE BLAMER. A score of 29 or HIGHER suggests your rely somewhat heavily on the blaming style.

If your score for the RIGHT COLUMN is from 21 to 28 you fall in the moderate problem-solving style category. A score of 29 or HIGHER indicates a strong leaning toward problem solving as your dominant technique.

<u>SOURCE</u>: O'Connell, Sandra W. *The Manager as Communicator* (1979), p. 25. Harper & Row Publishers, Inc.

Types of Communication

Communication exists on two levels: verbal and nonverbal. To better understand communication, you must first understand the differences between the verbal and nonverbal processes of communicating. Whether a person acts in the capacity of police officer, district attorney or judge, recognizing the subtle differences conveyed through nonverbal communication can secure arrest, conviction, and punishment for the offender. The old adage, "It's not what you say but how you say it," is as true today as it ever has been.

The person who believes that nonverbal communication is an unimportant component in this process is ill informed. Nonverbal communication makes up 93 percent[5] of the information exchanged in a face-to-face situation. The old adage, "It's not what you say but how you say it," is particularly relevant because of its reference to the use of paralanguage as a nonverbal communication technique. Therefore, law enforcement officials, like all other people, must make sure that spoken words and nonverbal cues complement each other.

Verbal Components

Verbal communication is not only comprised of the spoken word but of the written word as well. Reports, memoranda, and directives are all vital to the transmittal of information within a law enforcement agency. They provide the network by which individuals convey information and messages essential to the efficient operation of the department or agency. Chapter 6 will deal with these components in more detail.

The oral aspect of verbal communication is more spontaneous in nature and generally considered easier by most people. The reason for this belief is because we learn to speak long before we learn to write, and we spend a majority of our adult life engaged in conversation. While there is a great deal of difference between the casual conversation and a public presentation, they also share some commonalities. Generally there are three purposes associated with either casual conversation or public speaking: to inform, to persuade, or to entertain. While law enforcement officials are frequently seen in the role of informing the public or persuading individuals to comply with various legal requirements, seldom are they placed in a position to entertain. Even though many officers have been placed in a particularly entertaining situation, this was not intentional on the part of the law enforcement officer. Chapters 2 and 3 will discuss further aspects of public presentations in greater depth.

KISS/Verbal Obfuscation

> Early in my career, I had occasion to hear a radio transmission which advised all units to be on the lookout for a suspect in a particularly nasty malicious wounding described as a "corpulent Caucasian female with a recently deviated septum." Of the 30 units that received this transmission, only 2 were able to decipher the encrypted message: "Heavy-set white woman with a broken nose."
> [Actual example from Dr. Grubb's career as a police officer]

KISS is an extremely effective acronym. "Keep it Short and Simple" is not an indicator of a lack of intelligence or professionalism but rather an efficient way to communicate. Some police officers, through a sense of misplaced importance, feel compelled to use language that is inappropriate for the situation—inappropriate in the sense that it does not fit well in the context of the conversation or in the message that the officer is attempting to convey. In an effort to create or enhance an already established air of authority, officers may talk "above the heads" of suspects, witnesses, the general public, etc. Given that approximately 25% of the adult population has a bachelor's degree and that most local newspapers are written on a secondary reading level, these language skills could serve as barriers to the communication process. The ability to utilize speaking skills on a continuum ranging from the most basic elementary levels to a more sophisticated professional status distinguishes the stereotypical police officer from the truly effective law enforcement officer.

<u>Jargon or Slang</u> Another common error is the use of jargon or slang in an attempt to ingratiate or include the police officer in the closed or cloistered community. Young police officers frequently endeavor to master the local jargon in an effort to solicit information or develop informants at the local level. While in some instances this may be effective, it is a matter of ensuring that the police officer's personality meshes well with the local language pattern. A Caucasian police officer with military bearing or persona would experience a great deal of difficulty in being accepted by a minority community. Even mastering the lingo would prove fruitless in this situation. For example, this officer might state, "I followed the dude to his crib and Homey tried to rabbit out the back." Rather than being accepted as a peer or ingratiating himself/herself to the community, this type of officer would be viewed as offensive if he/she did not possess the concomitant demeanor. In fact, the minority community might be insulted at his/her attempt to fit in because they would see it as a form of mockery and this would serve to further alienate the community and the officer.

<u>"Legalese"</u> The incorporation of legal phrases or legal terms in general conversation with the community, witnesses, or suspects may be ill advised. There are occasions on which, in order to comply with local, state, or federal codes, that a specific phrase or warning/advisement may be necessary. However, these legalistic terms generally serve to confuse or cloud the individual's

understanding of the officer=s message. An illustration of this caveat may be clarified by the following example:

> **Police Officer (to suspect)**: "You are under arrest for robbery, and I want you to listen carefully as I read you your rights."

as opposed to

> **Police Officer (to suspect)**: "You are under arrest for violation of Section 18.2-3 COV, and I am going to advise you of your Constitutional rights under the *Miranda* decision."

As evidenced in this example, the use of legal terms serves only to add to the confusion of the arrest situation. Generally the suspect is already either feigning or actually experiencing confusion or embarrassment at this point, and this use of legal terminology only enhances the confusion, making matters worse.

Nonverbal Components

Police academies teach young men and women to look, act, and behave like police officers. A variety of means is utilized to achieve this transformation, but one of the more important aspects of this socialization is the mastering of the command presence concept. In essence, recruits are instructed how to establish and maintain control of a situation by their mere presence, and nonverbal communication plays a major role in establishing this command presence. Nonverbal communication is comprised of body language, voice, proxemics, gender, and gestures and touch[6].

Body language Body language is formally identified as kinesics. The use of the eyes, the head, posture, and stance convey meanings that sometimes might prove to be the antithesis of the verbal message. Federal law enforcement and corrections agencies instruct their investigators and correctional officers to use eye movement as one indicator of possible deception. For instance, suspects who look down and to the left may be deceptive in their description of an incident. The importance of body language in interviewing and interrogation situations has been well documented. However, the interpretation of body language is bi-directional (the suspect may be scrutinizing the officer's body language during the interview as well).

Voice Vocal characteristics are considered to be a type of nonverbal communication called paralanguage. The speed with which an individual speaks is sometimes perceived as an indicator of truthfulness or intelligence. Individuals who speak quickly are often thought of as having something to hide. Stereotypically, individuals who speak more slowly, particularly those individuals from the Deep South, are considered to be less intelligent because of their dialect.

Pitch is another voice characteristic that may be revealing. Individuals who speak in a high, shrill voice may be experiencing fear, while those who speak in a deep, booming voice exude confidence and control.

Proxemics The use of objects, clothing, etc., in communication is known as proxemics. Police officers already present a strong nonverbal image—one that may be construed as contradictory in nature. The color blue is associated with trust. The blue uniforms and the squad cars of police officers are supposed to engender trust and integrity in the community. On the other hand, police officers are armed with guns, pepper spray, batons, and badges, which are all recognized symbols of authority and aggression. Basically, the community receives a mixed message with regard to the police officer's role as protector or warrior in the neighborhood.

<u>Gender</u> Men and women do not speak the same language. While they may use the same vocabulary, their interpretations may be radically different. Typically female officers do not evoke or promote the "defensive response" from a male suspect. No posturing occurs with respect to establishing a sense of dominance; and therefore hostility is not met with hostility. Rather than a combative atmosphere, a neutral atmosphere exists which frequently dissipates the suspect's anger, particularly in domestic disputes.

Female victims in domestic disputes may be more disposed to an open dialogue with a female officer than with a male officer. This is not always the case, but female officers may be perceived as more empathetic in these situations. Some female victims may find the presence of a male officer to be more comforting because it provides them with a sense of paternalistic protection and security. On the other hand, male suspects may prefer female officers to speak with them because they perceive these officers to be less judgmental and critical in certain situations. The understanding of the role of gender in communication is important in determining which officer may need to take the lead role in interviewing a witness, a suspect, or a victim. More information on this topic will be provided in a later chapter in this text.

<u>Gestures and Touch</u> The significance of gestures and touch in nonverbal communication should not be overlooked. The grip and duration of a handshake may be a nonverbal signal that communicates a sense of being open and friendly or clandestine and antagonistic.

Many individuals feel that a violation of their intimate personal space, which occurs with any type of touching automatically, creates a fight-or-flight response. Not only does the definition of personal space vary from individual to individual, but the level of comfort also varies from culture to culture. Therefore, while a pat on the back may be an attempt on the part of the officer to provide comfort and assurance, this act may be perceived by the recipient as a threatening gesture.

Law enforcement officials in cities with gang populations need to be aware of the nonverbal cues used by individuals to identify or signify membership in a particular group (flashing gang signs, wearing gang colors, and graffiti). The use of these cues frequently denote the targeting of certain individuals for acts of violence or retaliation as well as marking certain areas as gang turf. Officers also need to be knowledgeable concerning nonverbal communication with these groups so as to avoid misunderstandings and to make the communication process as effective as possible.

Flow of Communication

Communication in organizations, whether public or private, tends to follow two succinct channels: **formal** or **informal**[7]. **Formal communication** follows the chain of command in an organization, as seen in Figure 1.5. Information concerning policies and procedures is most often communicated from the top of the organizational structure to the bottom (**downward**) through this formal channel. Formal communication flow, however, is not limited to downward but may also be upward or horizontal. **Upward** communication in organizations may take the form of employee feedback through memoranda, reports, departmental meetings, suggestion systems, and exit interviews. **Horizontal** communication occurs when workers at the same level share information. Horizontal communication may take place through e-mail, personal contact, memoranda, or meetings.

      Informal communication takes place in organizations through the unofficial communication channel called the "grapevine." A recent study indicated that as much as two-thirds of an employee's information comes from the grapevine.[8] While social situations lend themselves toward discussions of organizational problems and processes, heavy reliance on the grapevine to disseminate detail suggests that insufficient information is being released through formal channels.

Barriers to Communication

      As in any act of communicating, there are likely to occur incidences of misunderstanding in the law enforcement field. No matter how attentive, empathetic, or effective an individual is during the course of communication, certain barriers will arise which impede the flow of or the correct interpretation of information. These barriers or distractions to effective communication may be reduced or eliminated if the officer is aware of their existence. Having the knowledge to recognize and compensate for these differences may also allow the officer to acquire information that may have eluded him or her previously.

      <u>Bypassing</u>[9] Because individuals are different, they attach different meanings to the same words. Most people attempt to understand messages based on the context in which they are delivered. In essence, they decide what the words mean by the way in which they are used in conversation or in written documentation. Unfortunately, the meanings attached by the receiver are not always the ones intended by the sender. For example, an examination of the English language produces an overwhelming number of meanings ascribed to the word "fast." As shown in Figure 1.6, fast has as many as eight different meanings. In order to avoid bypassing, the sender and receiver must attach the same meanings to words. When faced with the task of creating understanding, law enforcement officials must assist the public in applying the appropriate meaning to statements delivered to the community. One way to avoid semantic bypassing is to define any terms that could be misunderstood. Another method for creating a common understanding is to use words properly in sentences. Most of the meaning behind our language comes from the way we arrange our sentences and paragraphs. We derive an understanding of what is said from the surrounding descriptions and concomitant arrangement of words.

Formal Communication

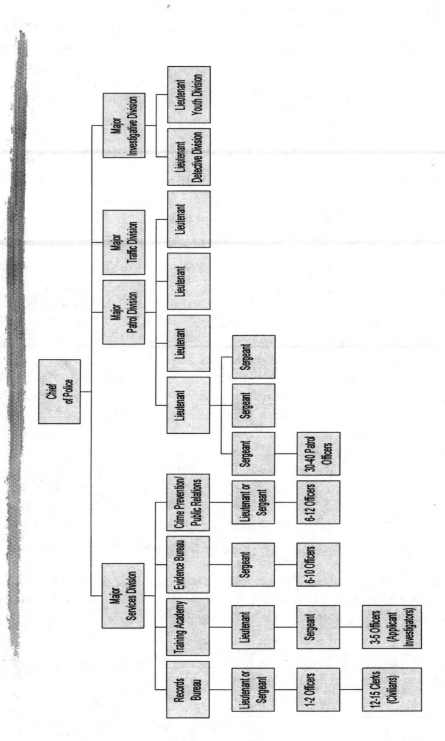

The Meanings of "Fast"[10]

A man is **fast** when he can run rapidly.
But he is also **fast** when he is tied down and cannot run at all.
And colors are **fast** when they do not run.
One is **fast** when s/he moves in suspect company.
But this is not quite the same thing as playing **fast** and loose.
A racetrack is **fast** when it is in good running condition.
A friend is **fast** when s/he is loyal.
A watch is **fast** when it is ahead of time.
To be **fast** asleep is to be deep in sleep.
To be **fast** by is to be near.
To **fast** is to refrain from eating.
A **fast** may be a period of non-eating – or a ship's mooring line.
Photographic film is **fast** when it is sensitive to light.
But bacteria are **fast** when they are insensitive to antiseptics.

Listening Most individuals are able to process the spoken word at a rate of 400 words per minute[11]. Unfortunately, the average speaker has a rate of only 125-185 words per minute. This creates a critical gap during which the receiver may be distracted by a variety of sources. Daydreaming, forming a response or an answer, forming a question or rebuttal, noise, time factors or constraints all serve to cloud or block effective listening. This cloud not only obscures the complete receipt of information but also obscures the interpretation of information.

Listening is an active process that requires an individual to be alert to both verbal and nonverbal cues. An active listener will note an increase in blood pressure, an increase in pulse rate, and a tendency to perspire. This physiologic response is indicative of a situation where an individual is observing nonverbal behaviors and processing verbal information such as one would see in a therapist's office. By its very nature, law enforcement requires officers to be active listeners not only in seeking the truth but also in providing them a means of protection.

Cultural/Language Most law enforcement agencies actively seek recruits who possess a fluency in a second language as it enables them to be more effective in communicating with a specific minority community. However, fluency in a language is not necessarily sufficient in and of itself to overcome cultural barriers. This knowledge of the language must be accompanied by an understanding and appreciation of the associated culture. The significance here is that the officer does not send or receive mixed messages but effectively communicates with citizens in the community.

Psychological (Defensiveness) Traditionally police officers have been wary of change as it creates a new environment in which they must operate. Law enforcement officers feel a certain level of comfort and security with measures that have withstood the test of time. When officers are forced to change, it creates a sense of anxiety because the environment is unfamiliar and may present new obstacles or dangers. Typically fear and anxiety evoke a defensive response. This defensive response may be transmitted to the community. A prime example of this type of reaction would involve community policing and the use of citizen police academies. Police officers who believe that involving the community in the prevention or detection of crime will be resistant to acceptance of these types of associations. Purely philosophical differences may be at the crux of the issue; however, in most situations the law enforcement officers view community involvement as a loss of control for departments and officers. This loss of control results in the adoption of a defensive stance, thus creating a barrier to communication surrounding this issue.

Physical The environment (light, heat, cold, wind, rain, noise, etc.) frequently competes with an individual trying to convey a message. The officer's attention may be distracted by any number of elements. Large groups of people milling about and talking, cars passing, and dogs barking serve as impediments to the communication process.

Experiential When most individuals converse, they do so from a platform or base of experience. Unfortunately, not all individuals share the same experiences or view the same experience in the same manner; therefore, bias is built into the communication process. These differences or biases in experience serve to hinder effective communication and understanding. For instance, officers frequently experience difficulty in communicating with each other because of the wide gap created by varying levels of rank, seniority, income, education, previous military experience, and social class. Resentment may occur among senior officers due to perceived opportunities or privileges afforded younger officers prior to their entering the law enforcement profession. This resentment may also be transferred to citizens within the community.

Officers may also find it difficult to communicate with citizens whose prior experiences are not synchronous with those of the officer. The ability to empathize with and understand others decreases when shared experiences are not present. Since most law enforcement personnel view life through the window of their individual experience, adapting that perspective to the background of suspects, victims, or witnesses is difficult. Nevertheless, protecting the public and upholding the law is the responsibility of any officer, and part of that obligation encompasses the communication process.

Overcoming Communication Barriers

In addressing the barriers to the communication process, we must also identify methods for overcoming those barriers. As you plan your communication, ask yourself the following questions to ensure that you have anticipated communication obstacles:

1.   Have you anticipated problems in communication? People are different and in these differences, communication problems thrive. Be proactive in planning communication so that you address the needs of the receiver. Just knowing that things can and do go wrong will help you to prepare appropriate communication strategies to reduce any misunderstanding caused by bypassing.

2.   Have you focused on the receiver and his or her frame of reference? Experiential barriers occur because people engaged in the communication process are inherently different, coming from different backgrounds, and having varied outlooks on life. Question what the receiver knows about your subject matter. Ask questions like, "What does the receiver know about my message?" "Does he or she know as much as I do about the subject?" "How is the receiver likely to respond to my message—will he or she be happy, angry, frustrated, etc.?" The

more often you put yourself in the receiver's place and attempt to anticipate questions he or she might have, the better you will be at successful communication. Remember to put yourself in the shoes of the receiver and to look at the subject matter from his or her perspective, and you will achieve effective communication.

3.   Have you planned to listen? Unfortunately, most people are not taught to listen. If anything, families and schools teach us that we get more response if we talk. We learn at an early age that if we ask someone to repeat what was said—whether it was an assignment for homework or a name or telephone number—that he or she will repeat the requested information. This positive reinforcement of a bad behavior, poor listening, carries us into adulthood with little ability to hear and process information. In law enforcement, listening is often the key to a successful conclusion to a case. Often, witnesses or suspects do not verbalize every detail of a case in straightforward terms. The police officer must rely on his or her ability to hear what the suspect or witness is not saying. The only way to "hear between the lines" is to actively listen. Active listening requires you to focus on the speaker and to hear what is being said as well as to process the nonverbal cues of the speaker. Overcoming the listening barrier to communication is not easy, but you can learn some techniques that will help you to be a more productive listener.

Checklist for Improving Listening[12]

▶ Stop talking. Accept the role of listener by concentrating on the speaker's words, not on what your response will be.

▶ Work hard at listening. Become actively involved; expect to learn something.

▶ Block out competing thoughts. Concentrate on the message. Don't allow yourself to daydream during lag time.

▶ Control the listening environment. Turn off the TV, close the windows, and move to a quiet location. Tell the speaker when you cannot hear.

▶ Maintain an open mind. Know your biases and try to correct for them. Be tolerant of less-abled and different-looking speakers.

▶ Provide verbal and nonverbal feedback. Encourage the speaker with comments like "yes," "I see," "Okay," and "Uh-huh," and ask polite questions. Look alert by leaning forward.

▶ Paraphrase the speaker's ideas. Silently repeat the message in your own words, sort out the main points, and identify supporting details. In conversation sum up the main points to confirm what was said.

▶ Take selective notes. If you are hearing instructions or important data, record the major points; then, verify your notes with the speaker.

▶ Listen between the lines. Observe nonverbal cues, and interpret the feelings of the speaker. What is really being said?

▶ Capitalize on lag time. Use spare moments to organize, review, anticipate, challenge, and weigh the evidence.

4.   Have you created a psychologically appealing environment? When you are communicating with people, try to ensure that any defensiveness is eradicated as soon as possible. When people assume a defensive posture, they may fail to adequately listen or to communicate with you. As a law enforcement officer, you should try wherever possible to create a climate of acceptance and concern. If a suspect or witness is anxious or defensive, you will be unlikely to garner any cooperation from him or her. Try questioning witnesses in their own environment, in particular their homes. People are more willing to speak with an officer on their own turf. Merely having to go to the police station can cause witnesses to assume a defensive stance, which you will find difficult or impossible to overcome.

5.   Have you eliminated physical barriers? Physical barriers such as loud competing sounds or background noise, heat, cold, wind, rain, etc., cause communication mishaps. People will often get distracted by loud noises or inclement weather conditions. When possible, law enforcement personnel should move into an area to question witnesses or suspects where no physical barriers to the communication process exist. Something as simple as having a witness sit in the patrol car during questioning may be enough to eliminate noise distractions. Another example of a physical barrier to communication is distance. If a witness is not located in the same area as the police officer that is investigating a case, the officer should do whatever is possible to reduce the distance when speaking with the witness. This distance problem may mean that the officer has to travel to speak with or to interview the witness. Eliminating the distance means that the officer also eliminates a physical barrier to the communication process.

The remainder of this handbook will apply the principles from Chapter 1 to situations that might occur in the criminal justice profession. A sound knowledge base in relation to the concepts presented here will allow students, trainees, and law enforcement officials to become better communicators and thus, better law enforcement officers.

Summary

In this chapter we examined the process and cycle of communication. Communication is a process that involves at least two people, the sender and the receiver, who exchange information through a system of shared symbols or language. The sender encodes the message and sends it through an appropriate channel or medium to the receiver who then decodes the message and provides feedback to the sender. This process continues until such time as the sender and receiver have completed their communication. Barriers to communication exist in such areas as bypassing, listening, cultural differences, experiences, physical differences, and psychological problems.

Individuals have different styles of communication—blaming, directing, persuading, and problem solving. The old style in law enforcement would be most comfortable with the blaming and directing dimensions, but with the advent of community policing, persuading and problem solving are rising to the forefront.

Communication is either verbal or nonverbal. The verbal components of communication were identified as both the oral and written word. Verbal obfuscation, the use of jargon/slang or legalese were identified as problem areas in verbal communication. Nonverbal communication is composed of a variety of aspects: the body (kinesics), the voice (paralanguage), objects (proxemics), gender, and gestures and touch (haptics).

Communication also flows through formal or informal channels. Formal communication follows the chain of command in an organization and either flows upward, downward, or horizontally. Informal communication in organizations takes place through the unofficial communication channel called the "grapevine."

Barriers to communication are experiential, listening, bypassing, cultural, psychological, or physical. Understanding that these obstacles are present in the communication process is important, but developing methods for removing these barriers is tantamount to the success of any communication. Experiential, cultural, and bypassing barriers can be removed or reduced if you attempt to practice empathy in your communication process. Looking at the situation from another's perspective will allow you to provide answers to questions that might arise and to address the particular needs of the other party. Practicing active listening skills will help you to be able to hear and process more information. Active listening is a difficult task that requires practice. Learn to paraphrase what has been said, to link new information to existing information, and to question the speaker so that you can be sure you have received the correct communication.

Key Terms

Communication	Sender
Receiver	Communication Channel
Encoding	Decoding
Feedback	Bypassing
Noise	Blaming
Directing	Persuading
Problem Solving	Community-oriented policing
Problem-oriented Policing	Nonverbal Communication

Verbal Communication	Kinesics
Proxemics	Paralanguage
Gender	Haptics
KISS	Legalese
Gestures	Formal Communication
Downward	Upward
Horizontal	Informal Communication
Experiential Barriers to Communication	

Discussion Questions

1. What role does communication play in the criminal justice process?
2. Describe the process and cycle of communication.
3. Why is it important for criminal justice professionals to be aware of the various communication styles?
4. Why are the formal and informal channels of communication so important to the criminal justice professional? Give examples of the formal and informal communication channels in a criminal justice agency.
5. List and discuss barriers to communication.
6. Observe a police officer directing traffic at an intersection. Where applicable, discuss the nonverbal components you observe occurring between the officer and the motorists.
7. Using the same scenario, discuss the officer=s reaction to inattentive motorists or defiant motorists who ignore his/her direction.
8. Discuss the appropriateness of an officer using neighborhood slang or jargon in a conversation with the public.
9. **Ethical Issue:** Should criminal justice professionals be allowed to express their personal feelings even if they conflict with their professional position?
10. **Ethical Issue:** Should personal bias be reflected in the way in which a criminal justice professional addresses other individuals?
11. **Ethical Issue:** Should criminal justice professionals be permitted to join or hold membership in organizations that have an expressed or implied racial or sexist creed?
12. **Ethical Issue:** Should police officers be allowed to express their displeasure or disgust through (a) the use of nonverbal signals or (b) the use of profanity? Explain.
13. **Ethical Issue:** Should criminal justice professionals use their knowledge of nonverbal behaviors to determine if their colleagues are being deceptive?
14. **Ethical Issue:** Should criminal justice professionals with advanced education use words or phrases which are unclear or confusing in their discussions with their colleagues or subordinates?

Notes

1. "The Detective's Story,"*Vanity Fair*, February 1997.
2. Guffey, M. E., *Business Communication: Process and Product.* Cincinnati, OH: South-Western College Publishing, 2000.

3. Lahiff, J. M., & Penrose, I. M., *Business Communication: Strategies and Skills* (5th ed.), Upper Saddle River, NJ: Prentice Hall, 1997.

4 *Pittsburgh Post Gazette,* Febrary 13, 1997, p. A.

5. Mehrabian, A., *Silent Messages*. Belmont, CA: Wadsworth, 1971.

6. Mausehund, J., & Timm, S. "Teaching Strategies for Nonverbal Skills." *Instructional Strategies: An Applied Research* Series. Little Rock, AR: Delta Pi Epsilon. Volume 10, Issue 3, 1994.

7. Guffey, M.E., *Business Communication: Process and Product*. Cincinnati, OH: South-Western College Publishing, 2000, pp. 20-23.

8. "Who Told You That?" *The Wall Street Journal,* May 23, 1985, 33.

9. Guffey, p. 13.

10 Haney, W.V. (1992). *Communication and Interpersonal Relations: Text and Cases* (6th ed.). Burr Ridge, IL: Richard D. Irwin, Inc.

11. Guffey, p. 46.

12. Ibid, p. 49.

CHAPTER 2

THINK BEFORE YOU SPEAK: THE VERBAL COMPONENT

Learning Objectives:

1.   To identify the two components of verbal communication.

2.   To explain the importance of listening in oral communication.

3.   To differentiate between hearing and listening.

4.   To describe the different types of listening behavior.

5.   To identify the critical behaviors in active listening.

6.   To recognize examples of poor listeners.

7.   To identify barriers to active listening.

8.   To recognize the types of written communication.

9.   To compare letters and memoranda and to identify appropriate uses for each.

10. To understand the importance of word selection in written communication.

11. To understand sentence and paragraph development.

> *A marked departure in foreign policy was observed at the beginning of George W. Bush's administration. While former President Clinton had promoted reaching an agreement with North Korea that would have ended its development and export of ballistic missiles and related technologies, Bush expressed criticism. In addition, National Security Advisor Condoleeza Rice described North Korea as the "roadkill of history[1]." However, Security of State Colin Powell, when questioned about the administration's policies, stated that "we do plan to engage with North Korea to pick up where President Clinton and his administration left off. Some promising elements were left on the table and we will be examining those elements.[2]" While apparently part of the same administration, these three individuals clearly expressed differing ideas regarding foreign policy concerning North Korea.*

Even though its name implies speech, verbal communication actually consists of all oral *and* written communications. The life and work of a criminal justice professional involves both aspects of oral and written communication. Preparing reports that are grammatically sound while providing all essential information is an imperative. By the same token, the oral component of verbal communication requires careful planning and thoughtful preparation prior to speaking. Chapter 3 will address issues related to public speaking and the use of visual aids in presentations while Chapter 4 explores the role nonverbal communication plays in oral communication's authenticity and acceptance.

Verbal Communication: The Oral Component

Consider how limited we would be as a society if we could not verbally ask questions or give instructions. Oral communication is the only way we have of receiving immediate answers to questions or of providing feedback to others. How would you know if you had performed a job well or if you required further information if you and others around you could not speak? Another facet of oral communication involves listening skills. Speaking and listening are reciprocal parts of the communication process.

Three Myths of Listening[3]	Three Truths of Listening
Listening cannot be learned; it is a natural occurrence.	Listening is not a natural activity; it is learned.
Hearing and listening are the same.	Telling someone something is not the same thing as communicating.
When you speak, everyone listens.	You speak to one person at a time—even in an audience situation.

Listening

Just as important to the oral component of communication as the spoken word is our ability to listen. Listening skills are vital in any profession, but in matters of law enforcement, listening effectively is a top priority. Consider that on average, we remember approximately 25 percent of what we hear in any conversation. If we remember only one-fourth of the information, then three-fourths of the content of that conversation is lost.

Listening and speaking are part of a natural process that should occur together. Most of the time we converse and listen; rarely are we required to do only one or the other. Five concepts of listening underscore the reciprocity involved in speaking and listening: **attending, understanding, remembering, analyzing critically,** and **responding empathically**.[4]

The **attending** concept of listening refers to the process of selecting or focusing on specific stimuli from amongst the countless number of stimuli we receive. In order to effectively listen, the attending process gives us parameters to follow.

1. Prepare yourself, both physically and mentally, to listen. Compel yourself to focus on what is being said.

2. Give the speaker the appropriate time to complete his/her statement(s) before you react. In other words, do not rehearse what you are planning to say in response to something the speaker said–LISTEN to what is being said until the speaker's intent is complete.

3. Adjust your listening to the goal of the situation. Determine the goal of your communication. Do you need to understand, to evaluate, to respond, or to comfort? Depending on your goal in the communication situation, your listening will range from "pleasure listening" (i.e., listening without much intensity) to "critical analysis."

A second aspect of listening is **understanding**. When we decode (or translate) a message accurately by assigning appropriate meaning to it, we are able to understand the message. To fully understand what another individual says requires **active listening**. When we engage in active listening, we use specific techniques of empathizing, asking questions, and paraphrasing. More discussion on active listening will follow later in this chapter.

Remembering, the third concept of listening, is being able to process information and store it for later retrieval (or recall). Unfortunately, our ability to remember is very limited. Often we cannot remember the name of person to whom we have been introduced merely moments earlier. Several techniques are available which can assist us in remembering information: repetition, mnemonics, and taking notes.

1. **Repetition** helps listeners store information in long-term memory. Repetition refers to saying something two, three, or even four times to reinforce the information. If we do not engage in repetition, whatever we hear will be held in short-term memory for approximately 20 seconds and then discarded.

2. Constructing **mnemonics** is another technique we can use to help us remember information. "A mnemonic device is any artificial technique used as a memory aid" (Verderber, 1999, p. 141). When attempting to remember items in a sequence, you can try to form a sentence using the

words themselves, or you can take the first letter of a list of items you are trying to remember and form a word.

3.   **Note taking** provides an additional venue for retaining information. While you would not want to take notes during a casual interpersonal encounter, telephone conversations, interviews, interrogations, etc., would benefit from this powerful tool for increasing your recall of information.

Critical analysis, the fourth concept of listening, is the process you engage in when attempting to determine whether information you hear is truthful, authentic, or believable. Critical analysis requires you to be able to distinguish between facts and inferences. You also have to be able to evaluate the quality of inferences. **Factual statements** can be verified or proven. **Inferences**, on the other hand, are assertions or claims that are based on observation or fact but that are not necessarily true. As an effective listener, you have to be able to distinguish between statements that can be accepted at face value as truths and statements that require proof (inferences).

The final concept of listening involves **responding empathically**. When we respond empathically to give comfort, we are indicating that we have understood a person's meaning but also affirming that the person has a right to his or her own feelings. Offering support to others shows that we care about them and what happens to them. As an effective listener, you will want to offer supporting statements to demonstrate that you empathize with the person's feelings, regardless of intensity or direction.

The Listening Process

We are taught as young children that listening is a passive activity that requires no effort on our part. Our educational institutions, families, etc., condition us to believe that we do not need to work at listening. Remember when you were in elementary school and the teacher gave you an assignment? That assignment would most likely be repeated several times or in frustration, the teacher would simply write it on the board to avoid the need to repeat it. Your parents would often have to call you several times for dinner or remind you repeatedly to take out the garbage or to clean your room. When confronted about your behavior, you might even have said, "I didn't hear you."

Listening and Hearing. Is there a difference between **hearing** and **listening**? **Hearing** involves the perception of sound; a physiological process whereby sound waves strike the eardrum and cause vibrations that travel to the brain.[5] **Listening** means we attach a meaning to the sounds that have been transmitted to our brain. When we listen, we go beyond the sound itself. We discern various sounds and ideas and comprehend and attach meanings to them. Listening, therefore, is an active skill.

Much like speaking, reading, or writing, listening requires us to be engaged both physically and psychologically. Physical responses to listening involve an increased pulse rate, higher blood pressure, and a slight elevation in body temperature. When counselors and negotiators proclaim that they are exhausted at the end of a day's work, they are merely stating a fact. Their responses to the listening process have effectively rendered them physically drained—much as if they had been performing a type of manual labor.

Psychological responses to listening are much harder to identify. Since we each have our own beliefs or perceptions of the world, we find it difficult (sometimes impossible) to truly listen to others. If listening to another means that we would have to change, most of us would prefer to maintain the status quo and to avoid a variation in our beliefs. After all, change is frightening; so listening could involve considerable risk that we would have to examine what we think or feel and perhaps how we act.

Types of Listening. Three general types of listening have been consistently noted in research. However, the level or intensity of listening activity in which you engage varies with the conversation topic, the relevancy of the subject matter to your needs, and the people involved in the conversation. The three types of listening are **casual or marginal listening**, **attentive listening**, and **active listening**[6].

Casual or marginal listening occurs when listening is secondary in importance to some other activity in which you are engaged. The listener in this situation is not required to learn, comprehend, or remember any materials for later recall and action. An example might be the off-duty police officer that has a scanner running in his home. The officer is not actively listening to what is being said on the scanner when he is engaged in watching television or interacting with his family; he simply has the scanner on in the background. A similar scenario would occur when an individual is driving to work with the radio on in the car. The major focus would be on driving and watching for other vehicles, not on listening to what is being said on the radio.

Attentive listening occurs when there is a need to obtain some information that might be required for a future action. To follow through with the example of the off-duty police officer and his scanner, if he is watching television and suddenly he hears an emergency come through such as "officer needs assistance" or "officer down, needs assistance," then he would suddenly be compelled to listen attentively to the scanner to determine the location of the officer in trouble. The scenario where the individual is driving to work and listening to the radio could become one requiring attentive listening if an emergency broadcast were suddenly to be issued. The driver would then be motivated to hear, understand, and remember what was being said in the broadcast.

The final type of listening is **active listening**. This type of listening occurs most frequently in counseling, interviewing, and interrogating situations. In these situations you are required to listen for more than just the words or the content of the message. You need to pay attention to the nonverbal language and emotions of the speaker. Active listening is most difficult because it requires you to put aside personal preferences and to physically and psychologically listen.

Active listening also requires you to demonstrate four types of behavior: **acceptance, congruence, empathy,** and **concreteness**. **Acceptance** says to the speaker that the listener will not pass judgment or will not criticize the speaker. An important first step in getting a speaker to trust you is to demonstrate acceptance. Once the speaker trusts you, he or she will feel free to share feelings or thoughts.

Congruence is defined as agreeing or harmonizing. In active listening, congruence refers to the agreement or harmony between the speaker's experience, the way he or she feels about the experience, and what the speaker then conveys to others about that experience. In law enforcement, a sergeant is required to take the lieutenant's examination to be placed in line for promotion. For example, Sergeant Mary Smith takes the exam and achieves a score of 93. She is ranked number one in the line for promotion to lieutenant. When the next available lieutenant's slot opens, the sergeant is promoted. She has worked very hard for this promotion and feels very good about it. As a result, Sergeant Smith tells her friends and co-workers about the promotion and how excited she is. At this point, there is total harmony between her experience, her feelings, and her communication to others. As an active listener, you have to be aware of the congruence or absence of congruence in a speaker. When congruence is not present–when no harmony exists between the speaker's experience and feelings, communication will not take place.

In active listening, congruence becomes problematic when an individual is lacking harmony or agreement in his or her experience, feelings, and communication. To use the foregoing example, if Sergeant Smith were to be passed over for the promotion and the person who was ranked second were to be promoted in her place, she would find it very difficult to assist the new lieutenant with his or her duties. Sergeant Smith would be angry that her belief in hard work was ill founded. She would then find it difficult to listen to the new lieutenant when he or she discussed loyalty and duty among the department.

Empathy refers to "putting yourself in another's position." In order to be empathetic toward another, you must attempt to vicariously experience his or her feelings, thoughts, and emotions. When a listener is successful in practicing empathy, he or she is better able to respond appropriately to the concerns or needs of the speaker. Empathy is particularly important in situations of cultural diversity. We must learn to subordinate our opinions and emotions and to approach situations with an open mind. This task is especially difficult given our tendency as humans to judge people. However, the only way to be successful in communication is to listen with empathy.

The final critical behavior for active listening is **concreteness**. Concreteness refers to the speaker's need to concentrate on actions over which he or she has control. We have all heard statements such as "I don't know what to do about Mary. She used to be such a good worker." Nothing the speaker says here has any specific meaning. An active listener would encourage the speaker to give definitive statements about the problem with Mary's work. In this way, a plan of action can be formulated to help Mary work through whatever issues are involved in the situation.

Types of Ineffective Listeners[7]

Through research, we have come to recognize several types of listeners: the **faker**, the **continual talker**, the **rapid-writing note taker**, the **critic**, the **"I'm in a hurry"** the **"hand on the doorknob,"** the **"make sure it is correct,"** the **"finish the sentence for you,"** and the **"I've done one better,"** listeners. Each of these listeners has characteristics you will recognize from your own or others' actions.

Barriers to Listening

Mental and emotional distractions. One of the greatest deterrents to listening involves mental distractions. We can comprehend information at a rate three times that at which most people speak. Because we have a "gap" between the time the words are spoken and the time we

Type of Listener	Characteristics
The Critic	1. Listens merely for points of fact which he or she can take issue with. 2. Waits only to hear something that he or she finds emotionally charged and then proceeds to formulate a mental argument, neglecting to continue listening to the speaker.
The Faker	1. Appears for all intents and purposes to be paying close attention to what is being said. 2. Nods his or her head at all the right places, makes appropriate eye contact, and appears to be following the conversation closely. 3. In reality, this type of listener is merely faking—doing what is necessary to convince another that he or she is listening intently.
The Continual Talker	1. Find it very difficult to listen to anyone since they never stop talking! 2. Always has something to say, interrupts conversations to talk, and rarely allows anyone else to contribute to the conversation.
The I'm in a Hurry	1. Too busy to stop whatever he or she is doing and look at the speaker. 2. This listener is usually performing some other task while "listening" to others—shuffling papers on a desk, searching for a lost object, etc.
The Make Sure it is Correct	1. The person who listens for facts and who will be the first to point out mistakes or errors. 2. Seems to thrive on pointing out the mistakes of others. 3. Will interrupt in order to make a point and cause the speaker to look bad.

The I've Done One Better	1.	Listens only for the points of action in a story and then proceeds to intrude with statements of his or her own.
	2.	Always climbed a higher mountain, captured a more violent criminal, drove faster in a high-speed chase, etc., than the speaker.
	3.	Doesn't really process what the speaker has said since he or she believes that the speaker's story is not nearly as dangerous or adventurous as his or her own.
The Hand on the Doorknob	1.	Always in a hurry and has little time to waste listening.
	2.	He or she will signal when the conversation is at an end by reaching for the doorknob or placing his or her materials away, regardless of whether or not the speaker has actually completed the conversation.
	3.	Once the listener has indicated that he or she has finished listening, to continue speaking would be futile— nothing is penetrating the "hand on the doorknob" listener's brain.
The Finish the Sentence For You	1.	Will intrude on a speaker to complete the sentence if the speaker pauses.
	2.	Impatient.
	3.	Sure he or she knows what the speaker was going to say next.
The Rapid-Writing Note Taker	1.	Attempts to write everything down on paper that is being said.
	2.	Unfortunately, in attempting to write verbatim what the speaker has said, this individual misses the entire point of the conversation. In the legal field, court reporters are charged with creating verbatim transcripts of depositions, testimony at trials and hearings, and sworn statements. However, other than this profession, few exist which require individuals to

| | write down everything that is being said. |
| | 3. In attempting to write down everything in a presentation or conversation, this listener is missing the main points because he or she is so busy writing that he or she does not have the mental capacity to process the information. |

hear and process them, we have a tendency to let our thoughts drift. We take a mental vacation, perhaps picturing ourselves lying on the beach in the warm sunshine, or tallying a list of items we need to get done today, or even preparing for our next meeting or activity. While we wander away from the speaker, we often lose track of what is being said and have trouble returning our concentration to the matter at hand. Consequently, we find that our efficiency as listeners is very low. In fact, we forget as much as 80 percent of what we hear within the first 24 hours of hearing it.

Emotional distractions are very similar to mental distractions. However, emotional distractions refer more to our overreaction to the words or message that the speaker is delivering. Each of us has a "buzz" word that is capable of diverting our attention away from the message. We then concentrate on the word or phrase and become so preoccupied that we neglect the speaker. A police officer that detests being called a "pig" would become incensed by a perpetrator's use of the term in an interrogation. The question and answer session would be hindered by the officer's emotional response to the use of the word "pig."

<u>Common frame of reference</u>. Another barrier to effective listening stems from the absence of a common frame of reference. The speaker and the listener must have a level of shared knowledge. In other words, they must have a common vocabulary. A probation and parole officer, if using legal terminology, would find it difficult to speak with an individual unfamiliar with the court system. For that reason, the officer would have to use words or phrases common to the individual.

<u>Physical distractions</u>. We have all been in situations where the room was too warm, the noise in the hall outside the door was too loud, or where our stomach was growling from hunger. These are physical distractions that impede our ability to listen actively. Even though it may be difficult to return to listening following one of these physical disruptions, we should try to consciously move back to the speaker as quickly as possible.

<u>Evaluation/Judgment</u>. Unfortunately, we as human beings have a tendency to judge others by their appearance, opinions, or knowledge. Even though we know that you "can't judge a book by its cover," we still make assumptions about others without knowing all the facts. When we make a rush to judge someone, we cease to listen to anything that person has to say. In effect, we shut down and close our minds.

<u>Miscellaneous</u>. Several conditions also exist which might affect our ability to listen. Examples of these conditions are

♦ our interest in the topic or activity

♦   our attitude toward the presenter and subject
♦   any distractions we face, whether emotional, mental, or physical
♦   the nonverbal behavior of the speaker
♦   the time of day for the activity or presentation

Guidelines for Effective Listening

Instruction in listening skills has been neglected in our educational institutions. As mentioned earlier, if we are taught anything about listening, we are taught that we **really don't have to listen**. Educational facilities need to incorporate programs of instruction in listening. However, we may still acquire good listening skills on our own. Some steps for improving your listening ability are as follows:

> **Stop Talking!** Remember, you cannot listen if you have your mouth open.
> **Pay Attention!** Give your full attention to the speaker. You cannot communicate if both parties are not actively involved in the process.
> **Read Nonverbal cues.** Along with hearing and processing the words of the speaker, you should pay careful attention to the nonverbal language being communicated. Watch for eye contact, expressions, gestures, and so on.
> **Ask Questions.** A good way to ensure that you have accurately understood the message is to ask questions of the speaker.
> **Resist Distractions.** Stop doodling! Do not shuffle papers, draw, or doodle when you are listening.
> **Don't Interrupt!** Even though you may get angry or upset by something the speaker says, do not interrupt. Let the speaker finish and resist the temptation to focus on your emotional response to the speaker's words.
> **Open your Mind.** Try to look at the situation from the speaker's point of view and not just your own. Be flexible.
> **Paraphrase.** Use your own words to mirror what you have heard. Restating information in your own words helps you to remember what you have heard.

Criminal Justice Professionals and Oral Communication

Criminal justice professionals are involved in five primary areas of oral communication: responding, reporting, interviewing, interrogating, and testifying. Each area has both a formal and an informal aspect. In the same vein, each component may be delegated to a different level of supervision within the agency. For instance, only in the most extreme cases, or in very small agencies, would the Chief of Police be involved in a suspect interview and/or interrogation. By the same token, rarely do patrol officers make presentations to the city council or mayor. However, every member of a law enforcement agency should be able to speak publicly and to present the agency in the best light possible. Interviewing and interrogating will be discussed further in Chapter 8.

Responding

Two methods are employed for responding to complaints or inquiries from the general public: formal and informal. These responses are also ascribed a certain priority depending upon the nature of the complaint and, unfortunately, the status of the complainant.

The most common type of citizen inquiry or complaint is one made to the chief of police concerning either a local problem (i.e., parking on the street in neighborhoods, barking dogs, etc.) or a complaint about an officer's conduct or behavior. Generally, these issues necessitate a formal written response from the chief or corresponding head of the local law enforcement agency. The chief or other agency head will usually delegate this matter to a first-line supervisor (sergeant) for investigation. However, if the complaint or inquiry is of an extremely sensitive nature, it may be delegated to a mid-level manager or shift commander (lieutenant).

The investigation then follows an established procedure whereby the investigating officer will frequently travel to the area to observe firsthand the nature of the complaint, if possible. This visit may include a personal contact with the complainant as well as interviews with witnesses or neighbors affected by the complaint. The officer will review the local ordinance and/or law specific to the complaint, if such exists, and offer an opinion based upon the officer's interpretation of the statute. At this point, the investigating officer will prepare a formal written report to the chief detailing the findings and analysis of the problem. The officer may make a recommendation based upon a careful examination of the issue. The report is then forwarded to the chief who will review the provided information, formulate an opinion, and prepare a written response to the complainant's inquiry or complaint. The chief is the only person who will issue an official response to the complaint or inquiry.

Informal complaints are generally handled via the telephone or by personal contact with a local or district patrol officer. These issues may be just as significant to the complainant; however, they do not carry the same sense of importance since they are not in written form. Some of the informal issues police officers are asked to resolve involve alien abductions, directions to certain locations, requirements for becoming a police officer, and other sometimes amusing requests. Frequently, the officer will make a spontaneous decision concerning the nature of the problem and the best manner in which to resolve the issue. If the complainant initiates no further contact, the officer considers the problem to have been solved.

Verbal Communication: The Written Component

As explained earlier in this chapter, verbal communication is comprised of two parts—oral and written. Writing is more difficult than speaking because you do not have access to immediate feedback. In essence, you have to be able to communicate your message without the benefit of being able to see the person with whom you are communicating. Written communication may take the form of letters, memoranda, e-mail, or reports. Each of these types of messages has an appropriate use and a corresponding purpose.

1. **Letters**. Letters are used to communicate outside the agency. Typically a criminal justice agency will have an existing letterhead on which all letters must be typed.
2. **Memoranda**. A memorandum is a written message used to communicate within the agency. Traditionally, a memorandum includes the headings "To," "From," "Date," and "Subject."

3.   **E-Mail** (electronic mail). E-mail is a message transmitted electronically via the use of a computer network. E-mail may be sent either within the agency or outside the agency. E-mail's appearance is very similar to a memorandum with the same headings, "To," "From," "Date," and "Subject." E-mail should be given the same considerations as other forms of communication. The rules of grammar, punctuation, and spelling also apply to E-mail.

4.   **Reports**. Reports are documents written in an organized manner used to communicate findings or developments and to provide updates for projects, etc.

While oral communication is important in obtaining and maintaining interest, the written document serves as a permanent record for others to review in the future. In the criminal justice profession, written documentation is vital to the success of any agency.

Writing Techniques: Choosing the Right Words

Our choice of words in written documentation is very important to the effective transfer of information. Improper or inappropriate word choice can hinder even the best attempt at communication. The following principles of word choice should guide you in developing your written documentation.

1.   **Write clearly.** You must write in a complete, accurate manner. Give the reader a message he or she can understand and act on.

A.   <u>Accuracy</u>. As a writer, you must use your integrity to make sure your communications are ethical. Your credibility is the most important facet in communication with others, and if you damage or destroy the trust of your reader through misleading information, you may never be able to repair the damage.

B.   <u>Completeness</u>. Your message must contain all necessary information for the reader to make an informed decision. A good place for you as the writer to start is to develop the five **W's**: who, what, when, where, and why.

C.   <u>Jargon and Word Familiarity</u>. Every field has its own special vocabulary. When communicating with others in your area, the use of jargon is appropriate. However, you should remember that the use of jargon is inappropriate when you are writing for the reader outside your agency. You should strive as a writer to use terms that are familiar both to you and to your reader.

2.   **Use Simple Words**. Using long words in communication is not necessary to achieve your purpose. Short, simple words are a better choice. Your reader is less likely to become confused when you opt for words that convey the precise meaning you desire. You want your readers to focus on the information you are presenting, not on the words themselves.

3.   **Use Concrete Language**. Concrete words give the reader a mental picture of what you mean in your writing. Try to avoid using words such as *several, a number of, a few, a lot of, substantial*, etc. Give definite numbers or specific information.

4. **Avoid the Use of Clichés and Slang.** A **cliché** is an expression that has been overused in our language. Examples might consist of "according to our records," "if you have any further questions," "if I may be of further assistance," "please find enclosed," etc. **Slang** is informal word usage usually identified with a specific group of people. For this reason, you should avoid the use of slang in your writing.

5. **Avoid Wordiness.** Because people are exceedingly busy in today's society, you should strive to be concise in your writing. When one or two words will suffice, why would you use four or more to say, in effect, the same thing? Examples of excessive wordiness would be "enclosed herewith," "enclosed you will find," "a long period of time," "continuous and uninterrupted," and others.

6. **Use Positive Language.** You are more likely to build goodwill with your reader if you write using positive as opposed to negative language. You should attempt to avoid the use of negative or negative-sounding words in your writing. For example, eliminate or minimize the use of words like *cannot, will not, failure, refuse, deny, mistake*, etc.

Developing and Writing Effective Sentences and Paragraphs

In addition to selecting appropriate words, using a variety of sentences in your writing is important to the complete development of logical paragraphs. When we vary our sentence types between simple, compound, and complex, we keep our writing interesting and our reader interested.

➢ A **simple sentence** is one in which you present a single idea.
➢ A **compound sentence** contains two or more independent clauses, each of which presents a complete idea.
➢ A **complex sentence** contains one independent clause and at least one dependent clause. Typically the dependent clauses present additional information that is not as important as that contained in the independent clause.

A **paragraph** is defined as a group of sentences that focus on one main idea or topic. Paragraphs must be unified and give information which is directly related to the topic. This information must be organized in a logical manner and contain all relevant details. Paragraphs also must be cohesive. That is, they must integrate the words together in such a way as to create a relationship between the sentences. Transitional words should be used to join sentences for a step-by-step movement. These "road signs" tell your reader where your message is heading.

You should attempt to control the length of your paragraphs so that you have enough information to support your main idea or topic, but not so long that your important information or ideas get buried in the middle of a long block of unbroken text. Effective paragraphs typically fall somewhere between the 60 to 80 word range.

```
┌─────────────────────────────────────────────────────────────┐
│                   Transitional Expressions                    │
│         also, besides, furthermore, in addition, moreover, too,│
│      as a result, because, consequently, hence, so, therefore, thus, likewise,│
│         although, nevertheless, still, for example, in other words, at last,│
│               finally, in conclusion, meanwhile, since, next   │
└─────────────────────────────────────────────────────────────┘
```

Criminal Justice Professionals and Written Communication

Reporting

The situation or scenario of reporting in a paramilitary organization can be one of the most delicate and politically sensitive actions taken by an agency member. No matter what position you occupy in the chain of command, reporting can always be filled with hazards. The individual department member needs to be aware of the nature of the reporting situation and whether it is formal or informal.

Generally when making a report, the recipient is a "higher" authority in the chain of command. Therefore, the presenter is put at a psychological disadvantage in this reporting situation. For that reason, the presenter must be prepared and rehearsed, when possible. The agency member should be aware of the topic for discussion prior to the actual formal meeting and should attempt to control the environment in which the reporting occurs. In addition to giving the advantage to the presenter, this allows time to properly prepare the report and to rehearse the presentation. The presenter should pay particular attention to any areas that may be sensitive or offensive to the recipient. While certain comments may seem innocuous to the presenter, they may produce or provoke an inadvertent response. An example might occur when an officer must report to the shift commander regarding matters of impropriety with respect to gender or ethnic issues. In this scenario, the officer must be cognizant of the lieutenant's biases in these areas. Occasions have arisen in which inadvertent remarks later impacted an officer's opportunities for promotion or transfer. Every opportunity should be taken to eliminate biased or sexist language from the vocabulary.

Testifying

"In the Fall of 1990, before the Senate Judiciary Committee, chaired by Joseph Biden, when queried on his response to casual drug users, Chief Gates responded the casual drug user ought to be taken out and shot."

. . . .

"They ought to be taken out and shot because if this is a war on drugs, they are giving aid and comfort to the enemy."[8]

Testifying is a recitation of facts or information, under oath, gained during the course of an investigation. Testifying usually involves only those facts of which the officer has direct knowledge. However, in some instances, under specific guidelines officers are allowed to proffer an opinion. Law enforcement officials may be called upon to testify in courtroom proceedings, in depositions, and in sworn statements. Furthermore, in certain select instances, criminal justice professionals may be called upon to testify before governmental bodies such as the Senate Judiciary Committee mentioned in the quote above.

The Officer Speaks in the Courtroom. When an officer testifies in court, he/she is in a confrontational setting. Obviously, the defendant's attorney, in an attempt to seek the best defense possible for his/her client, is going to question the officer's recollection of the facts, gathering of the evidence, procedural propriety, or professional integrity. Frequently, the officer is at a distinct disadvantage in the courtroom setting from an educational standpoint. The major participants in the courtroom all have law degrees or three years' post-graduate education while the typical police officer has a high school diploma or, at most, an associate's degree from a local community college.

Any discrepancy noted in the officer's written reports or testimony will be thoroughly examined. When testifying in a court action, an officer must carefully review all materials prior to taking the stand. Oftentimes, the officer will be prepared by the prosecuting attorney for the types of questions he/she can expect to be asked both by the prosecution and by the defense. The officer has the opportunity to cast him/herself in the best light possible at this point by being prepared.

The Officer gives a Deposition. The courtroom is the legal arena for fact-finding and the determination of guilt or innocence. A deposition, however, is an opportunity for discovery or a "fishing" expedition. The latitude in a sworn deposition with regard to questioning is much broader in scope. Queries made of the officer need not be limited to the parameters of the case at hand. Therefore, an officer's performance in previous cases, matters of professional or career development (with particular regard to previous disciplinary actions due to poor performance or inappropriate behavior), and matters involving an officer's personal life are all open for examination in a deposition. Delving into the officer's life in this way is an attempt to discover any biases or prejudices, which would alter or affect his/her testimony or perception of facts as they relate to the case.

Depositions are stress inducing and frequently confrontational in nature. Even the most patient officer may find that a deposition tests the limits of that patience.

The Officer makes a Sworn Statement. Sworn statements are typically written documents that serve in lieu of an officer's personal appearance in a legal proceeding. More information on sworn statements will be discussed in Chapter 8.

Verbal Communication: The Video Component

Up to this point, the discussion has focused on face-to-face verbal communication. Face-to-face communication is indicative of the old adage, "You can't unring a bell." Once a statement has been made in a one-on-one situation, the information can never be retrieved nor the statement recanted. However, in videotaped communications, the opportunity exists for misstatements or faux pas to be retaped prior to distribution.

While law enforcement officials predominantly rely on face-to-face communication, certain instances exist in which videotaped presentations are more efficient and most cost effective. This is particularly true with regard to training tapes. With the increase in costs associated with training and given that training is essential due to the high incidence of litigation against law enforcement agencies, training tapes are vital to insulating a department against excessive civil judgments.

Training tapes are routinely prepared or created by officers who have a certain area of expertise. Training tapes are also generated quite by accident through the recording of officer/citizen interaction on the street. The use of these tapes allows training officers to continue with their normal duties rather than having to interrupt a busy schedule to instruct in the academy. Furthermore, if travel is involved, these tapes eliminate the costs associated with transportation, room and board for the sponsoring department.

Aside from training tapes, recorded prepared statements to the news media are often used to inform the public of ongoing investigations or critical incidents. The advantage of using recorded statements is that the officer is given the opportunity to review a list of questions the media will ask, to prepare appropriate responses, and to rehearse those responses. The officer must confine his/her responses to only those questions that have been previously submitted. He/She should not attempt to or be lured into responding to questions outside the scope of the current issue. Spontaneity at this point could be extremely detrimental to the integrity of the investigation or the reputation of the department.

Media Relations and Law Enforcement: The History. In the early decades of the twentieth century, law enforcement employed unparalleled support and popularity. With the creation of the FBI, and under J. Edgar Hoover's tutelage, high profile arrests were frequently documented in newspapers across the country. Violent gangsters were arrested by well-dressed and well-educated "G-men" personally selected by the Hoover machine. The media was seldom critical of federal law enforcement. This support may have been the result of good personal relationships between government agents and local newspaper reporters or the result of some government control exercised by local field offices in an attempt to ensure the agency was always portrayed in a positive manner.

Local law enforcement was not as fortunate, however, since scandals involving police officers and deputy sheriffs were frequently reported, and wire services would publish these improprieties nationwide. While Hoover had the wisdom, foresight, and personnel to orchestrate public relations opportunities, local law enforcement was left to its own devices. The chief or sheriff either failed to recognize the public relations value of the local department success or would not fully capitalize upon the success, preferring instead to opt for humility and let the "deed speak for itself." While noble in its sentiment, the humility only garnered brief coverage, which was at best covered only by the local newspaper.

During the 40s and 50s, law enforcement began to lose some of the respectability and credibility associated with federal agencies, and scandals continued to plague cities such as New York, Chicago, and Los Angeles. The media became more sophisticated technologically and procedurally. Local events of note were no longer relegated to just local or regional coverage. Radio and television were able to produce remote broadcasts and taped delays bringing good and bad news to the consumer's living room. Reporters, while still dependent upon police sources, were becoming more dependent upon research. Journalism schools were turning out increasingly better-educated and more sophisticated graduates (interviewers). These interviewers were able to glean significant amounts of information from witnesses and bystanders, and in some cases, became more proficient in gathering information than their law enforcement counterparts.

The civil strife and social unrest of the 60s and 70s set the stage for some of law enforcement's most publicized disasters. Videotapes of Bull Conner in Montgomery, Alabama, allowing police dogs to attack peaceful protestors, Governor George Wallace surrounded by Alabama State Police making his infamous (Segregation now … Segregation forever" remarks, and Chicago police officers clubbing protestors at the 1968 Democratic National Convention all served to embarrass and degrade law enforcement. These agencies "circled the wagons" and attempted to shift the blame to the populace and the situation rather than to attempt damage control by accepting responsibility and promoting new training programs for handling civil disobedience.

In a 1973 *Police Chief* editorial, Don R. Derning, IACP president, stated "The foundation of police/public relations is built on public trust. It cannot be demanded or bought. It must be earned with efficient police service. Communication with the public is a never-ending process and should be viewed as the lifeline between the police and the communities they serve."[9] Furthermore, he advised administrators that only through open and productive lines of communication will support for law enforcement be established. Yet less than five years later, the New York City Police Department, failing to heed Derning's advice, was attempting to minimize the damage of a massive corruption scandal. Frank Serpico, an honest cop and typical of New York's Finest, was on the front page of every New York newspaper in an effort to divert attention from the real issue, the depth and breadth of departmental corruption. Perhaps admitting that the department had serious corruption problems and instituting enforceable sanctions would have been more advantageous to the reputation of the organization, which underwent another massive scandal a decade later.

In October 1978, Mike Brake, a police reporter for the *Oklahoma Journal,* outlined the essential responsibilities for the Public Information Officer as follows:

1. Media accessibility to answer inquiries on matters of public interest.
2. Assistance to the media in developing feature and documentary items.
3. Monitoring media contacts with other agency personnel, and moderately controlling information disseminated by such contacts.
4. Advice to the Command Staff in formulating press policies.
5. Service to the agency in matters requiring journalistic skill, such as the publication of an internal newsletter or the publication of public service materials.[10]

Having created this list, Brake admonished law enforcement executives not to confuse the roles of the PIO and the Community Relations Officer as they are both unique and need to be separate. The PIO needs to maintain continuity of identity as a media liaison in order to sustain efficiency and integrity. Brake believed that the PIO must have the full support of the administration and receive cooperation from all levels of the agency.

In order to staff such a position, officers must possess certain characteristics that promote a rapport with people and establish an aura of credibility. Brake suggested that perhaps civilian personnel would be an excellent choice to fill this position since they possess certain journalistic skills not found in the rank and file of most police agencies and would be intimately familiar with the inner workings of the media. Furthermore, the media may be less likely to view civilian personnel as people with an extraordinary stake in the image of the agency and, therefore, more credible.

Brake concluded that the positive characteristics of a PIO should include

1. A commitment to the free press philosophy, and an aversion to the unfair suppression of information concerning the agency.
2. The ability to work with minimal supervision and control, and a willingness to use the initiative and imagination in dealing with the media.
3. A strong respect for facts, to avoid the slipshod dissemination of erroneous information.
4. A command of written and spoken English, to ensure that press releases, interviews, and other materials distributed to the media and to the public are clear, readable, and not open to misinterpretation.
5. Patience and tactfulness, valuable tools in dealing with an often demanding press.
6. An overview of the agency's structure, policies, operating techniques and personnel, and a thorough knowledge of the criminal justice system.
7. Loyalty to the agency first, then the administrator, to avoid an image as a press agent for the executive.
8. Personal integrity.

Brake's article provided sage advice since nearly twenty years later, in 1995, Ray Surette examined the use of civilian versus sworn personnel in the role of Public Information Officer. His article in the *Journal of Criminal Justice* explored the backgrounds of PIOs and discovered that most civilian PIOs tend to be female with education backgrounds and have prior media-related experience. While their sworn counterparts were male with criminal justice degrees who had little or no media-related experience. Furthermore, the civilian PIOs were more satisfied with their role.

According to Surette, it was not until the 1980s that agencies began to establish formal media relations units.[11] As late as April 1997, Tim McBride, commanding officer of community affairs at the Los Angeles Police Department, announced the hiring of a public relations practitioner stating, "We're cops, we're not PR people."[12] In the wake of the Rodney King beating, the O.J. Simpson trial, and Willie Williams' public dispute with the L.A. Police Commission of the non-renewal of his contract and his threat to sue, the LAPD could use professional public relations assistance.

In 2002, Don Kelly stated "the luxury of deliberation and reflection is disappearing, as the traditional news cycle erodes into a continuous blur. We find ourselves inundated with broad requests, even demands, for information from varied sources, all conditioned to expect immediate answers."[13] With this tremendous demand for information and an omnipresent news media, more and more agencies have come to rely on full-time professional PIOs. Every agency should consider this position a funding priority since the support of the public is essential to the law enforcement mission. An informed and content public will be much more likely to increase funding for local agencies through increased taxes or funding referendums. No police or sheriff's department is without blemishes or problems, but the manner in which they handle these negative events will determine how they are accepted or rejected by their local community. A vital goal and essential quality of law enforcement agencies should be that they are viewed as a community partner and not an occupying force.

Law Enforcement Professionals: Responding to the Media. Aside from training tapes, recorded prepared statements to the news media are often used to inform the public of ongoing investigations or critical incidents. The advantage to the use of recorded statements is that the officer is given the opportunity to review a list of questions the media will ask, to prepare appropriate responses, and to rehearse those responses. The officer must confine his/her responses to only those questions that have been previously submitted. He/She should not attempt to or be lured into responding to questions outside the scope of the current issue. Spontaneity at this point could be extremely detrimental to the integrity of the investigation or the reputation of the department.

On occasion, officers are confronted by news media at the scene of a crime or critical incident. At this point, no opportunity for advance preparation is present. Therefore, the officer must be extremely guarded in his/her response to questions from the media. Officers should inform the media that the investigation is in the preliminary stages and specific details at this time are not available or may serve as a barrier to a successful investigation. The officer should attempt to be candid in his/her statements, but should not allow the media to force a hasty or inappropriate response. Officers need to be wary of the "60 second sound bite." Some reporters or news agencies will attempt to create or capture a headline in order to make the early evening or late news.

Regardless of whether the interview situation is spontaneous or planned, the responding officer should maintain proper decorum and adhere to the fundamentals of proper speech. A short film clip provides the opportunity for an officer to greatly enhance or to rapidly destroy the image of the department due to the tremendous number of viewers. More damage can occur in that 30-second sound bite than the department could incur in 30 years of service to the public. Unfortunately, the adage that may be most appropriate is "often an ounce of perception is worth a pound of performance." Following the guidelines for effective oral presentations affords opportunities for the law enforcement community to enhance its image. As important as good oral communication skills are, communication is a bi-fold process involving both verbal and nonverbal skills. If what the officer says is contradicted by inappropriate nonverbal cues, then the officer's credibility is questioned. Chapter 4 introduces the concepts of nonverbal communication and explains how these skills supplement or complement the spoken word of the officer, and Chapter 3 addresses the visual component of presentations.

Summary

Verbal communication involves both the oral and written facets of communication. Oral communication is a reciprocal process that involves both listening and speaking. Listening is a vitally important skill because we get the information we need to cope with our environment through listening. However, hearing and listening are not synonymous terms. Hearing involves the physiological response to sound while listening is both physical and psychological processing of sound. Many barriers exist to listening, but we should try to overcome our tendency to close our minds to new information.

The written aspect of verbal communication typically involves the preparation of letters, memoranda, e-mail, and reports. In our writing, we should remember to chose our words carefully, trying to maintain clarity and conciseness in our selections. The reader must be able to understand our message, and he or she will not be able to do so if we use jargon or slang inappropriately.

Sentences and paragraphs are important to the logical transfer of information. Simply choosing the appropriate word will not suffice when preparing written communication. Our sentences must vary in length between simple, compound, and complex styles; and our paragraphs should logically develop our main idea or topic while holding to a 60 to 80-word maximum. We should remember to use transitional words in paragraph development so that our sentences flow in a progressive and understandable manner.

Key Terms

Listening	Hearing
Casual or Marginal Listening	Attentive Listening
Active Listening	Acceptance
Empathy	Congruence
Concreteness	The Critic
The Faker	The Continual Talker
The "Hand on the Doorknob" Listener	Letters
The "Make Sure it's Correct" Listener	Memoranda
The "Finish the Sentence for You" Listener	E-Mail
The "Rapid Writing Notetaker" Listener	Reports
The "I'm in a Hurry" Listener	Simple Sentence
The "I've Done One Better" Listener	Compound Sentence
Complex Sentence	Paragraph
Clichés	Slang

Discussion Questions

1.   Differentiate between listening and hearing.
2.   Describe in detail the types of listening. As a criminal justice professional, which type of listening behavior should you engage in and why?
3.   Identify the most important factors that influence our ability to listen.
4.   Identify a word or words that might elicit an emotional response from you and cause you to "tune out" a speaker. Why do you believe this word(s) has the ability to affect you in this way?
5.   As a criminal justice professional, you are often called upon to produce written communication in the form of incident reports, memoranda, etc. Give an example of one way you will attempt to avoid negative language in this written communication.
6.   As a police chief you are in charge of preparing a press release announcing the establishment of a Citizens Police Academy in your city. This press release will appear in the local newspaper and will be recorded for delivery by radio stations in the area. Think about how you can use words, sentences, and paragraphs to explain this addition to your police department.
   A.   What do you want to accomplish with this press release?
   B.   What should you know about your audience(s) before you start to write?

     C.   What jargon or technical terms should you define in this press release? Why?

     D.   Will you use any negative language in this press release? Why or why not?

     E.   Write a concise headline for this press release.

7.   **Ethical Issue:** Should an officer knowingly withhold information in a statement to the press that could later affect the prosecution of a suspect?

8.   **Ethical Issue:** Should an officer attempt to correct a mistake in his notes when giving a deposition?

9.   **Ethical Issue:** When giving a deposition, is it improper for an officer to knowingly withhold information if not specifically asked for that information?

10.   **Ethical Issue:** Should an officer ignore a mistake in previous testimony when the mistake is not specifically brought to the attention of the defense or the court?

11.   **Ethical Issue:** Since a good Public Relations program is built upon trust, would it be appropriate for the Public Information Officer (PIO) to deliberately mislead the press if the information offered would aid in the capture of a suspect or aid in the prosecution of a suspect?

12.   **Ethical Issue:** Would it be improper for the PIO to release information to one reporter prior to releasing the same information to other reporters allowing the first to "scoop" the others on a local newscast?

13.   **Ethical Issue:** Good Public Information Officers know how to "set the stage" for interviews or press releases. Is this sound professional work or manipulating the press?

Notes

1. "Bush Shows Cold Shoulder Across the Pacific." Guardian Unlimited. (n.d.). September 3, 2002 <http://www.guardian.co.uk/korea/article>.

2. "Missile Negotiations." Center for Arms Control and Non-proliferation. (n.d.). September 3, 2002 <http://www.armscontrolcenter.org/prolifproject/southeast_asia>.

3. Marshall, T.A., and Vincent, J., *Improving Listening Skills: Instructional Module for Business Communication Classrooms. Methods, Activities, Evaluations, and Resources.* Published in conjunction with Dr. Mary Ellen Guffey, South-Western College Publishing, 1998.

4. Verderber, R. F., *Communication in Our Lives.* Belmont, CA: Wadsworth, 1999, pp. 130-155.

5. Wood, J. T., *Communication in Our Lives.* Belmont, CA: Wadsworth, 1997, p. 95.

6. Wood, J. T., pp.110-115.

7. Johnson, I.W., and Pearce, C. G., "Assess and Improve your Listening Quotient." *Business Education Forum,* March 1990, pp. 22-27.

8. Gates, D., *Chief: My Life in the LAPD.* Los Angeles: Bantam Books, 1992, p. 286.

9. Derning, D.R., "The True Measure of Police/Public Relations." *The Police Chief,* March 1973, p. 8.

10. Brake, M., "Establishing a Public Information Officer." *FBI Law Enforcement Bulletin,* October 1978, pp. 22-25.

11. Surette, R., "Public Information Officers: A Descriptive Study of Crime News Gatekeepers." *Journal of Criminal Justice, 23,* 1995, pp. 325-336.

12. Statement, A., "LAPD blues." *Public Relations Tactics, 4 (4),* April 1997.

13. Motschall, M., and Cao, L., "An Analysis of the Public Relations Role of the Police/Public Information Officer," *Police Quarterly,* Volume 5, issue 2, pp. 152-180.

CHAPTER 3

PREPARING TO SPEAK:
PRESENTATIONS AND VISUAL AIDS

Learning Objectives:

1.   To compare and contrast formal presentations and everyday speech

2.   To describe the different types of speeches

3.   To develop guidelines for effective speaking

4.   To produce techniques for organizing presentations

5.   To identify methods for developing the speaker's voice

6.   To explain the steps in making an effective oral presentation.

7.   To identify techniques for introducing a speaker's subject

8.   To understand the purpose for using visual aids in a presentation

9.   To identify the types and appropriate uses for visual aids in presentations

10.   To develop guidelines for designing visual aids

11.   To understand how to use visual aids effectively

12.   To understand stage fright and to learn ways to overcome it

President Theodore Roosevelt, a master at garnering the support of the public through his use of language and imagery, was one of the most influential and dynamic leaders of the free world. President George W. Bush, seizing upon this theme, used the backdrop of Mount Rushmore in an attempt to rally the American people in this time of national disaster and recovery following the terrorist attack of September 11, 2001. With Teddy Roosevelt apparently smiling over his shoulder, President Bush returned to the tactics of the "bully pulpit." In a speech made August 15, 2002, before a crowd gathered in front of one of America's most notable national monuments, President Bush made his case to the American people for overriding Congressional restrictions and allowing him to move forward with his vision for America. "But, what a magnificent place on such a beautiful day to talk about America and the challenges we face. I mean, after all, standing here at Mount Rushmore reminds us that a lot of folks came before us to make sure that we are free…. A lot of our predecessors faced hardship and overcame those hardships, because we're Americans.

…

And that's what's going to happen in this era, too. We've got problems, we've got challenges…and we're going to meet those challenges head on. We've got the challenge of fighting and winning in a war against terrorists and we're going to win that war…."

> *President Talks Homeland/Economic Security at Mount Rushmore*
> *The White House Office of the Press Secretary*
> *August 15, 2002*

As children, we all learn that speaking gains us attention. Speaking is how we receive information about our environment, how we garner feedback about our own actions, and what we do to interact socially with others. We control our own and others' behaviors through speaking.

Considering that each of us speaks every day to friends, colleagues, and superiors, you might be prone to wonder why it is that the idea of making a formal presentation is met with such hesitation, angst, and fear. In an examination of anxiety-inducing situations where participants were asked to rank a list of items on the basis of personal fear, public speaking came out as the number one response—even surpassing the fear of death[1]. Despite the shortcomings of speech making, though, researchers and the public alike agree that a charismatic speaker can captivate an audience, communicating logically, clearly, and confidently.

Can good speakers be created or are they born with some innate ability to control an audience? First of all, we must examine the components of formal speech and everyday communication. Everyday speech and formal presentation share several similarities. When we communicate with friends and family, we organize our speech pattern in an orderly fashion. We would never place words in a random order. When we describe our new job, we would not say "officer police to hired start week in a was as I one." Our thoughts must be organized in a logical way so that we can communicate with others. Then we must construct our conversation using a common language. Even if our thoughts and words are organized logically, in order to communicate with another, we must share a system of language.

We speak to tell a story, building from the least important fact to the most important fact. Consider how you tell a funny story or joke to your friends. Do you start with the punch line? No, you begin with the main points of the story or joke and build the momentum of your conversation so that when the punch line is delivered, your audience is hanging on your every word in order to get the full value of the story or joke.

	Everyday Speech versus Formal Presentations
Similarities	1. Orderly 2. Builds from least important to most important 3. Common language
Differences	1. Time constraints 2. Formal language 3. Location 4. Topic 5. Posture

Just as similarities exist between everyday conversation and formal presentation, so too do differences. In a formal presentation or speech, you are usually required to adhere to certain guidelines concerning the location of the presentation, the amount of time available for you to speak, and the topic you must speak on. For example, a corrections officer asked to speak at one of the weekly meetings of the local Rotary Club will be told the date and place of the meeting as well as the amount of time he or she will be given to speak and a selection of topics the membership has expressed interest in. The officer will then be required to put the information into a formal speech, allowing for time and audience constraints.

While everyday speech is often filled with "colorful metaphors," a formal presentation is much more restrictive. Profanity and "off-color jokes" are inappropriate in this setting. Also, in everyday communication, we tend to be very relaxed in our posture and often to lean on desks, chairs, and any available object. In formal situations, however, you should remember to stand up straight and not to rely on any "crutch" when delivering your speech.[2]

Purposes of Speeches

The first step in preparing a speech is to determine the purpose–what you want to accomplish with your speech. Speeches predominantly have three purposes: **to inform, to persuade, or to entertain**. In each situation, however, the subject matter, the situation, and the persons involved vary.

After deciding the purpose of your speech, the second step in your preparation involves analyzing the audience. You will need to know whether you will have a large, medium, or small audience and what the age, gender, educational levels, experience, and attitudes of the audience are, particularly as they relate to your topic.[3]

To accommodate the varying levels of involvement, four basic speech formats exist—the **impromptu style**, the **extemporaneous style**, the **manuscript style**, and the **memorized style**[4].

Impromptu Style Speech

An impromptu speech is one that involves little or no preparation. This style of speech is spontaneous and occurs commonly in small groups and one-on-one situations. Rarely are we asked to give an impromptu speech in a large group or public gathering. When we are asked to deliver an impromptu speech in a large group, the situation often dictates that we are asked to "say a few words" or to "offer a comment."

Impromptu speeches present a challenge to the speaker—to be able to "think on your feet.[5]" Since you have no preparation time, you must be able to adjust your comments and material for the audience, time, and place.

Extemporaneous Style Speech

Extemporaneous speeches are both spontaneous and planned. They are planned because you know ahead of time that you are going to be asked to speak on a certain topic. They are spontaneous, however, from the standpoint of delivery. You do not memorize your speech, nor do you read it; you deliver the speech and make adjustments in your remarks to meet the needs of the audience and the situation. For example, the speaker might prepare a brief outline on his or her topic using index cards. The speaker then proceeds to speak from the outline, filling in the information as he or she moves along. This type of speech allows the speaker to have a great deal of interaction with the audience and to concentrate more on sharing ideas with the audience rather than on delivering the message. And since it involves a conversational and interactive manner that is generally very effective with listeners, the extemporaneous style of speech is the most popular of all the presentational styles.

Manuscript Style Speech

Many people are afraid of trying to speak spontaneously. They are also afraid of memorizing a speech because they tend to sound wooden and to create the impression in the audience that the speech is memorized. Therefore, they choose what they consider to be the next best thing to memorization—reading the speech in its entirety.

Adults dislike nothing more than having an entire speech **read** to them. When a speaker engages in this type of speaking, he or she is implying that the audience is too unsophisticated to be able to properly read and comprehend the speech themselves. Or, perhaps the speaker is indicating that the audience is incompetent or incapable of reading at all! If you plan to read your speech to the audience, just hand out copies and forget about the presentation. Let the audience read the speech for themselves.

In addition to the implied problems already mentioned with a manuscript style speech, a speaker who chooses this type of presentation loses the ability to interact with the audience. In fact, no eye contact can occur between the speaker and the audience when the speaker's eyes are focused solely on the material being read. If by chance the speaker does attempt to make some eye contact during the speech delivery, he risks the possibility of losing his place and becoming embarrassed as he searches to regain it.

The old expression, "never say never," is true about the speech that is read, however. If I were to advise you to **never** read a speech, you would be receiving some faulty advice! If you must present very technical data that cannot be properly committed to memory or which cannot be spoken about spontaneously, you should read that portion of your speech containing the technical facts. In addition, if you are required to address a controversial topic where the need for precision is vitally important, you should write and then read your comments. A good example in police work involves the media questioning a department representative concerning a crime. The officer's best response is to plan ahead. Write down as many details of the crime as can be legally and ethically released and then read the statement to the reporters. In this way, the officer ensures the proper release of information in a precise manner without fear of being caught off guard or ill prepared.

Memorized Style Speech

A memorized speech really needs no definition since it is exactly what its name implies—a speech which you, the speaker, memorized prior to its delivery. A memorized speech has many disadvantages, the most important one being that a speaker who uses this method of delivery loses the ability to change or modify the speech to accommodate the audience. Also, if for some reason the speaker needed to deviate from the memorized speech, he or she would have difficulty returning to the original point—possibly even forgetting everything and being unable to continue. The major weakness with the memorized speech is that the speaker is so obsessed with simply getting the words of the speech out, that he or she cannot pay attention to details such as delivery style and listener interaction.

Guidelines for an Effective Oral Presentation

Many things affect the preparation and delivery of an effective speech or presentation. The purpose of the speech, the audience, the location, your choice of vocabulary, your voice control and gestures all play a role in the process. The most important things to remember in any presentation, however, are your purpose and your audience. To whom are you speaking and why are you speaking to them?

Your Purpose

You cannot prepare for a presentation without first knowing what you want to accomplish in that presentation. Do you want to persuade the members of your community to increase the number of police officers in your district? Do you want to inform your subordinates of important ways to prepare written communication within the department? Regardless of the goal of your presentation, you must have a plan of direction for your speech. A good rule of thumb is to ask yourself, "At the conclusion of my presentation, what do I want my audience (listeners) to remember or do?"

Your Audience/Listeners

Since the audience is one of the first priorities in the development of the presentation, you must have as much background information as possible in that regard. Language skills, biases, educational backgrounds, and other demographics play a major role in the acceptance and/or rejection of your ideas, concepts, or findings. Also, you must be aware of the existing knowledge of your audience as well as how vocal the audience is likely to be concerning your topic of presentation. Some specific questions to consider concerning your audience are as follows:

> ➢ How will this topic appeal to this audience?
> ➢ How can I relate this information to their needs?
> ➢ How can I earn respect so they accept my message?
> ➢ Which of the following would be most effective in making my point? Statistics? Graphic Illustrations? Demonstrations? Case histories? Analogies? Cost figures?
> ➢ What measures must I take to ensure that this audience remembers my main points? (Guffey, 1997, pp., 482-83)

Knowing something about the general characteristics of your listeners may suggest what type of evidence and which authorities will be most effective with them. For example, citing statistics may bore many listeners, but if you are speaking with a group of criminal justice professionals interested in the United States' increasing crime rate, you will find them to be interested in your topic. While demographic information does not offer precise insight into any particular individual, this analysis can offer you some general information about groups of people.[6]

Organizing Your Presentation

Once the purpose of your speech and the characteristics of your audience have been identified, steps toward the preparation of your oral presentation may be initiated. Your presentation must be clear, concise, and complete. However, in some situations, in order to protect the integrity of an ongoing investigation or because of the sensitive nature of certain personnel matters, the presentation of some facts may need to be selectively screened or omitted. The selective screening or omission of information is not intended to deceive but merely to ensure the preservation of these matters.

The Perception of the Speaker

The audience in any presentation looks to the speaker for information. That information must be given in a manner that is easily understood by the audience. In that regard, speakers must be aware of several aspects of speech development: language, biases, and delivery. Language patterns should be appropriate for the average educational background and knowledge levels of the audience. Jargon and slang may be appropriate in certain agency presentations but may be inappropriate or offensive to general audiences. Also, grammar and pronunciation skills are vitally important to the audience's perception of the speaker. If an officer responds with an air of confidence, "Nobody done nothing wrong," certain audiences would likely disregard the statement believing the officer to be ill- or under-educated and, therefore, ill-informed or even deceptive. In essence, the officer's veracity is in question. However, the officer who boldly states, "At this time, proper procedure appears to have been followed," not only enhances individual credibility but departmental integrity as well. This officer is perceived by most audiences to be competent and truthful.

The Speaker's Voice

The quality of the speaker's voice and the way a speaker moves during a presentation are elements of the delivery. In order to deliver a successful presentation, loudness, pitch, rate, pauses, articulation, and pronunciation must be considered.

Loudness refers to the volume of the speaker's voice. An audience must be able to hear the speaker, but the speaker must be able to project his/her voice without shouting. However, the speaker must remember to regulate the loudness of his/her voice based on the size of the room and the acoustics.

Pitch defines how high or low the speaker's voice sounds. Appropriate modulation of the pitch enhances certain elements of a presentation. A monotone voice does not denote severity or the gravity of a situation. Frequently, law enforcement officers, in an effort to project a serious image, utilize a monotone. The use of a monotone voice only serves to guarantee that the listener will be easily distracted and that the content of the message will be weakened or lost.

Rate deals with the speed with which the speaker talks. Speakers who speak too rapidly give the impression that they are deceptive or attempting to "gloss over" certain facts. On the other hand, speakers who talk too slowly give the impression of being dim-witted or poorly prepared. Varying the rate of speech is particularly appropriate and effective when the speaker is attempting to emphasize a certain point or to recount familiar material.

Pauses can add emphasis, power, and effective timing to the delivery of presentations. Pauses may add dramatic effect to particular points in a story and may influence the impact of a joke or a series of rhetorical questions, a quotation, or a visual aid. These pauses should be planned in advance for maximum impact in your presentation. Unplanned vocal pauses (umms, ers, you know, ahs), however, detract from the presentation and reduce the speaker's credibility.

Articulation and pronunciation refer to the manner in which the speaker vocalizes words in the presentation. While certain variations in pronunciation exist due to international or regional dialects, mispronunciation may hinder an otherwise effective speaker. Southerners have a tendency to drop the "g" from the endings of words. This speech pattern, though, is not representative of mispronunciation but is part of the colloquialism pattern associated with the Southern dialect. However, if a person used the term "dashhound" instead of "dachshund" to refer to a particular breed of dog, this would be indicative of a mispronunciation.

The Parts of an Oral Presentation or Speech

Speeches and oral presentations have many things in common with written reports and other documentation. First of all, they all have a beginning, a middle, and an ending. As such, the parts of an oral presentation or speech include an introduction, the body of the speech, and a conclusion. In essence, you should introduce the topic, tell your audience what you plan to say; effectively say what you intended to say; and then conclude with a review of what you just said.

You should also remember to include **verbal signposts** in your speech. Since your audience/listeners cannot flip back through the pages of your speech to review the main points, many of them get lost along the way. A good way to ensure that your audience is able to identify the main points of your presentation is to include verbal signposts. These "notices of information to come" help your listeners to follow the presentation. The following verbal signposts are some examples of previews, summaries, and transitions:

> ➢ **To Preview**
> The next portion of my presentation discusses five reasons . . .
> Let's now examine the problems associated with . . .
> ➢ **To Summarize**
> Let's review the major issues I've just addressed . . .
> As you can see, the most significant contributions are . . .
> ➢ **To Switch Directions**
> Thus far we've discussed . . .; now let's examine . . .
> I have argued my position that . . . but an alternate view is . . . (Guffey, 1997)

The use of transitional words or phrases also helps to improve your oral presentation. Words like *therefore, moreover, however, on the other hand, in conclusion, first, second, next,* and *in conclusion* emphasize your points and lead your audience/listeners in the direction you are headed.

The Introduction. The introduction to a speech or oral presentation should account for no more than 10 percent of the entire presentation. In the first 60 to 90 seconds of the presentation, the audience decides whether the speech has any merit and whether or not to pay attention to the speaker. "The opening of your presentation should strive to accomplish three specific goals:

> ◆ Capture listeners' attention and get them involved.
> ◆ Identify yourself and establish your credibility.
> ◆ Preview your main points." (Guffey, 1997, p. 483)

Some techniques for effectively introducing your subject are as follows:
1.   Ask a question. As a speaker, asking a rhetorical question encourages the audience to think of responses without actually answering your question aloud. Generally a speaker proposes rhetorical questions to an audience because he or she plans to answer those questions during the course of the presentation.
2.   Tell a funny story or joke. Using humor is one of the most effective ways of capturing the attention of an audience. Humor establishes an immediate connection between the audience and the speaker.
   3.   Use an anecdote. Recount a short, entertaining account of some event.
   4.   Make a startling statement. Say something unexpected. Remember, however, there is a difference between the effective startling statement and

the offensive shock tactic. Using profanity or telling offensive jokes reduces credibility.

5.   <u>Quote someone</u>. Quoting a well-known authority on your subject matter adds credibility to your speech or presentation.

6.   <u>Demonstrate something</u>. Bring in prototypes or samples to demonstrate a process or product. Demonstrations are attention-grabbers.

<u>The body</u>. The body is the heart of your speech or presentation and should receive the most attention and should account for the most speaking time. Support your main points through evidence, statistics, brief or extended examples, testimony, quotations, or analogies. An important point to remember is that listeners have a limited ability to absorb information. As a rule, limit your presentation to between two and five main points. Support each of those points with a minimal amount of explanation and detail. Remember to keep the information simple and to the point. Unlike a book, a speech offers the audience no material or pages to review. One caveat to remember—always prepare more material than you think you will need. Experienced presenters know that it is important to have something in reserve in the event that they finish earlier than anticipated.

<u>The conclusion</u>. The conclusion of a speech or oral presentation serves four important functions: to summarize your message, to place your message in a broad context, to personalize your message, and to call for specific future action. The conclusion should, like the introduction, take about 10 percent of the presentation time. The speaker may use the same techniques in the conclusion as in the introduction—anecdotes, rhetorical questions, quotes, demonstrations, startling statements, and humor.

You should never end a presentation with a statement such as "I guess that's all I have." Remember that the conclusion is your last chance to make sure that audience gets your main points. Use this opportunity to review your major points and focus on the goal of your speech. You should specifically concentrate on what you want your audience to remember, to do, or to think. Use some of the remaining time to ask for questions. If the audience is hesitant, you could offer to take individual questions following the completion of the presentation.

Using Visuals in Your Presentation

The impact of a visual aid should never be underestimated. Visual aids can be an exciting and dramatic addition to any speaker's presentation. If properly prepared, the visual aid may increase the speaker's ability to establish a point and may enhance retention by the audience members.

Visual aids serve two basic purposes: (1) to enhance a presentation by reinforcing the important points covered in the presentation and (2) to provide the speaker with an alternate delivery method or system. The use of visuals in a presentation gives the speaker an opportunity to redirect the audience's attention away from him/her so that any anxiety (stage fright) can be minimized. Visuals may be utilized in the form of an introduction or segue or as a conclusion to a presentation.[7]

Types of Visual Aids

The choice of visual aid for a presentation may vary widely, anything from models and objects to overhead transparencies and slides are possible. In selecting visual aids, the speaker must adhere to certain guidelines with regard to the purpose of the speech, the size of the audience, the environment or location of the presentation, and the speaker's skill and expertise in utilizing the selected medium. Remember that visual aids complement a presentation, not stand in the place of the presentation.

Objects and Models. In order to use objects or models as visuals in a presentation, the environment or location must be small in scope. Attempting to pass an object or model around a room of several hundred people would be ill advised. Attention would be focused away from the speaker and on the object/model and its position in the audience. However, in intimate group settings, the utilization of models or objects is entirely appropriate when the presentation would be enhanced by their use.

Flip Charts, Chalk- and Marker Boards, and Posters. These media are most useful when presenting information to small interactive groups. They provide an excellent opportunity for problem-solving or idea-generating discussions. These media enhance speaker/audience interaction by allowing the speaker to ask questions and then to record key ideas as they are contributed.

Handouts. Speakers often use handouts as reference materials for the audience. However, timing of the distribution of handouts is important to the success of the presentation. Many speakers hand out printed materials as they speak so that the audience may refer to them. If the material is particularly complex, then the distribution of the handouts at the beginning of the presentation might be beneficial. When the handout is merely to reinforce the important points covered in the presentation, however, delaying the distribution until the conclusion of the presentation would be the better option.

Overhead Transparencies. Overhead transparencies are the most popular presentation medium. They are easy to create, do not require the room to be totally darkened in order to project them, and are flexible in that you can supplement or highlight a concept while it is being shown.

Computer-Generated Presentations. Software packages such as Microsoft's PowerPoint and Corel's Presentations have allowed speakers to create computer-generated slides. These packages offer the speaker options such as embedding sounds, animation, and video clips to enhance the quality of their presentation. A drawback, however, to the use of these types of media is the cost factor. Using software for presentations requires the purchase of a variety of hardware and software. Furthermore, the speaker must be well trained in the integration of the various hardware and software components.

Table 2-1 compares the features of some of the visual aides that we have examined in this section.

Designing Visual Aids

In today's technological society, some speakers have a tendency to become dependent on the use of visuals in a presentation. However, the excessive use of visual aids detracts from the effectiveness of the message. A caveat to keep in mind is that visuals should supplement your presentation and should reinforce important points. Also, be aware of your description of the visual. Do not repeat everything contained on the visual when it is displayed. Allow the audience to scan the information projected on the visual by pausing after the initial main point. Speaking on top of the visual only forces the audience to choose between what you are saying and what the visual is projecting. In essence, you are competing with your own visual for the audience's attention.

The following guidelines are useful in the development and design of effective visual aids:

Simplicity. In the design of visual aids, particularly computer-generated slides and transparencies, the speaker should remember to adhere to the "6 x 6" rule. This rule states that, per slide or per transparency, a maximum of six lines of text containing six words per line should be utilized. For a majority of individuals, processing more than seven points of information at any given time may be too complex or even impossible. In order to insure that the speaker's message is communicated in a simple and direct manner, visuals should be limited to a series of related concepts.

Table 3-1. <u>Some Examples of Visual Aids used in Presentations</u>[8]

Type of Visual	Audience/ Environment	Advantages	Disadvantages
Flip charts, chalk- and marker-boards	Small (2-200) Informal	1. Aids in organization 2. Helps to summarize 3. Low human error 4. Informal 5. Flexible	1. Not very dramatic 2. No "bells and whistles"
Overhead Transparencies	Medium to Large (2-200) Formal or Informal	1. Portable 2. Flexible 3. Easily tailored to different groups 4. Easy to use	1. Limited visual impact 2. Can be distracting
Computer-Generated Presentations	Medium to Large (2-200) Formal or Informal	1. High impact 2. Easily tailored to different groups 3. Flexible 4. Very persuasive 5. Able to show motion or animation and to use sound bites	1. Expense 2. Requires technical skills 3. May overshadow the speaker or the topic being presented 4. May provide more flash than substance 5. Not easily transportable 6. Requires equipment
Handouts	Any size (Unlimited)	1. Easy 2. Portable 3. Relatively	1. Not flexible 2. Can be bulky 3. When to distribute

	Formal or Informal	inexpensive 4. Aids in organization 5. Serves as reminder of presentation	4. Generate minimal impact

<u>Size</u>. The total size of the audience is equal to the total size of the visual plus the total size of the print/font used in the visual. The larger the audience, the greater the overall size of the visual and the greater the size of the print/font within the visual. In this manner, all audience members are afforded an opportunity to clearly see and to process the information contained in the visual.

<u>Color</u>. Color can enhance the effectiveness of a visual when it is used correctly, making the visual easier to read and more attractive. However, when used incorrectly, color has the opposite effect on the visual, making it more difficult to read. Research has indicated that blue backgrounds for computer-generated presentations are the most effective. Using a yellow or white type on the blue background produces the best results among all audiences. Since more males than females are color blind, the use of colors like red and green or red and blue as contrasting background and print selections, may render those visuals useless to a significant portion of the audience. Remember to use the same color palette for every visual and to maintain the same print type or style throughout.

Points to Remember in Using Visual Aids Effectively

Visual aids are an enhancement to any presentation and should be used whenever possible. However, a few rules apply which will make your presentation run smoother.

- **Avoid overdoing it.** Some people believe that if a few visuals are good, then a lot of them must be better. You should refrain from adopting this attitude. Visual aids should be used only for major points or for information requiring clarification. Too many visuals will impact their effectiveness. If your audience would find a visual helpful in understanding a particular point in your speech or in remembering important ideas, then a visual aid at that point in the presentation would be appropriate. However, if the use of a visual (regardless of how exciting it would be) does not contribute to your overall presentation in terms of the audience's understanding, then do not use the visual.[9]
- **Refrain from cramming too much information on each visual**. Remember the 6 x 6 rule: Use only 6 lines of text per slide/transparency and include only 6 words per line of text. Each visual should headline one major point.
- **Use appropriate text/type styles**. Remember that everyone in the room needs to be able to see and read your visuals. Be sure you use the correct size type (font) so your visual can be seen from any point in the room
- **Allow appropriate time for the audience to read and digest information on the visual**. Put the visual up so the audience can see it. Then give them time to read and digest the information before you begin explaining it to them. You should paraphrase what the visual says and not read it word for word.
- **Practice, practice, practice!** When you rehearse your presentation, include the use of visuals in your preparation. Make sure you know how to use the equipment properly and

that you allow sufficient time for the audience to read the visual. **Remember**: Always speak to your audience—not to your visual.

- **Prepare for problems!** The best intentions of every speaker in the use of visuals are often sidetracked by failures in technology, air carriers who lose or misdirect luggage, mail and/or package services that "fail to deliver," and any number of incidents or accidents outside the realm of the speaker's control. The best plan of defense for these types of problems is an adequate offense: **have a backup plan!**

A. In the instance where you have chosen to use a Power Point presentation as the visual in your speech, a good rule of thumb to remember is that in the event of computer failure, disk destruction, and/or incompatible software packages, you can always rely on transparencies and handouts. Therefore, as the speaker you should always prepare

    1. a set of transparencies of your Power Point presentation (usually an overhead projector is available at most sites where public speeches are scheduled),

    2. enough sets of handouts of your presentation to give to each attendee at your speech, and/or

    3. one full copy of each slide you would project through your Power Point presentation printed on regular computer paper using a color printer. In the event that the venue where your speech is scheduled has a document camera and projection unit, you would be able to project each slide onto a screen, thereby giving the audience the full effect of the color presentation they would have gotten through Power Point.

B. A good point to reinforce here is that you should always keep your visual with you. If you are traveling by air, you should make sure your visual (whether a presentation that is stored on a disk or on the hard drive of your laptop computer, an object, handouts, etc.) is included in your carry-on luggage. This small acquiescence to discomfort at being unable to check your briefcase or laptop case will ensure that your presentation arrives at your destination at the same time you arrive. Thus, you eliminate the possibility of the "lost" or "misdirected" luggage problem. Additionally, if you carry your own visual with you to your speech destination, you also eliminate the need for a mail or package carrier service. Again, you are planning ahead by handling your own visual needs and not relying on others to ensure its/their arrival.

C. Another means of insuring your speech will occur without problem is to get an adequate estimate of the number of attendees at your presentation. By having an accurate count of those individuals who will be present at your speech, you will be able to photocopy enough handouts to distribute at your presentation so that each person gets his or her own copy. Always err on the side of too many handout copies rather than too few. If you are given an estimate of 30 attendees, make 40 copies of your handouts to take with you. Again, you will be better prepared with too many copies than too few.

Overcoming Barriers to Effective Presentations

Stage fright is a natural occurrence. Nearly every person suffers from some form of stage fright. Being afraid results from physiological responses or changes in our bodies that occur when we are faced with threatening situations. The "fight-or-flight" syndrome provides your body with increased energy to deal with those situations. The dry mouth, sweaty hands, increased heartbeat, and butterflies in your stomach are all responses to your body's perceived threat.

Ask any speaker if he or she suffers from stage fright, and you will find that the honest ones all admit they do. Consequently, all effective presenters know that successful presentations do not just happen; they require practice. By thoroughly preparing and rehearsing presentations, stage fright can be lessened. Realize that fear is not an either-or matter, but more a matter of degree. Most of us fall between the two extremes of no nervousness at all and total fear.[10] According to research conducted by Gerald Phillips[11], a speech scholar, nervousness helps us to do our best job. If we are unconcerned about a presentation, we will probably not put forth our best effort and thus, we will not do our best job. Keep in mind these reassuring facts about stage fright:

a. Very few people are unable to make it through a speech, despite their nervousness. You may not enjoy your experience, but you can still deliver an effective speech.

b. Members of an audience are not as likely to recognize your stage fright as you might think.

c. When you are well prepared, your nervousness will be lessened. You show more nervousness when you are not well prepared or when you believe you are not well prepared.

d. Speak as often as you can. Volunteer to make speeches or presentations whenever possible. Experience is the best teacher and offers you an opportunity to gain confidence in your ability.[12]

Checklist for Preparing and Organizing Oral Presentations[13]

Getting Ready to Speak

□ *Identify your purpose*. Decide what you want your audience to believe, to remember, or to do when you finish. Aim your speech toward this purpose.

□ *Analyze the audience*. Examine the demographic make-up of your audience and adapt your message toward their knowledge and needs.

Organizing the Introduction

□ *Get the audience involved*. Begin your speech with an attention-getting opener. You can ask a question, tell a story, give a startling fact, use a quote, make a promise, or tell a self-effacing joke.

□ *Establish yourself*. You need to identify yourself, your position, your expertise, knowledge, and qualifications so that you establish your credibility.

□ *Preview your main points*. Introduce your topic and give a summary of the principal parts of your presentation.

Organizing the Body

- ❑ *Develop two to four main points*. Focus on two to four major issues so that you can streamline your overall topic.
- ❑ *Arrange the points logically*. Sequence your points either chronologically, from most important to least important, by comparison and contrast, or by some other strategy.
- ❑ *Prepare transitions*. Use bridge statements between each major point so that you connect each item to the next item. Use transitional words or expressions as verbal signposts (to tell your audience where you are going to take them next). Examples of transitions include *first, second, then, however, consequently, on the contrary,* etc.
- ❑ *Have extra material ready*. Always be prepared for the unknown. Be prepared with more information and/or visuals in case you have additional time to fill.

Organizing the Conclusion

- ❑ *Review your main points*. Emphasize your main ideas in the conclusion so that your audience will remember them.
- ❑ *Provide a final focus*. Close by telling your audience how they can use the information you have provided, why you have spoken, or what you want them to do.

Designing Visual Aids

- ❑ *Select your medium carefully*. Consider the size of your audience, the degree of desired formality in this presentation, the cost and ease of preparation of visuals, and potential effectiveness.
- ❑ *Highlight main ideas*. Use visual aids to illustrate major points only. Keep them brief and simple.
- ❑ *Use aids skillfully*. Talk to the audience–not the visuals. Paraphrase the content of the visuals; do not read their content to the audience.

Developing Electronic Presentations

- ❑ *Learn to use your software program*. Know the basics of using the software such as template and slide layout designs and how you can adapt them to your needs.
- ❑ *Select a pleasing color palette*. Work with five or fewer colors for your entire presentation.
- ❑ *Use bulleted points for major headings*. Make sure your points are all parallel and follow the 6x6 rule.

Prior to your Presentation

1. **Prepare!** Thorough preparation is one of the most effective ways to reduce stage fright. When you know your subject matter, you feel more confident. People who try to "wing it," are the ones who suffer the worst butterflies—and the ones who make the worst presentation.[14]

2.   **Rehearse.** Rehearsing involves practicing your entire presentation. You can use note cards on which to place your topic sentences. Use your cards as you practice, and remember to include visual aids in your practice sessions as well.

A good way to check your presentation savvy is to videotape or audiotape your practice sessions. Make your practice session as similar to the speech situation as possible. When you view your videotaped practice session, concentrate on your message and delivery style. In particular pay attention to

- ➤ **your speed**. Are you speaking too fast? Too slow?
- ➤ **your volume**. Are you speaking too softly? Can everyone in the room hear you?
- ➤ **your nonverbal message**. Are you engaging in any annoying habits such as jingling the coins or keys in your pants pocket, tugging on your clothes, swaying, puling on your hair (or ears), stroking your beard or mustache, etc.?
- ➤ **your enthusiasm**. Are you excited and animated during your presentation? Are you speaking in a monotone and boring the audience?

3.   **Time your presentation**. When you are given the opportunity, you want to limit your presentation to no more than 20 minutes since most audiences tend to lose interest if you go longer than that. However, the length of your presentation will depend on its purpose. Are you trying to inform, persuade, or entertain your audience? What is the message you want your audience to remember from your presentation? When your goal has been decided for your speech, all preparation has been concluded, and you are ready to begin practice, you should use a kitchen timer to practice your presentation. Begin speaking and continue speaking until your presentation is complete in its entirety, even if the timer sounds. You will need to know exactly how much time your speech takes so that you can modify areas where you can eliminate excess material to keep your presentation within the allotted time period.

4.   **Check your location**. You have spent a great deal of time and effort in the preparation for your presentation. You have researched your topic and your audience, planned and drafted your speech outline, and practiced your delivery. Now comes the next step—checking out the location of your presentation. You need to know what to expect in the room where you plan to present. As soon as possible, you should either visit the site of your presentation or contact the person who arranged for you to speak and ask for details. You need to know how large the room is so you can plan most adequately for the appropriate visuals. You also need to know what type of audiovisual equipment is available in the room and whether you will need to wear a microphone or to stand behind a podium or lectern. On the day of your presentation, you should plan to arrive at least one hour before your presentation to double check the room, to correct any problems, and to mentally prepare yourself.

5.   **Breathe!** While waiting to begin your presentation, use deep breathing techniques to help you relax. Take in deep breaths and let them out slowly. Count to 10 as

you inhale and exhale. Realize that you are prepared for this speech. Feel confident of your ability.

The Presentation

The moment has arrived for you to make your presentation. The following list of guidelines will help you make the best out of your speaking opportunity.

1. Calmly walk to the podium, lectern, or the front of the room. Take a moment to gather your thoughts and to take a deep breath. **Relax!**

2. Begin your presentation with direct eye contact. You can establish a rapport with your audience when you establish eye contact and maintain it. You also appear confident and knowledgeable. Try to maintain eye contact through your entire presentation. Remember not to pick out one or two people in the room to focus on. You will make these individuals very uncomfortable if you look only at them and others may feel uncomfortable from the message you are conveying. Try to establish eye contact with several members of your audience around the room. Try to hold eye contact with your audience members for a few seconds and then move on to others.

3. Moderate your speed and vocalics. Sometimes speakers have a tendency to rush or to talk rapidly because they are nervous. Another noticeable sign of unease are fillers like *um, ah, er*, and *you know*. You can just remain silent while thinking of your next idea since silence is preferable to a speech punctuated by ah, um, and er.

    If you happen to stumble in your presentation, just move on. Do not apologize or confess to being nervous. The audience might not have noticed your faux pas anyway, and if they did, they tend to quickly forget mistakes.

4. If you plan to move around during your presentation, do so naturally and casually. Just remember not to pace—otherwise you will resemble one of the shooting games at the fair and **you** will be the target people are trying to hit! Pacing is not a natural or casual movement!

5. Remember to use your visual aids and to follow the outline for your speech. Summarize your presentation and conclude when you say, "In conclusion." The audience does not appreciate your talking for 5 or 10 more minutes after you have announced your intent to conclude.

6. When you have finished your presentation, ask for questions—when the situation allows. Try to repeat a question when it is asked so you can be sure everyone in the room heard it. Repeating the question also gives you time to formulate your response.

7. If you have prepared handouts for the audience, you should wait until the conclusion of your presentation before distributing them. If you offer handouts to the audience in advance of or at the beginning of your presentation, you risk losing a high percentage of your audience. The distraction of pages turning and audience members reading ahead and ignoring the speaking are not conducive to an effective presentation.

8.   At the conclusion of your presentation, remember to express appreciation to your audience for allowing you the opportunity to speak with them.

Summary

Planning and delivering formal presentations is an important facet of your work life, regardless of your position. Police and corrections officers are often asked to appear at civic organizations' meetings to discuss a topic of concern to the membership. The media expects interviews to discuss criminal occurrences in the community. Officers must testify in court and at depositions. Understanding how to handle these situations can make your presentations run more smoothly and can produce a better rapport with your peers, subordinates, and superiors.

Terms to Remember

memorized speech	verbal signposts
impromptu speech	objects and models
speech that is read	flip charts
extemporaneous speech	handouts
loudness	simplicity
pitch	size
rate	color
pauses	stage fright
articulation	pronunciation

Discussion Questions

1.   As a juvenile detention officer, you have been asked to make a presentation at the local Rotary Club luncheon. You have been told that your time frame will be 20-30 minutes. The meeting will be held at the local Holiday Inn in Meeting Room C. The membership of the organization would like to hear about the new juvenile detention facility being constructed in the county. What steps should you take in developing your presentation?

2.   Two criminals escaped from the maximum-security prison located in your community. As the Warden of the prison you have been contacted by the media for a statement. Your investigation has revealed a possible location for the escapees, but you are not absolutely sure of their whereabouts. Prepare a statement for the media taking into consideration the information you have available and being careful not to divulge too much in case the escapees are listening to the transmission.

3.   As a city police officer, you have been invited to the elementary school (grades K-5) to talk to the students about crime and how to protect themselves. Several recent occurrences where a strange man attempted to entice children into his van after school has led the school board to request that you specifically talk to the children about these types of situations. How would you develop your presentation? Prepare an outline of the speech you would give to the students. Would you use visuals? Why or why not?

4.   **Ethical Issue**: As the Chief/Sheriff of your department, you have been invited by a civic group to make a speech on the community's declining crime rate to a very affluent body

of corporate leaders. Realizing that your officers need bulletproof vests, would be inappropriate for you to attempt to solicit funds during your speech to this group for the purchase of these vests?

5. **Ethical Issue**: As the Shift Commander, you have been asked by the Chief to make a few remarks at the retirement dinner of one of your officers. You have had conflicts with this officer's style of policing and you have had to discipline this officer on three recent occasions. How should you approach your assignment? What should be the content of your speech?

Notes

1. "Speaking Effectively to One or One Thousand," CRM Films, 1995.
2. Lucas, S.E., *The Art of Public Speaking.* New York: McGraw-Hill, Inc., 1995.
3. Guffey, M.E., *Business Communication: Process and Product.* Cincinnati, OH: South-Western College Publishing, 2000, p. 462.
4. Wood, J. T., *Communication in Our Lives.* Belmont, CA: Wadsworth, 1997, pp. 398-400.
5. Ibid, p. 398.
6. Ibid, p. 336.
7. Guffey, pp. 467-473.
8. Guffey, p. 468.
9. Verderber, R. F., *Communicate!,* Belmont, CA: Wadsworth, 1999.
10. Ibid, pp. 391-92.
11. Phillips, G. M., *Communication Incompetencies: A Theory of Training Oral Performance Behavior,* Carbondale, IL: Southern Illinois University Press, 1991.
12. Verderber, pp. 393-94.
13. Guffey, pp. 478-80.
14. Ibid, p. 475.

CHAPTER 4

ACTIONS SPEAK LOUDER THAN WORDS: NONVERBAL COMMUNICATION

Learning Objectives:

1. To identify the functions of nonverbal communication.

2. To describe the different types of nonverbal communication.

3. To classify the categories of body language.

4. To interpret nonverbal behaviors in criminal justice settings.

5. To identify limitations and exceptions to nonverbal communication.

The O.J. Simpson case has been called "the Trial of the Century" for many reasons. Ms case was the first one in history in which a popular public figure was arrested and tried/or murder. The Simpson case also polarized the nation, placing those who believed in his innocence on one side and those sure of his guilt on the other. Allowing cameras into the courtroom provided the average American a glimpse into the lifestyle of the rich defendant, into the arena where the battle lines were drawn by Marsha Clark and Johnny Cochran, and into the theater where the actors were trying to prove beyond a reasonable doubt that Mr. Simpson was guilty or innocent.

During the course of the Simpson trial, an abundance of evidence was presented by both sides—prosecution and defense alike. Argument ensued as to what evidence would or should be allowed. One piece of evidence that received a great deal of heated discourse was the bloody gloves. Can anyone ever forget the day Johnny Cochran, Simpson's attorney, had him try on the bloody gloves for the jury? Mr. Cochran's statement, "If the glove doesn't fit, then you must acquit, " became a slogan for the defense.

The day Mr. Simpson was asked to put on the gloves, he was first gloved with sterile latex gloves. He then had the once bloody but now dry gloves placed on his hands, and they did not fit. Mr. Simpson went to great lengths to demonstrate to his audience through his nonverbal behavior that the gloves did not fit. He held his hands up to show that they were too small for him. His exaggerated physical behaviors were meant to illustrate to all who were watching that he was an innocent man because the gloves did not fit And the mantra continued for the remainder of the trial— "If the glove doesn't fit, then you must acquit."

As briefly discussed in Chapter 1, nonverbal communication involves more than merely "body language." Nonverbal communication includes the individual's use of personal space, gestures, touch, voice, and objects. While understanding nonverbal communication can be important to the average individual, the criminal justice professional should learn to interpret body signals as a means of protection, self-preservation, and deception.

The Functions of Nonverbal Communication[1]

Nonverbal communication's functions are both wide and varied—contradicting, complementing, substituting, accenting, or regulating verbal messages.

Contradicting nonverbal communication occurs when a person's words and actions do not express the same or similar meanings. An example would be a potential witness to a crime who says he or she saw nothing when questioned by an officer but who refuses to look the officer in the eye when making this denial. Contradicting verbal messages with body language, vocalics, gestures, etc., creates the potential for misunderstandings between the officer and the public. Distrust arises when people see that an officer's actions do not support the spoken message.

Complementing and **accenting** nonverbal communication are similar in nature. Complementing behaviors occur when the actions expressed complete the picture created by the verbal message. Normally the complementing behaviors are widely accepted ones such as a hug when telling a parent you love him/her. The nonverbal hug complements or completes the verbal message of the expression of love.

Accenting nonverbal communication is the result of actions which stress the underlying meaning of the verbal message. Using an upraised hand to signal a driver to stop is one example of an accenting behavior. Also, following an anger-producing scene, if an officer slams the door on the cruiser when loading a prisoner, he or she is expressing the rage or frustration caused by the arrest. The slamming of the door is an accenting behavior which emphasizes the officer's feelings of anger.

Substituting nonverbal communication involves the use of symbols to replace the verbal message. Law enforcement officials utilize substituting nonverbal communication through uniforms, badges, night sticks, blue lights, etc. No words have to be spoken in order for a police officer to be identified if he/she is wearing a uniform or driving a marked vehicle. Substituting nonverbal communication also occurs in the use of certain street signs (pedestrian crossing, merging traffic, right lane/left lane ends, etc.). The universal symbol for "No" (see figure at right) is also a substituting nonverbal communication tool.

Regulating nonverbal communication serves as a governor in verbal communication. To fully understand this concept, picture a presidential debate with the two candidates and the moderator. The moderator acts as the official timekeeper and lets each party know when his or her allotted time to speak is finished. In interpersonal communication, no moderator is present when two parties converse. Therefore, nonverbal cues serve as the regulator in the conversation. A pause in the conversation, a raised hand, a quizzical look—any of these behaviors may signal a desire by one of the parties to speak.

Regardless of its function, nonverbal communication is composed of a variety of aspects: the body (kinesics), the voice (paralanguage), objects (proxemics), and touch (haptics). Each component is a distinct facet of any communication process.

Kinesics: The Science of Body Language

Rarely do we convey our messages verbally. Instead, we use gestures involving the body to indicate disbelief, puzzlement, protection, indifference, intimacy, impatience, or forgetfulness. Most of our gestures are conscious-we realize we are raising our eyebrow in disbelief, tapping our fingers for impatience, and shrugging our shoulders for indifference. While these acts are predominantly deliberate, some gestures are mostly unconscious-we do not always realize that we rub our nose when we are puzzled, or that we clasp our arms to protect ourselves from a perceived verbal or physical threat. Nonetheless, these "signals" can be vitally important in the interpretation of messages between two individuals.

Kinesics, the study of body movements in communication, has been classified into nine categories: **emblems, illustrators, affect displays, regulators, adaptors, body size and shape, posture and gestures, the face and head,** and **eye movement.**

- ► **Emblems** approximate sign language and are intentional gestures which have a universal meaning. Examples of emblems in our culture would be the "V" sign for peace or the hitchhiker's thumb.

- ► **Illustrators** help to support or underscore the verbal message we are attempting to deliver. For example, a witness describing the size or shape of an object used by a suspect during the course of a crime might use his or her hands to form the shape or dimensions of the object.

- ► **Affect displays** typically involve the face and are movements which show the emotional condition of the person speaking. Affect displays are impossible to intentionally control because they involve our facial expressions. Since affect displays are truthful reports of what we are feeling, they often contradict our verbal message. Wide eyes and pursed lips in a witness conveys that he or she is frightened or anxious. An astute criminal justice professional would recognize this affect display and make arrangements to reduce the witness's fear and/or anxiety.

- ► **Regulators** involve head and eye movements and vocalizations which are use to regulate a conversation. Rapid head nodding coupled with an upheld palm signal to the speaker to pause so that me listener can comment. On the other hand, slow, periodic nods from the listener indicate that he or she is listening and understands the message, and further, that the speaker should continue talking.

- ► **Adaptors** are unconscious motions, tics, or gestures we use as a means of dealing with stress or anxiety, or to adjust to an unusual situation. Examples of adaptors would be drumming fingers, tapping feet, shaking leg, cracking knuckles, stroking the chin or the beard, smoothing or twisting the hair, and tugging at the ears.

- ► **Body** size **and shape** have long been associated with certain stereotypical characteristics or traits. Three body types identified through previous research are **endomorphs, ectomorphs,** and **mesomorphs.** Each of these body types has distinctive behavioral attributes affiliated with it. In the same vein as body size and shape are other body features that convey nonverbal cues. These features include skin color, gender, physical handicaps, blemishes, hair color, and body odor.

Body Type	**Characteristics**
Endomorphs **Description**: short, fat, round	► Sympathetic ► Warm ► Sociable ► Soft-hearted ► Content ► Affable
Ectomorphs **Description**: tall, thin	► Shy ► Tense ► Cautious ► Serious ► Self-conscious
Mesomorphs	► Active ► Cheerful

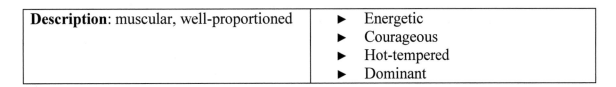

Description: muscular, well-proportioned	▶ Energetic
	▶ Courageous
	▶ Hot-tempered
	▶ Dominant

Posture and gestures are learned responses-which-we acquire throughout our early socialization. This category of body language tends to be bound to the culture in which we are raised. In other words, we tend to lean forward toward a speaker when we like and are interested in the speaker. If we lean backward, away from the speaker, however, we are expressing dislike or disinterest. Posture also is a status indicator. Persons of high status in criminal justice agencies typically assume a more open and relaxed posture when in the presence of lower status individuals.

The face and head are probably the most expressive nonverbal communicators. Since we tend to have the remainder of our bodies clothed, the face and head are the most exposed body parts, thereby drawing the most attention to them. The face tends to communicate the most information because emotions tend to be intensified through facial expression. The position of the head also conveys many nonverbal signals. For example, cocking the head back slowly indicates disbelief or doubt. A bowed head reveals a shy, withdrawn individual; whereas an upright head indicates confidence and interest.

Eye movement is one of the most important facets of nonverbal communication. The eyes can provide many cues in conversation. They can be used to read the response of a listener, to regulate or control the speaker, to express interest or involvement. Two patterns of eye contact associated with doubt or suspicion are the **eye dart** and the slow **blink.** The **eye dart** occurs when an individual is unable to maintain eye contact for a reasonable amount of time (between 10 seconds and 1 minute or more). In essence, their eyes are constantly darting from place to place, usually conveying disinterest or dishonesty. The **slow blink** occurs when a person closes his or her eyes for 2 to 4 seconds and then slowly opens them. If a person is condescending or impatient, the slow blink conveys disinterest or superiority.

Paralinguistics: The Voice

When you speak, you add a dimension to your words. The way you speak can often change the meaning of the words you spoke—even contradicting their actual meaning. Paralinguistics deals with the way something is said rather than what the spoken words actually were. Essentially we are looking at the characteristics of the voice. Paralinguistics typically consists of four categories: **voice qualities, vocal characterizers, vocal qualifiers,** and **vocal** segregates.

> **Voice qualities** include things associated with the voice such as pitch, rhythm, tempo, and volume. Voice qualities can make a tremendous difference in theperception of the spoken word. For example, a high-pitched voice indicates anger, but moderate rate, pitch, and volume indicate boredom.

▶ **Vocal characterizers** include things such as grunting, clearing the throat, awning, and coughing. Characterizers should be avoided when speaking because they are very annoying.

> ▶ **Vocal qualifiers** refer to changes in tone or volume of speech. A good method for illustrating how vocal qualifiers can change the nonverbal meaning of a sentence can be obtained by repeating the statement, "I didn't say he stole your car," seven times; each time place the emphasis on a different word in the sentence.
> ▶ **Vocal segregates** are nonfluencies or periods of silence between words. Nonfluencies are identified as the ahs, urns, etc., which you utter in speaking.

Proxemics: Space and Objects[2]

People communicate much about themselves and their feelings or relationships with others by the amount of space they maintain between them. Our approach to personal space is tied to our culture. As long as we and others maintain what we consider to be the appropriate amount of personal space, we do not feel threatened. However, if these zones are violated, we become nervous and uncomfortable, causing communication to be inhibited. Most Americans observe the following space zones relative to the concomitant situation:

Intimate:	0 to 18 inches
Personal:	1½ to 4 feet
Social:	4 to 12 feet
Public:	more than 12 feet

In addition to space, proxemics refers to the use of objects in communication, one of which may be our personal attire. As humans, we have three basic reasons why we clothe ourselves:

1. To protect ourselves from the elements.
2. To obey the laws of civility and modesty.
3. To look good to others.

Our clothing reflects many characteristics such as image, power, wealth, authority, and mood. In essence, the way we dress communicates to others **who we are, what we are,** and **how important we are to the world.**

Haptics: Touch

Shaking hands has become a universal greeting. Giving someone a "high five" or a pat on the back communicates "job well done" or "good work." Perhaps no other form of nonverbal communication causes as much physical reaction as touch. We judge others based on the strength or weakness of a handshake. However, we reserve hugs for those persons closest to us (i.e., family, friends, significant others); and if we receive a hug from someone outside our inner circle, our response is vastly different.

The following table presents a list of the most common nonverbal cues and their "perceived meanings."

Nonverbal Behavior	Perceived Meaning
Bouncing your leg	▶ Impatience ▶ Urgency ▶ Lack of Interest
Nodding you head	▶ Approval ▶ Encouragement ▶ Understanding
Raising an eyebrow	▶ Disbelief ▶ Questioning ▶ Surprise
Remaining silent	▶ Concentration ▶ Interest ▶ Respect
Slouching shoulders	▶ Tired ▶ Unenthusiastic ▶ Discouraged
Looking away	▶ Impatience ▶ Distraction ▶ Lack of interest

Interpreting Nonverbal Body Language in Criminal Justice Professions

The eyes have often been called "the windows to the soul." When you consider the fact that so many of our personal feelings are unconsciously mirrored in our eyes, you can understand that statement much better. The key for a criminal justice professional is to learn to "read" those visual clues so that information is not overlooked.

Much research has been conducted in an attempt to understand nonverbal communication, and most studies have produced similar findings. From this information, conclusions have been drawn with regard to certain nonverbal cues and their concomitant meanings. In particular, the FBI has identified types of behaviors which occur spontaneously during interviews under stressful conditions. Body movements, personal distance, facial color, facial expressions, and paralanguage offer insight into a subject's truthfulness. Learning to interpret this nonverbal behavior correctly could result in a successful resolution of an ongoing investigation, whether through additional leads or clarification of a verbal statement.

Body Movements. Movement of various body parts is the least controllable nonverbal characteristic. You have probably met or know someone who finds it necessary to "speak" with his or her hands. In fact, if you were to tie that individual's hands to his or her sides, no communication would be possible. Just as these natural gestures occur unconsciously, so too do those movements which are deceptive in nature. A suspect or parolee who has a calm, emotionless face but who constantly shifts his hands, arms, legs, and feet is conveying a message of deception. A witness, suspect, or parolee who does not lean forward and who moves his or her legs and feet during an interview is not being entirely truthful.

Hands and arms also provide critical insight into an individual. Arms folded tightly across the chest signify refusal or defiance. Arms loosely folded convey relaxation. If this gesture is difficult to interpret merely from the arms, the hands provide additional information. If the hands are closed in a fist or tightly grasping the biceps, this supports the refusal or defiance state; open and relaxed means the individual is relaxed.

In addition, drumming or tapping fingers is indicative of nervousness and often associated with deceit. While a person who makes hand-to-chest gestures is generally considered honest, one who makes a hand-to-mouth gesture is communicating self-doubt and is believed to be lying. As a matter of fact, truthful individuals most often gesture away from their body while liars tend to gesture toward themselves.

Leg and knee movements also provide nonverbal signals. When an interviewer asks particularly probing, critical questions, he or she may notice an increase in movement in the suspect's legs, indicating nervousness. Individuals may also use their legs as barriers by crossing them. When their legs are crossed, suspects are erecting a barrier to the interrogator and his or her questions. A suspect feels much more comfortable in this protected environment he or she has created. Leg crossing behaviors are also used by the suspect to stall. The suspect may listen to the question, but before responding, he or she will break eye contact, cross or uncross the legs, and then after he or she is completely settled, respond to the question.

In addition, movement of the knees can be a means for handling a stressful environment. A suspect may wobble his or her knees back and forth in an effort to diffuse a tense situation. The more stress the person is under, the faster the knee movements.

As a final caveat concerning body movements, criminal justice professionals should keep in mind that deceitful people are often aware of delaying tactics involving nonverbal communication. Any grooming gestures or clothing adjustments that allow the suspect or witness to busy his or her hands and allow a delay in responding to any questions also provide the individual with an opportunity to release his or her anxiety before answering.

Proxemics-Space and Objects. As indicated earlier in the chapter, Americans have a zone of protective space with which we surround ourselves. This personal space varies from as far away as four feet to as close as six inches, depending on the relationship the individuals share. Criminal Justice professionals can make use of the personal space zone in interrogation and interviewing settings. A good interviewer creates high levels of anxiety by beginning an interrogation session at a comfortable distance from the suspect or witness and by asking for general information. As the questions begin to center more on the subject at hand, the interviewer moves closer to the suspect or witness and backs off during desired responses. In this manner, the interviewer is programming the witness or suspect to provide the desired information in a cooperative manner. A psychologically normal person experiences a high level of anxiety when his or her personal space is invaded in this manner. Moreover, an individual finds it increasingly difficult to lie in this type of situation.

In law enforcement, objects such as tables, chairs, books, and other items that may be found in an interrogation or interviewing room may unfortunately aid the suspect or witness. Any kind of obstacle of this nature may give the suspect or witness a certain amount of confidence and relief. These obstacles prohibit invasion of the individual's personal space zone, thereby preventing the officer from achieving the goals of an interview or interrogation.

Facial Color. When an individual lies, the body responds through physiological changes. Perspiring, flushing or paleness of the skin, an increased pulse rate, and the appearance of veins in the head, neck, and throat are all signs that the individual is not being truthful. Also, if the person stutters, appears to have a dry tongue or mouth, exhibits changes in breathing, licks his or her lips, and has thickening speech, the officer should view these as indicators of deception.

Dramatic changes in facial color signal that our bodies are under stress. In an interview, criminal justice professionals may notice that a suspect's face and the sides of his neck turn chalky white. In a "fight or flight" situation, the body's response is to cause the cutaneous capillaries on the surface of the skin to constrict in order to provide more blood flow to the deep muscles and the core of the body. Since the blood in the cutaneous capillaries is what contributes to our skin tone, the removal of this pigment will make the skin appear lighter.

Conversely, in a situation where the interrogator is asking "hot" questions, he or she may notice that the suspect's neck and face begin to redden. The suspect's blood pressure has become elevated and the same cutaneous capillaries are now dilated. The interrogator may notice the reddening crawl up the suspect's neck and face. The whites of the eyes may even become red, as may the insides of the ears.

Facial Expressions. Facial asymmetry is a noticeable fact. The two halves of an individual's face are not identical-one nostril may be larger or one eye may sag more. When a person smiles or makes another facial expression, one side of the mouth may droop more than the other or one nostril may flair more. Spontaneous facial expressions tend to produce muscle movements which are about the same on both sides of the face. When a subject is attempting to be deceitful, the muscles on the left side of the face move more than those on the right.[4] Using these facial cues, an astute law enforcement officer may be able to detect whether a person is being sincere.

What accounts for this difference in facial muscular movement? When a person exhibits a spontaneous facial movement, such as a smile, it bypasses the brain's cognitive centers. When an individual attempts to regulate a facial movement, the signals to move the required muscles pass through the cortex of the brain, the center of conscious decisions. Because the portion of the cortex involved in this process has close ties to the left side of the body, the greater movement of facial muscles occurs on the left.[5]

Aside from the asymmetrical facial cues an officer may receive in an interview or interrogation, the eyes are also particularly helpful in ascertaining deceit and truthfulness. When an individual is being intentionally deceitful, "the eye-blink rate will increase significantly from one blink every few seconds to one to two blinks per second."[6] Internal stress will also cause a suspect's eyes to open wider than usual. Of course, the usual avoidance of direct eye contact, or looking away when responding to questions, provides additional clues to a suspect's deceit. Remember that a certain amount of eye movement is normal, but you may spot a trend when you probe into specific areas. Eyebrows are another facial feature that communicate nonverbally. The eyebrows enhance the expressions of the eyes and the rest of the face. When the subject is responding in anger, the eyebrows form a "V" shape with the tips of the eyebrows pointing downward toward the nose. When the subject experiences shock or surprise, you will notice the eyebrows raise high on the brow. The interviewer may have caught the suspect off guard by the particular area of inquiry you were pursuing. The interviewer should then vigorously continue along this line of questioning since there appears to be some unresolved issue surrounding this specific area.

Another part of facial expression involves the nose. In fact, the nose is the most stress sensitive part of the body. During the same "fight or flight" response as we have discussed previously, the nose also undergoes several physiological changes. The tissue in the nose will become engorged with blood when an increase in blood pressure occurs, and this same tissue will constrict as blood pressure drops. Since an interrogation involves constant changes in heart rate and blood pressure, the resulting response is a stimulation of the nasal membranes. The only way a suspect can deal with this stimulation is by touching, scratching, pinching, or massaging.

Paralanguage (the voice). Everyone at one time or another has heard the expression, "It wasn't what he said; it was how he said it." Paralanguage refers to the manner in which an individual speaks and of all the characteristics of the voice. The focus is not on the words themselves but rather on the manner in which the words are spoken. Pitch, loudness, rate of speech, voice quality, vocal segregates, and nonfluencies are characteristics of paralanguage that can aid in the identification of deception. Suspects who attempt deception will be less fluent and stutter more often. Also, these individuals will provide answers that are less believable and longer, and they will use more nonfluencies and repeated phrases throughout their responses. In addition, as these suspects become more nervous, they often respond in a high-pitched voice with heightened quivering or other breakers, they have a slower rate of speech with a longer hesitation prior to answering, and they volunteer less information.

Limitations and Exceptions to Nonverbal Communication

Accurate interpretation of nonverbal communication comes with experience and practice. Since nonverbal communication is as individualized as a person's speaking style, the longer you know an individual, the more adept you become at correctly interpreting his or her nonverbal signals. However, nonverbal communication is not the same for all cultures. In addition, nonverbal behaviors of mentally disabled individuals also vary. In Chapter 10 of this text, we will offer a full discussion on communication issues (including nonverbal) between criminal justice professionals and special populations such as the mentally handicapped, the elderly, youth, and those from different cultural and ethnic backgrounds.

No dictionary of nonverbal cues exists from which you might learn all you need to know about this issue. Observing an experienced successful interviewer is a good place to start your learning process, though. Nonetheless, an important note to remember is that nonverbal communication has limitations and exceptions just as any other form of communication. Keep the following in mind when interviewing or interrogating suspects and witnesses:

1. The intelligence of the suspect. The higher the intelligence of the suspect, the more reliable the behavior exhibited. Low intelligence individuals may not completely understand the questions and their behaviors are less reliable.

2. Emotional stability of the suspect. When the suspect has serious emotional or psychological problems, you cannot place reliability on the individual's behaviors.

3. Children and juveniles. These individuals may not have a developed sense of social responsibility, and the lack of fear of the consequences of their actions leads to the lack of reliable behavior.

4. <u>Drugs and alcohol.</u> The use of drugs and alcohol modifies the behavior of suspects. If possible, the investigating officer should wait until such time as the individual is free from the influence of these agents before questioning him or her.

5. <u>Cultural differences.</u> In revealing findings from his research, Fast stated that "the average man, unschooled in cultural nuances of body language, often misinterprets what he sees."[7] The best advice to the investigating officer is to know the culture with which you are dealing.

As a criminal justice professional, increasing your awareness and understanding of the impact of nonverbal communication can ensure continued success in the area of interviewing and interrogation. Again, you should avoid the belief that nonverbal behaviors mean the same across all cultures; and you should refrain from stereotyping individuals based on nonverbal qualities. Practice in recognizing the importance of nonverbal behavior in communication will promote success in all areas of criminal justice. The first step in identifying and understanding nonverbal communication comes through recognizing your own behaviors. The checklist below provides you with some tips for improving your nonverbal communication.

Checklist for Improving Your Nonverbal Communication

✓ **Establish and maintain** eye contact. Appropriate eye contact indicates interest and credibility.

✓ **Use posture to indicate interest.** Lean forward, sit or stand erect, and look alert so that you show interest in the subject.

✓ **Reduce or eliminate physical barriers.** Where possible, remove desks, chairs, and any other barriers. Step out from behind the desk unless you are engaged in an interrogation where the desk is serving an environmental purpose.

✓ **Improve your decoding skills.** Watch facial and body language to process and comprehend the entire message.

✓ **Probe for more information.** If nonverbal cues contradict the spoken message, you should politely seek more information.

✓ **Avoid assigning nonverbal meanings out of context.** Understand a situation or culture before you make nonverbal assessments.

Summary

Nonverbal communication is not an exact science. No dictionary exists in which we can search for the meaning of a gesture or touch. We predominantly rely on the socialization we have received as children to teach us the meanings of nonverbal communication. As such, our nonverbal behaviors vary from culture to culture. Americans have a great need for personal space and feel threatened when that space is invaded by "outsiders." We also place a great deal of emphasis on eye contact, believing that deception is conveyed by those who fail to meet and maintain eye contact with us.

In the criminal justice profession, nonverbal communication plays a vital role in determining the truth or falsehood of suspect and witness statements. A novice investigator may experience great difficulty in recognizing the nonverbal behaviors of suspects or witnesses. The only way to improve your skill and enhance your ability to reach the truth is to work with others who are more experienced in the interpretation of nonverbal behaviors.

Key Terms

Contradicting	Complementing
Accenting	Substituting
Regulating	Kinesics
Emblems	Illustrators
Affect Displays	Regulators
Adaptors	Endomorphs
Ectomorphs	Mesomorphs
Eye Dart	Slow Blink
Paralinguistics	Voice Qualities
Vocal Characterizers	Vocal Qualifiers
Vocal Segregates	Proxemics
Haptics	Paralanguage

Discussion Questions

1. Compare and contrast verbal and nonverbal communication.
2. List the specific functions of nonverbal communication and give an example of each. Discuss the limitations of nonverbal communication. Give a criminal justice example of how misinterpretation of a message can be traced to one or more of these limitations.
3. A suspect has volunteered to take a lie detector test to prove his innocence concerning a recent homicide. What role will nonverbal communication play in this lie detector test? Can the nonverbal behavior of the suspect have an impact on the outcome of the lie detector test? Why or why not?
4. Each courtroom has pre-established boundaries and barriers, a part of nonverbal communication called proxemics. List and explain each object and its corresponding nonverbal purpose. *Example: The judge's robe; communicates professionalism, power, authority.*
5. How might nonverbal communication assist a probation and parole officer when he or she is assigned a new parolee? What behaviors would the officer need to look for?
6. List as many nonverbal behaviors as possible. Create "definitions" for these behaviors. In other words, list the nonverbal action and describe what you believe the action indicates.[8]
7. Your Opinion: Do you believe nonverbal communication is more important, as important, or less important in the criminal justice professions than it is in everyday life. Why or why not?
8. **Ethical Issue:** When a uniformed officer approaches a vehicle or a citizen what distinguishes confidence from arrogance?

9. **Ethical Issue:** Should officers be allowed to use psychological ploys to secure information from reluctant or hesitant suspects?
10. **Ethical Issue:** Should nonverbal cues, without verbal confirmation, be allowed as sufficient probable cause for an arrest? Can you identify situations where this might occur?

Notes

1. Galle, W., Nelson B., Luce, D., and Villere, W. *Business Communication.* Columbus, OH: McGraw-Hill/Irwin. 1997.
2. Mausehand, J., & Timm, S. "Teaching Strategies for Nonverbal Skills." *Instructional Strategies: An Applied Research Series.* Little Rock, AR: Delta Pi Epsilon. Volume 10, Issue 3, 1994.
3. Chang, R Y. *Success Through Teamwork.* Richard Chang Associates.
4. Goleman, D., & Freeman, J. *What Psychology Knows That Everyone Should.* Lexington, MA: Lewis Publishers. 1982.
5. Goleman, D. "Can You Tell When Someone is Lying to You?" Psychology Today, 17. 1982.

CHAPTER 5

GRAMMAR: A LESSON IN THE BASICS

Learning Objectives:

1. To identify the parts of speech.

2. To identify the different categories of nouns.

3. To explain the types of pronouns and their corresponding uses.

4. To recognize irregular verbs and to identify how their past tenses are formed.

5. To understand errors in verb usage and how to avoid them.

6. To differentiate between adjectives and adverbs.

7. To recognize prepositions and errors to avoid in their usage.

8. To identify parts of a sentence.

9. To define sentence fragment and run-on sentence.

10. To understand how to correct comma splices.

11. To recognize frequently confused words.

Incident reports are one type of written communication investigating officers are required to prepare. Just as details of the incident must be accurate, so too must the words used to describe the situation. Consider the following example of a robbery incident report:

> "I, Officer Jackson, arrived at the location of West 47th and 17th Streets at 05:30. And apon my arrivel I spoke to the victim a Mr. Mike Parks. I asked Mr. Parks what had happened and Mr. Parks stated that he was walking home from work, when he crossed the alley way between Little's Bookstore and Dr. Greens florist a noise startiled Mr. Parks so he turned to see what the noise was and at that momement Mr. Parks states that a man with a gun pulled Mr. Parks into the alley way and toled Mr. Parks to give him all of his money and watch. The man then pistol wiped Mr.Parks. After taking his statement I called in the detectives and waited for their arrivel. I cleared the scene upon their arrivel."

After reading this excerpt from an actual incident report, do you know what took place? Between the misspelled words and the run-on sentences, this incident report makes virtually no sense. Imagine the impression your department would create if this document were to be introduced as evidence into a court of law. Imagine if you were Officer Sharf; how would you feel if your superior officer asked you to explain your report since he or she could not understand it?

A review of grammar and the role that it plays in written and spoken communication is essential to this text. Criminal justice professionals must be able to write clearly and coherently. Excerpts from reports are often introduced into court proceedings, and superiors review them as part of the investigative process. While entire books have been devoted to the subject of grammar, this chapter will merely review some of the most important aspects of grammar as well as introduce some commonly misused words in the English language. Criminal justice professionals frequently prepare reports, memoranda, and other intra- and inter-departmental documentation. These documents may be reviewed by judges, attorneys, the mayor, and other city officials who form their impressions of you and your organization or department from this writing sample. Therefore, it is imperative that you make the best impression possible by ensuring that your writing sample is grammatically sound and free from error.

Parts of Speech

The eight traditional parts of speech are nouns, adjectives, adverbs, pronouns, conjunctions, prepositions, verbs, and interjections.

Nouns. A **noun** is typically referred to as a person, place, thing, or idea. Most nouns are **common** nouns. They name any one of a class or kind of people, places, or things. A **proper** noun is the official name of a particular person, place, or thing and should always begin with a capital letter. Proper nouns include personal names, names of nationalities and religions, geographic names, names of holidays, and names of time units (i.e., months, days of the week).

Proper Nouns	**Common Nouns**
We'll go to the mall **Saturday**.	What **day** would you like to go?
I was born in **March**.	This **city** is beautiful!
My horse is in **Mexico**.	What is your **religion**?

Nouns are also categorized as **concrete** or **abstract**. Because the things they name are physical, tangible, and visible, they are **concrete nouns**. On the other hand, **abstract nouns** name a mental quality or concept, something that exists only in our minds. A review of the following list reveals that many criminal justice concepts fall into the category of abstract nouns.

Concrete Nouns	**Abstract Nouns**
Book	Truth
Plant	Justice
Court	Mankind
Sentence	Idea
Magazine	Love

Up to this point, we have examined nouns in their singular forms. Another example is a noun used to describe a group of people or things that is considered a single unit. This unit is referred to as a **collective noun**. Some examples of collective nouns follow:

orchestra	family	band
herd	flock	chorus
gang	Congress	audience
team	majority	bunch
group	personnel	crowd

The difficulty with collective nouns is in deciding what form of the verb to use with them in a sentence. Is the collective noun singular or is it plural? The answer depends on the meaning of the sentence and where the emphasis is placed. For example, if you are referring to individual members of the group, the plural verb is required. If you are focusing on the group in its entirety, the singular verb is used.

Singular: The **chorus** meets at noon every day.
Plural: The **chorus** are unable to work together.

Collective nouns also can be used in the plural form—i.e., orchestras, teams, audiences, etc.—when you are referring to more than one group.

In fact, most nouns can be either singular or plural. The greatest majority of them will form their plural by adding an "s" to the end of the word.

Singular	**Plural**
Desk	Desks
Boy	Boys
Letter	Letters
Report	Reports
Book	Books

However, four exceptions to this rule for forming plural nouns exist.

1.   **If the word ends in "y" and is preceded by a consonant**. Change the "y" to "i" and add "es."

Forty	Forties
Country	Countries
Lady	Ladies
Category	Categories
Baby	Babies

2.   **If the last sound in the word is "s," "z," "ch," "sh," or "x,"** then "es" is added to form the plural so that the word is easier to pronounce.

Class	Classes
Fish	Fishes
Kiss	Kisses
Match	Matches

3.   **If the "ch" ending to a word is pronounced "k,"** only "s" is added.

Stomach	Stomachs
Monarch	Monarchs

4.   **If a one-syllable word ends in "f" or "fe,"** then form the plural by changing the "f" or "fe" to "ves."

Half	Halves
Wife	Wives
Life	Lives
Leaf	Leaves

Of course, there are always exceptions to the rule. In this case, **chief and roof** form their plurals by simply adding "s" to the end.

Pronouns. **Pronouns** are used to refer to people, places, or things that have already been mentioned in the sentence. They usually replace some noun. The noun for which the pronoun stands (or replaces) is called an **antecedent**. The antecedent usually comes before the pronoun in the sentence or paragraph. The pronoun and its antecedent must agree in number, gender, and person. That means if you have a plural noun (antecedent), then your pronoun should also be plural. Further, if you have a feminine noun, your pronoun must also be feminine in gender.

> I heard **one dog** barking **his** loudest.
> I heard **three dogs** barking **their** loudest.
> The **man** raised **his** hand to ask a question.
> The **men** raised **their** hands to ask questions.
> The **woman** read **her** magazine.
> The **women** read **their** magazines.

About 50 pronouns exist in the English language. In fact, of the 25 most frequently used words, 10 of them are pronouns. Pronouns are traditionally divided into 6 groups or categories: **personal** pronouns, **relative** pronouns, **interrogative** pronouns, **demonstrative** pronouns, **indefinite** pronouns, and **reflexive** pronouns. In addition to its name, each category has its own definition and special function.

The group of pronouns most frequently used are the personal pronouns. Because of their many forms, however, this group can be troublesome.

PRONOUNS					
Number	**Person**	**Subject**	**Object**	**Possessive**	**Possessive Adjective**
Singular	First	I	me	mine	my
	Second	you	you	yours	your
	Third (masculine)	he	him	his	his
	Third (feminine)	she	her	hers	hers
	Third (Neutral)	it	it		**its***
Plural	First	we	us	ours	our
	Second	you	you	yours	your
	Third	they	them	theirs	their

*ITS: Often confused with it's (it is).

Relative pronouns often assume the role of the subject of a sentence. More often, though, they refer to nouns that have preceded them. Relative pronouns are **who (for persons)**, **whom (for persons)**, **whose (for persons)**, **that (for persons and things),** and **which (for things)**.

Mr. Smith, **whom** I know well, came by my office yesterday.
The boy **who** lived down the street was injured in an accident today.
The car, **which** was red, was his favorite.

Interrogative and demonstrative pronouns are easy to recognize. Interrogative pronouns are **who, what, which, whom, whose, whoever, whichever,** and **whatever**.

Who is on the phone?
What do you need me to bring to dinner?
Which kind of soft drink do you prefer?
Whom did you stay with last night?
Whatever you mean by "star-crossed lovers," I don't know.

Demonstrative pronouns are used to point to something or someone clearly expressed or implied: **this, that, these,** and **those**.

That is the car I want.
These are the shoes I've been looking for.
Give **this** to my sister for me, please.

Indefinite pronouns acquired their name because the noun for which they are standing in is indefinite: **everybody, somebody, anybody, nobody, everyone, someone, anyone, no one**.

Everybody joined in the race.
No one took more time than he did.
Is **anyone** home?

Reflexive pronouns are those pronouns that end in "self" or "selves:" **myself, yourself, yourselves, himself, herself, itself, ourselves,** and **themselves.** The main purpose of reflexive pronouns is to reflect back on the subject of a sentence.

She cut **herself** with the knife. (*herself refers to "she"*)
I bought **myself** a new car this week. (*myself refers to "I"*)
You are just not **yourself** today, are you? (*yourself refers to "you"*)

Reflexive pronouns may also serve to provide emphasis in a sentence. When they serve this purpose, they appear at the end of the sentence.

I will go to the store **myself**.

I suppose I will have to write the paper **myself**.

Errors To Avoid with Reflexive Pronouns

You should avoid using reflexive pronouns when your sentence calls for a personal pronoun such as "I," "me," or "you." Remember that a reflexive pronoun should "reflect back" on the subject of the sentence.

NO: Both Officer Smith and **myself** plan to go.

YES: Both Officer Smith and **I** plan to go.

NO: Either Captain Jones or **yourself** will prepare the report.

YES: Either Captain Jones or **you** will prepare the report.

<u>Verbs</u>. Every sentence **must have** a verb. Verbs express action or a state or being. Verbs can be either singular or plural, depending on the subject of the sentence. Verbs and subjects are like the black and white keys on a piano keyboard; they complement or support each other in the harmony of the sentence. Verbs change tense (time) to tell us when the action is occurring or when the action has occurred as well as what action is occurring. The two main forms of any verb are the present and past tense. The past tense is usually formed by adding "ed" to the end of the basic verb.

PRESENT	**PAST**
achieve	achieved
administer	administered
analyze	analyzed
apply	applied
approve	approved
arrange	arranged
assess	assessed
assist	assisted
brandish	brandished
chair	chaired
complete	completed
conduct	conducted
consult	consulted
control	controlled
coordinate	coordinated
decide	decided
design	designed
develop	developed
enter	entered
establish	established
evaluate	evaluated

examine	examined
guide	guided
help	helped
hire	hired
identify	identified
inspect	inspected
investigate	investigated
manage	managed
monitor	monitored
operate	operated
organize	organized
plan	planned
produce	produced
provide	provided
punch	punched
research	researched
schedule	scheduled
select	selected
serve	served
shout	shouted
slap	slapped
solve	solved
stab	stabbed
supervise	supervised
talk	talked
train	trained

As with almost everything in grammar, exceptions always follow rules. While most verbs, called **regular** verbs, follow the foregoing pattern of present and past tense, about 100 commonly used verbs **do not**. Verbs that do not form their past tense by adding "ed" are called **irregular** verbs.

<u>PRESENT</u>	<u>PAST</u>
am	was
cut	cut
shot	shot
flee	fled
run	ran
drive	drove
drink	drank
fight	fought
break	broke
hit	hit
spit	spat

dive	dove
lead	led
know	knew
leave	left
get	got
blow	blew
go	went
draw	drew
read	read
lie (to rest)	lay
lay (to place)	laid
swear	swore
write	wrote
lead	led
build	built
teach	taught

Errors to Avoid with Verbs

1. Learn the irregular verbs. Do not add "ed" to irregular verbs.

    NO: He **hitted** the car with his fist.
    YES: He **hit** the car with his fist.
    NO: I **sweared** to tell the truth.
    YES: I **swore** to tell the truth.

2. Do not use the present tense of the verb for the past tense.

    NO: Yesterday, he **sees** her twice.
    YES: Yesterday, he **saw** her twice.
    NO: Tuesday, I **says** to my friend, "Let's go to the store."
    YES: Tuesday, I **said** to my friend, "Let's go to the store."

3. Do not shift tenses in the same phrase, sentence, or paragraph.

    NO: He **runs** into the room and **pointed** the gun.
    YES: He **runs** into the room and **points** the gun.
    NO: The officer **forgot** the evidence and **runs** back for it.
    YES: The officer **forgot** the evidence and **ran** back for it.

4. Make sure that the subject and verb of the sentence agree in number (i.e., either both are singular or both are plural).

    NO: All the officers, including Captain Shields, **hopes** the criminal is arrested.

YES: All the officers, including Captain Shields, **hope** the criminal is arrested.
NO: Every one of you **know** your Miranda warning.
YES: Every one of you **knows** your Miranda warning.

Adjectives and Adverbs. Adjectives and adverbs are modifiers. They always appear in relation to some other word. An **adjective** modifies or describes a noun, pronoun, or any other word or group of words playing the part of a noun. Adjectives tell what kind of, which, or how many.

Living **well** is **the best** revenge.
The opposing team played **an aggressive, sophisticated** game.

Adverbs modify verbs, adjectives, or other adverbs. They tell how, when, and where.

Slowly he turned and saw her waiting **patiently there**.
The book is **more easily** understood if you read **quickly** through the **least** difficult chapters **first.**

Most adverbs end in "ly" but not all do. To add confusion to the situation, some **adjectives** end in "ly" also.

ADJECTIVES	**ADVERBS**
truthful	truthfully
intentional	intentionally
theoretical	theoretically
cowardly	cowardly
hourly	hourly
lovely	now
lively	quite
homely	soon
orderly	very
friendly	often
kindly	then
timely	when
lonely	down
jolly	yet
	still
	here
	too
	around
	almost

Rather than the way the word ends, the difference between adjectives and adverbs actually depends on the way the word functions in the sentence. If the word modifies or describes a noun, it is an **adjective**. If it modifies an adjective, adverb, or verb, it is an **adverb**.

Prepositions. Prepositions are connecting words which connect the word or words that follow them to the other part of the sentence. The preposition and the word or group of words that follows it are called a **prepositional phrase**.

Simple Prepositions

at the office	**by** the seashore
down south	**on** the desk
through the door	**about** the house
for your love	**like** her sister
over the top	**beside** the bed
except you	**across** town

Errors to Avoid in Prepositions

Do not overuse or omit necessary prepositions in formal writing. Remember that by the nature of their definitions, the words we "tack" prepositions to in overuse situations already mean what we are attempting to say. An example of overuse which occurs quite frequently involves "stand up." The word "stand" means to bring your body to an upright position; therefore, to tack "up" to this phrase is not necessary and redundant.

In the other extreme, the omission of necessary prepositions makes your writing nonparallel. Parallelism is an important quality in clear and coherent writing. When you omit prepositions, you allow your reader to interpret the writing; and his or her interpretations may not agree with your original meaning.

Overuse
NO: Let's divide **up** the paperwork.
YES: Let's divide the paperwork.
NO: When did they finally get **down** to the problem?
YES: When did they finally get to the problem?

Omission
NO: She was concerned **about** George and his many cats.
YES: She was concerned **about** George and **about** his many cats.
NO: **At** his office and home, he tried to be the same person.
YES: **At** his office and **at** home, he tried to be the same person.

Conjunctions. Conjunctions are also connecting words, much like prepositions. They connect words, phrases, and clauses. There are four kinds of conjunctions: **coordinating conjunctions, conjunctive adverbs, correlative conjunctions, and subordinating conjunctions.**

Coordinating conjunctions connect parts of a sentence that are equal. The following are commonly used coordinating conjunctions: **and, but, yet, for, or, nor, both, moreover, whereas**. Coordinating conjunctions may join a word to another word: Mom **and** Dad, Jill **or** Mary, firm **yet** kind, slowly **but** surely. They may also join a phrase to another phrase: out of sight **and** out of mind, running down the street **or** meandering through the traffic.

Conjunctive adverbs are used to connect independent clauses and to illustrate the relationship between these clauses. Clauses joined by a conjunctive adverb must be punctuated by either a semicolon or a period. Conjunctive adverbs often serve as transitional words connecting one paragraph to another. Examples of conjunctive adverbs are **therefore, however, consequently, accordingly, for this reason, for example, on the other hand, furthermore, besides, moreover, still, likewise, in addition, nevertheless, indeed, thus, on the contrary, hence**.

He won the choral competition; **consequently**, he went on to have a successful career.
I would like to visit my parents; **however**, I am extremely busy at work and have no time.
His testimony provided many fine insights. **Moreover**, it was eloquently spoken.

Correlative conjunctions always come in pairs: both—and, either—or, neither—nor, if—then, not only—but also, since—therefore. The parts of the sentence they join <u>must</u> be parallel.

Either the captain **or** chief must preside.
Since you were late, **therefore** I cannot seat you.
Neither your crying **nor** your protesting will change my opinion.

Since the sentence elements you join with correlative conjunctions must be equivalent, avoid the following mistakes:

NO: Her main interests were **that she succeed and running**.
YES: Her main interests were **success and running**.
NO: She loved him dearly **but not his dog**.
YES: She loved him dearly **but she did not love his dog**.

Unlike coordinating conjunctions which connect parts of the sentence that are equal, subordinating conjunctions are used to connect parts of a sentence that are unequal. Some examples of subordinating conjunctions are **as, since, provided that, in order that, until, how, where, because, although, after, when, if, so that, as though, though, before, while, unless, that**. Typically, subordinating conjunctions introduce descriptive clauses and connect to the main clause.

I'll go with you **provided that** you allow me to drive.
Because she did not run quickly, she arrived late.
He will call home **after** his meeting.

If you dislike the noise of the city, move to the country.

Having reviewed the parts of speech, we will now examine their placement in the sentence structure.

Parts of the Sentence

What is a sentence? A sentence may be as simple as two words: **He ran.** A sentence may also be a group or collection of words which may be complex. In either instance, a sentence is designed to convey a complete thought. It is the basis for communication. Every sentence has two parts: **a subject and a predicate**. The subject is the noun—the person, place, thing, or idea. The predicate is the verb—the action taking place. In order to form a complete sentence, you must have a subject and a verb. In some sentences, however, no apparent subject (noun) is present. In these instances, most often commands, the subject is understood to be "you."

> [**You**] Run as fast as you can!
> [**You**] Drop the gun!
> [**You**] Stop the car!

A sentence should have a certain order or design. This order may follow this sequence:

> SUBJECT-VERB-DIRECT OBJECT.
> James smokes cigars.
> Bill drives cabs.

A more complex design may follow this sequence:

> SUBJECT-VERB-INDIRECT OBJECT-DIRECT OBJECT
> Bill gave me some flares.
> The Captain promised me the promotion.

Sentence Errors. Two of the most common and confusing structural problems are dangling participles and misplaced modifiers. These errors create confusion because the sentence is unclear. The reader is forced to try and determine the writer's intent. This lack of clarity is particularly troublesome in police reports that rely on facts and accuracy. The investigator may not interpret the report in the same manner as it was written by the initial responding officer. Furthermore, this ambiguity may present a clever defense attorney with an avenue of attack in the officer's court presentation.

> NO: I saw two stores and a movie theater walking down the street.
> YES: Walking down the street, I saw two stores and a movie theater.
> NO: He found a black Labrador driving his truck through town.
> YES: Driving his truck through town, he found a black Labrador.
> NO: The officer saw the airplane pulling into his space.

YES: Pulling into his space, the officer saw the airplane.
NO: He climbed the ladder with a bad leg.
YES: He climbed the ladder even though he had a bad leg.
NO: I saw two boys running down the street with a television.
YES: While I was watching, two boys ran down the street carrying a television.

Sentence fragments, run-on sentences, and a lack of parallel structure are three other common errors. **Sentence fragments** are incomplete thoughts that occur because either a verb or a noun is missing. Sentence fragments frequently occur as a result of police officers writing like they speak in a conversation. Sentence fragments in conversation are acceptable since both parties are present and understand the context of the discussion. However, when only one part is privileged to the communication, sentence fragments damage the integrity of the writer.

NO: And danced for joy at the news.
YES: She danced for joy at the news.
NO: A tree as old as your father.
YES: The tree is as old as your father.
NO: No one. Not even the chief.
YES: No one, not even the chief, could do it.

Run-on sentences occur as a result of a lack of punctuation or an inability of the writer to organize thoughts appropriately. Run-on sentences are often a result of officers attempting to hurriedly write reports due to an increase in calls for service. Occasionally when officers save the report writing task for the end of the shift, run-on sentences are a natural result of this hurried attempt to complete the job and go home.

NO: You run too fast your side will hurt.
YES: You run too fast, and your side will hurt.
           OR
       You run too fast; your side will hurt.
NO: It was a beautiful day the sun was shining.
YES: It was a beautiful day because the sun was shining.
NO: The suspect said the gun was fired once I think it was fired more.
YES: The suspect said the gun was fired once, but I think it was fired more.

In an effort to eliminate run-on sentences or to correct them, many writers will simply insert a comma between the clauses. However, they are simply creating another error—**the comma splice**.

NO: Speak softly, someone is listening.
YES: Speak softly; someone is listening.
           OR
       Speak softly, because someone is listening.

NO: If you know, you must tell us, we will handle the investigation.

YES: If you know, you must tell us. Then we will handle the investigation.

Like ideas should be expressed in a like manner. **Parallel structure** in sentence writing means that like elements of a sentence are written in similar form.

NO: The suspect shot into the roof, wall, and floor.

YES: The suspect shot into **the roof, the wall, and the floor**.

NO: The drunk driver failed to properly perform the heel-to-toe walk, balance test, and the finger-to-nose test.

YES: The drunk driver failed to properly perform **the heel-to-toe walk, balance test, and finger-to-nose test**.

As mentioned earlier, punctuation is a way to organize thoughts and express those thoughts clearly to others. Punctuation serves as the ties that bind sentences together. Sentences form the foundation of paragraphs and paragraphs act as columns that support the crest or theme of the story the writer is attempting to relate or convey.

Punctuation

For purposes of this chapter, four basic components of punctuation will be discussed. These components are the **period, the comma, the semicolon, and the colon**. The period is the most powerful form of punctuation. It denotes the end of a complete thought. A **question mark** and an **exclamation point** are also used to end sentences. Question marks follow direct questions; exclamation points end emphatic statements.

Go get my newspaper.

Where will we go next?

Would you prepare that report for me?

Let go of me!

Help!

The **comma** is the most versatile form of punctuation. Commas are used to separate words in a series, in dates, and to set off direct quotations. However, one of the most important aspects of the comma may be to separate sentences with two main ideas (compound sentences). One of the ways to correct run-on sentences is to use the comma. A compound sentence has two subjects and two verbs that are typically joined by a conjunction (and, but, or, yet, for, nor). A comma should precede the conjunction in a compound sentence.

He is supposed to be released from prison tomorrow, **but** who knows if his parole will be approved.

She said she was separated from her husband, **yet** she allowed him to enter her apartment.

The **semicolon**, much like the comma, may be used to connect two main ideas in a sentence; however, unlike the comma, it requires no conjunction. A semicolon may also be used to separate items in a series when commas have been previously used in the same sentence. The use of the semicolon in this situation makes the meaning of the sentence clearer.

It was a dark and stormy night; a shot rang out.
Violent crimes rose in October, 15 percent; dropped in November, 10 percent; and in December, dropped 5 percent. This indicates no significant increase in violent crimes during the last quarter.

The **colon** is the least frequently utilized mark of punctuation. Colons most often are used to introduce a series or a list.

Only a few of the officers were at roll call: Sgt. Smith, Officer Jones, Officer Jackson, and Officer Johnson.
Please order the following supplies: 50 index cards, 20 envelopes, and 15 pens.

Colons are also used in place of a comma in the introductory salutation of a business letter.

Dear Sgt. Smith:
Dear Mayor Jones:

Proper punctuation is as crucial to the construction of a sentence as the use of the appropriate words. Unfortunately, not only are mistakes made in the choice of punctuation but also in the proper selection of words.

Frequently Confused Words

Mark Twain once said, "The difference between the right word and the almost right word is the difference between lightning and the lightning bug." As evidenced by this quote, selecting the inappropriate word changes the entire meaning of a sentence. In today's litigious society, the importance of word selection can be the difference between a dismissal and a judgment. Prior to the sophistication of the 90s, the 60s sitcom, "All in the Family," supplied a wide list of spoonerisms or malapropisms. Archie Bunker's verbal gaffes served as a platform from which to launch a variety of humorous commentaries concerning race, religion, and ethnicity. Today these culturally insensitive phrases would serve to alienate audiences. In this same light, criminal justice professionals need to be very conscious of the words or phrases they select in their spoken or written communication.

flee	flea
led	lead
its	it's
there	their/they're
passed	past
were	where

are	our
counsel	council
except	accept
affect	effect
know	now
no	know
knew	new
quiet	quite/quit
than	then
to	too/two
who's	whose
your	you're
personnel	personal
principal	principle

Abbreviations versus Full Words

Many abbreviations in writing are standard. We have used them so frequently that they have become second nature, and the full form of the words almost never appears. In other instances, however, abbreviations should be used in only certain circumstances.

Titles and Ranks

Mr., Mrs., and Ms. should be used when they appear before names.

Mr. John Doe
Mrs. Jane Doe
Ms. Jackie **Doe**

Jr. and *Sr.* should be used when they appear as part of a name.

Robert E. Grubb, Jr.

Dr. should be used when the title appears before a name.

Dr. Grubb

Civil and Military Titles

You may abbreviate civil and military titles when they appear before a full name. However, you should not abbreviate them when they appear before a last name **ONLY.**

CORRECT: Cmdr. Jim Terry
Capt. Mark Rhodes
Sgt. Angie Howell
Lt. Dickie Parker

CORRECT: Commander Terry
                    Captain Rhodes
                    Sergeant Howell
                    Lieutenant Parker

INCORRECT: Cmdr. Terry
                    Capt. Rhodes
                    Sgt. Howell
                    Lt. Parker

You may abbreviate **Reverend** and **Honorable** when they precede a full name and do not follow *the.* You may not, however, abbreviate these titles when they appear before a last name alone or when they follow *the.*

CORRECT: Rev. Phillip R. Hemby
                    Hon. Margaret Phipps-Brown
CORRECT: Reverend Hemby
                    the Honorable Margaret Phipps-Brown

INCORRECT: Rev. Hemby
                    the Hon. Phipps-Brown

Degrees and Certifications

Scholarly degrees (B.A., B.S., M.S., M.Ed., Ph.D.) can be abbreviated. An important point to remember is that no other title should precede a name when a degree follows it.

CORRECT: K. Virginia Hemby, Ph.D.

INCORRECT: Dr. K. Virginia Hemby, Ph.D.

Time, Days, and Months

Time designations such as a.m., p.m., EST, or CDT are not frequently utilized in law enforcement reports. Most agencies prefer to use the military designation of time (e.g., 0800, 1300, etc.).

CORRECT: The crime was reported at 8:32 p.m.

CORRECT: The crime was reported at 2032 hours.

INCORRECT: The crime was reported at 8:32 PM.

INCORRECT: The crime was reported at 2032 p.m.

Names of the days of the week and months of the year should be written in full in formal reports and correspondence. However, in officer's field notes or on field interrogation cards, abbreviations for the days of the week and months of the year are acceptable. A note here, though—not all months of the year have abbreviations (March, April, May, June, July).

<u>Days of the Week</u>
Monday	Mon.
Tuesday	Tues.
Wednesday	Wed.
Thursday	Thurs.
Friday	Fri.
Saturday	Sat.
Sunday	Sun.

<u>Months of the Year</u>
January	Jan.
February	Feb.
March	March
April	April
May	May
June	June
July	July
August	Aug.
September	Sept.
October	Oct.
November	Nov.
December	Dec.

Acronyms and Familiar Initials

The full forms of initials are often pronounced as words (or acronyms). The full words are almost never written out: *snqfu, tarfu, fubar, WYSIWYG.* The full forms of familiar initials in the law enforcement field are also rarely spelled out: FBI, DBA, ATF, ED, DUI/DWI, CCW, DL/OL, VIN, PI.

Address Abbreviations

In law enforcement, geographical locations are frequently cited. For example, *street, avenue, boulevard, road, building,* and *highway* are often used in both written and oral reports.

Street	St.
Avenue	Ave.
Boulevard	Blvd.
Road	Rd.
Building	Bldg.

Highway   Hwy.

In addition, compass directions are also a major component in offense reports and radio communications. In written form, when a compass direction precedes a street name, it is part of the name and is not abbreviated: *95 Southeast Hickory Street.* When a compass direction follows a street name, however, it indicates a city's section and is abbreviated: *95 Hickory Street, SE.*

Because the use of periods in abbreviations changes from time to time, always check current practice in an up-to-date dictionary. You will find that some abbreviations contain periods, some have optional periods, and some have none.

State Abbreviations

The United States Postal Service has designated two-letter codes for abbreviating the names of states. In all but the most formal writing, you have the option of using these abbreviations.

Alabama	AL	Montana	MT
Alaska	AK	Nebraska	NE
Arizona	AZ	Nevada	NV
Arkansas	AR	New Hampshire	NH
California	CA	New Jersey	NJ
Colorado	CO	New Mexico	NM
Connecticut	CT	New York	NY
Delaware	DE	North Carolina	NC
District of Columbia	DC	North Dakota	ND
Florida	FL	Ohio	OH
Georgia	GA	Oklahoma	OK
Hawaii	HI	Oregon	OR
Idaho	ID	Pennsylvania	PA
Illinois	IL	Rhode Island	RI
Indiana	IN	South Carolina	SC
Iowa	IA	South Dakota	SD
Kansas	KS	Tennessee	TN
Kentucky	KY	Texas	TX
Louisiana	LA	Utah	UT
Maine	ME	Vermont	VT
Maryland	MD	Virginia	VA
Massachusetts	MA	Washington	WA
Michigan	MI	West Virginia	WV
Minnesota	MN	Wisconsin	WI
Mississippi	MS	Wyoming	WY
Missouri	MO		

Capitalization

Everyone understands that the first letter of the first word in a sentence is capitalized. Additionally, we are aware that rules govern capitalization of proper names and titles. However, the rules for capitalizing proper names and titles are complex. Authorities disagree and conventions change. Add to the mix the fact that a word may be capitalized in one instance but not in another. What you need to know is the solution to capitalization problems can be found in standard up-to-date dictionaries or handbooks. "When in doubt, check it out!"

Capitalization of First Words

As mentioned in the previous paragraph, you should capitalize the first letter of the first word in a complete sentence.

CORRECT: Students broke the security of the computer system.

You should also capitalize the first letter of the first word in a quotation that begins a new sentence within a sentence.

CORRECT: Sergeant Jones asks, "Will all the witnesses be present in court?"

If the quotation does not begin a new sentence, however, the first letter of the first word in the quote is not capitalized.

CORRECT: Mussolini believed that only war put "the stamp of nobility upon the peoples who have the courage to face it."

Capitalization of Proper Names and Proper Adjectives

Proper nouns are the specific names of persons, places, or things. You should capitalize these nouns and any adjectives that are derived from them. The following are categories that illustrate the kinds of words considered proper nouns and adjectives.

Names of People and Animals (Real and Fictional)
Roy Rogers, James Bond, King Kong

Place Names (Natural and Artificial)
Australia, Delaware River, Washington Monument, Statue of Liberty, Mars

Organizations (Government. Business, Social)
Fraternal Order of Police, Department of State

Historical Names
Tonkin Resolution, Monroe Doctrine, Custer's Last Stand

Religious Terms
God, He, His, Him [referring to God in a religious context]. Palm Sunday

Names in Education
University of Southern Mississippi, Business and Interpersonal Communication, Graduate Record Examination

Awards. Medals, Prizes
Medal of Honor, Bronze Star, Silver Star, Distinguished Service Cross, Purple Heart

Calendar Terms (Days. Months. Holidays)
Friday, July, Memorial Day, Christmas

Product Names-Trade Names and Specific Names
Nissan Pathfinder, Volkswagen Jetta, Sony Walkman, Maytag washer [The common term of a product's name is usually not capitalized.]

Ethnic Terms-Nationalities. Races, Languages
English, Chinese, Sioux, African-American

Scientific Terms-Classifications (except species) and Chemical Abbreviations
0 (oxygen), Au (gold), Alligator mississippiensis

You also capitalize nicknames or substitutes for proper names.

Official Name	Nickname
Mississippi	Magnolia State
New York City	The Big Apple
Mayor Jones	Mayor

Capitalization of Titles of Honor or Rank
You should always capitalize titles of honor or rank when they precede names—whether the titles are governmental, military, ecclesiastical, royal, or professional. In instances where these titles do not precede names, usually you do not capitalize them.

CAPITAL: In Mississippi, Governor Kirk Fordice served two consecutive terms.

NO CAPITAL: Kirk Fordice of Mississippi served as governor of Mississippi after a public scandal involving a woman purported to be his mistress.

CAPITAL: In 1863, General William S. Rosecrans fought at Chickamauga.

NO CAPITAL: William S. Rosecrans, a general with the Union army, fought at Chickamauga.

CAPITAL: After a serious accident, Professor Hemby resigned from teaching.

NO CAPITAL: After a serious accident, Dr. Hemby, a professor of Business and Interpersonal Communication, resigned from teaching.

Capitalization of Academic and Professional Degrees

Academic and professional degrees should be capitalized only when they appear immediately after a name or when they are abbreviated,

CAPITALS;   John Henry, Doctor of Laws, died yesterday.

CAPITALS: John Henry, LL.D., died yesterday.

NO CAPITALS: Skip Grubb earned his doctor of laws degree in 2002.

CAPITALS: Matt Jackson completed his **B.S.** degree in 2002.

NO CAPITALS: Matt Jackson completed his bachelor of science degree in 2002.

CAPITALS: Mark Smith, CPA, handled the bookkeeping for the organization.

NO CAPITALS: An independent certified public accountant handled the bookkeeping responsibilities for the organization.

Inappropriate Capitals

The following should not be capitalized:

- Common nouns, even when they appear in phrases that contain capitals

    American history
    Dell computer
    Heinz ketchup

- Words referring to areas of study, unless they are titles of specific courses

    CAPITALS: Economics 121
    NO CAPITALS: economics
    CAPITALS: Algebra II
    NO CAPITALS: algebra

CAPITALS:	Microbased Computer Literacy
NO CAPITALS:	computer literacy

- Words expressing family relationships-mother, father, aunt, uncle, grandmother, grandfather-unless they precede or substitute for names

CAPITAL:	I learned to ride my bike by watching Uncle Ruben.
NO CAPITAL:	I learned to ride my bike by watching my uncle.
CAPITAL:	When he was fifty-two. Grandfather had a heart attack.
NO CAPITAL:	When he was fifty-two, my grandfather had a heart attack.

- The words north, south, southwest, and so on when they refer to compass directions. These words should be capitalized when referring to regions.

CAPITAL:	The South is changing its image.
NO CAPITAL:	Drive south.
CAPITAL:	The first trip I took to the Southwest was very exciting.
NO CAPITAL:	My house lies southwest of town.

Spelling Errors

Spelling errors are a common problem in written communication. As law enforcement professionals, you must read any documentation closely and slowly so that your eyes fall on each individual word. We have a tendency to "read into" our written documents. We know what we intended to say and when we breeze through our writing quickly with a minimal scan, we are very sure that our words are correct and are spelled correctly. When others read our written documents, however, they note misspelled words, improper word usage, poor grammar, and incorrect punctuation. A good rule of thumb to incorporate into your writing practice is to read each word of your document backwards; thus, you are reading isolated words and not "ideas" or "what you intended to say."

Another method for detecting misspelled words requires you to be alert to those words that have frequently caused you problems. Some of these words may be *received, occurred* and *commitment.* If you pay attention to those problem words, you can then take special care in spelling them correctly.

One electronic means of detecting misspelled words is found on your computer in your word processing program. Most programs (Word, WordPerfect) offer you an opportunity to "check your spelling" when you complete your writing process. These built-in **spell checkers** will check the spelling of words in an entire document or of just a single word. The computer can check hundreds of words in a short amount of time. Unfortunately, even the best of word processing program spell checkers cannot catch nor correct problems such as confusing words— *affect* for *effect, their* for *there, its* for *it's* - since the words are spelled correctly. The form of the word you chose is incorrect.

Suggestions for Improving Your Use of a Computer Spell Checker
- ✓ Keep a dictionary available to use in checking the definition of terms. Do not rely on the spell checker to tell you the correct spelling of a word. Many times the alternative spellings are not useful.

- ✓ Create a personal dictionary within your word processing program. Proper names, technical terms you use frequently, and other words that may not be included in the computer dictionary can be added. Make sure the words you add, though, are spelled correctly!

- ✓ Most spell checkers will not find words that are used in the wrong context. If the words are spelled correctly, the computer checker will ignore them. *I told them the dog was over* **their** *and* **Its** *my belief that time heals all wounds.*

Fifty Most Commonly Misspelled Words[1]

The following list includes the 50 most commonly misspelled words. The spellings given are the American spellings. Variants listed in your dictionary should **not** be used. Remember, just because it's included in the dictionary does not mean it's all right to use (i.e., "ain't" is listed in the dictionary but that doesn't mean it's correct).

1. Anoint	18. Cemetery	35. Repetition
2. Coolly	19. Subpoena	36. Battalion
3. Supersede	20. Definitely	37. Despair
4. Irresistible	21. Occasion	38. Irritable
5. Development	22. Consensus	39. Accidentally
6. All right	23. Inadvertent	40. Liaison
7. Separate	24. Minuscule	41. Memento
8. Tyranny	25. Judgment	42. Broccoli
9. Harass	26. Inoculate	43. Millennium
10. Desiccate	27. Drunkenness	44. Yield
11. Indispensable	28. Occurrence	45. Existence
12. Receive	29. Dissipate	46. Independent
13. Pursue	30. Weird	47. Sacrilegious
14. Recommend	31. A lot	48. Insistent
15. Desperate	32. Accommodate	49. Exceed
16. Liquefy	33. Embarrassment	50. Privilege
17. Seize	34. Ecstasy	

Summary

In summary, while most criminal justice professionals (police officers, deputy sheriffs, parole officers, bailiffs, etc.) are not particularly interested in nor overly concerned about grammar and sentence structure, these items are just as vital in the preparation and prosecution of their cases as physical evidence or the confession. Inappropriate grammar or sentence structure may jeopardize the credibility or competence of the officer's investigation or testimony. Judges and attorneys have had the benefit of and experience associated with writing courses in law school. Therefore, they may be particularly sensitive to or aware of errors in grammar and sentence structure. If the same amount of care and concern that went into an investigation is given to the spoken word and written report, the credibility of the officer and the organization will be enhanced immensely.

Key Terms

Noun	Proper Noun
Common Noun	Concrete Noun
Abstract Noun	Collective Noun
Pronoun	Relative Pronoun
Interrogative Pronoun	Demonstrative Pronoun
Indefinite Pronoun	Reflexive Pronoun
Personal Pronoun	Verb
Regular Verbs	Irregular Verbs
Adjective	Adverb
Preposition	Prepositional Phrase
Conjunctions	Coordinating Conjunction
Conjunctive Adverb	Correlative Conjunction
Subordinating Conjunction	Subject
Predicate	Sentence
Sentence Fragment	Run-on Sentence
Comma Splice	Parallel Structure
Period	Comma
Semicolon	Colon
Question Mark	Exclamation Point
Antecedent	

Discussion Questions

1. Underline all **nouns** in the following sentences and identify whether or not they are common, proper, concrete, or abstract.
    A.   Jonathon celebrated Memorial Day in Washington, DC, this year.
    B.   Spring vacation begins next Friday.
    C.   The jury found the defendant not guilty by reason of insanity.
    D.   In Plato's dialogue *The Crito*, the concept of justice is discussed.

2. Change the following words to the plural form.
    A.   Motto   F.   Stomach
    B.   Basis   G.   Idea
    C.   Fly   H.   Crisis
    D.   Deer   I.   Sheriff

E. Lady   J. Appendix

3. In the following sentences, choose the correct form of the pronouns given in parentheses:
   A. Both Mary and (I, me) went to the mall Saturday.
   B. They missed the bus because of (he, him).
   C. (We, Us) officers must be ready for combat at all times.
   D. You and (I, me) do not understand each other.
   E. Neither Sam nor (they, them) will be going to the FBI Training Academy.

4. Fill in the correct form of the verb in parentheses.
   A. I _____ sad to leave. (to be)
   B. They _____ to walk the dog occasionally. (to forget)
   C. We _____ in the concert. (to sing)
   D. I _____ 20 pages in my book this afternoon. (to read)

5. In the following sentences, underline the **subject** once and the **verb** twice.
   A. John, along with the rest of his family, is attending the picnic.
   B. Every student has a trip planned for spring break.
   C. There go the prisoners on their work detail.

6. In the following sentences, identify and label the adjectives and adverbs.
   A. Her grandfather is a jolly old man.
   B. Are they late?
   C. She almost passed the driving examination.
   D. Which gun did you buy?
   E. He answered the lawyer's questions honestly.

7. In the following sentences, underline the prepositional phrase.
   A. They wouldn't think of going without you.
   B. He sat in front of me in Psychology class.
   C. They went into the house to get a cup of coffee.
   D. According to the report, crime has gone down.

Notes

1. McAdams, M. (1995). A Spelling Test. September 16, 2002
<http://www.sentex.net/~mmcadams/spelling.html>

CHAPTER 6

WRITTEN COMMUNICATION:
AN AGENCY'S LIFELINE

Learning Objectives:

1. To establish the types of written communication encountered in law enforcement agencies.

2. To understand the purpose of General Orders and Standard Operating Procedures.

3. To understand the importance of accreditation to law enforcement agencies.

4. To learn writing principles for report development.

5. To understand the relationship of sentence development to paragraph development.

6. To identify topic sentences and to develop paragraphs from topic sentences.

7. To develop effective transitions in sentence and paragraph writing.

8. To explain the importance of note taking.

9. To insure credibility in the development of offense/incident and supplemental reports.

10. To differentiate between interdepartmental and intradepartmental memoranda.

"What'll it be, a root canal or report writing? In our post-literate society, many officers might gladly accept nearly any punishment if it would save them from the time and effort needed to craft a good incident report. But their lack of skills and enthusiasm in this regard can cost them dearly—especially in use-of-force cases where their failure to get across important messages can wreak severe personal consequences.... There is little doubt that officers will do the best they can to survive on the streets, but where we fail is when we have to document the incidents we're involved in. Deficiencies then can lead to the failure to survive in court."

Street Survival Newsline No. 356 (1999, March 21)

Communication occurs on many levels in criminal justice agencies. This chapter presents the most basic types of written documentation you may encounter in your employment. The most important fact to keep in mind when preparing written communication is to identify who will ultimately read the document. Your reader is the most important consideration in preparing your written communication. If your reader cannot understand your communication, the process has not been successful and you must begin anew—requiring additional time and effort.

Writing Principles for Report Development

Writing begins with word selection—appropriate word selection. Words are the building blocks of sentences and paragraphs, and ultimately of reports. We can view the writing process as a stair-step one where we begin at the bottom level with the category "Words." Here we begin with clear and concise writing, choosing short, simple words. The next step involves generating sentences. Your sentences should vary in type between simple, compound, and complex ones. You should also use passive and active voice appropriately. The final step in the writing process is paragraph development. You need to keep your paragraphs unified and coherent and to control their length.

Words

Word choice is vital to achieving the appropriate response to your writing. In planning and developing your writing, you always want to keep in mind that the "reader" is the most important element in this process. While each of us knows what we desire to express, our reader does not always have the benefit of questioning us if our writing is unclear. Also, if the reader fails to comprehend our message, our writing will not achieve its desired purpose.

Software packages allow us to select a synonym for any word of our choice with the click of a button. Unfortunately, the word selections available do not always serve your writing well. Some basic concepts to remember concerning the writing process and your choice of words follow:

1.   **Use familiar words**. In order for your message to be understood, you must use words familiar to both you and your reader. If you are in doubt as to whether your

reader will define a word the way you do, then you should make sure to thoroughly explain your meaning either by providing a definition or an appropriate synonym. In the example below, a brief definition has been included in parentheses to insure the reader's understanding will match your intended meaning.

My watch always seems to be running **fast** (ahead of time).

2.   **Avoid unnecessary jargon.** While the criminal justice professions have their own technical jargon or specialized words, you should be wary of using jargon in writing that will be read by persons outside the field. For example, a jury may have problems understanding a report containing numerous jargon references.

3.   **Use concrete, specific language.** If you use concrete words in your writing, you will be selecting terms that bring a mental image to your reader's mind. Be sure your words give the reader as much information as necessary so he or she can react appropriately.

4.   **Write concisely.** You should avoid redundancy and wordy expressions in your writing. A **redundancy** is the unnecessary repetition of a previously expressed idea.

> NO: Combine the ingredients together.
> YES: Combine the ingredients.

Wordy expressions are not necessarily writing errors, but they should be avoided since they tend to slow the communication process. The following are examples of wordy expressions you should avoid in your writing with the preferred one-word substitutes in parentheses:

> Due to the fact (because)
> For the purpose of (for **or** to)
> In the event that (if)
> With regard to (about)
> Came to an agreement (agreed)
> Gave an explanation (explained)

5.   **Use positive language.** Positive language helps to build goodwill between you, the writer, and the reader. You also are much more likely to achieve your purpose if you use positive words. In addition to avoiding words such as "cannot" or "will not," you should avoid negative-sounding words such as "mistake," "damage," "failure," or "refuse." However, in most situations in the criminal justice professions, you may have no alternative but to use negative wording. Since negative language is strong and emphatic, sometimes you will want to use it.

Sentences

Chapter 5 discussed the basics of grammar. Particular emphasis was placed on sentence fragments and run-on sentences and the appropriate means for eliminating these problem areas. In this Chapter, we will examine sentence development. Some sentences are very simple—having only a subject and a predicate. Still others are longer and contain more details. Regardless of its length, a sentence is meant to convey a complete thought. The sentence is the basic unit of communication. Sentences are the building blocks for paragraphs.

When you read something written using short, choppy sentences, you find yourself unable to mentally picture the scene. Writing in this manner usually indicates that the writer simply wrote each thought as it occurred to him or her. Although no grammatical problems exist with short, simple sentences, they often separate ideas that need to be brought together. Varying sentence length creates well-balanced writing that flows. The reader gets the feeling that the writer really knows the subject well.

Two problem areas exist in sentence development: wordiness and rambling. **Wordiness** refers to the cluttering of sentences with unnecessary words. As mentioned in the foregoing section on "Words," you should always attempt to write concisely. However, as long as a word serves a purpose, it should remain in your sentence. Notice the difference in the following pairs of sentences:

NO: The psychological examination that he gave me was entirely complete.

YES: The psychological examination he gave me was complete.

NO: It will be our aim to ensure the safety of each and every one of the citizens in the State of Pennsylvania.

YES: Our aim will be to ensure the safety of all Pennsylvanians.

A **rambling sentence** goes on and on and seems to never end. Consider the following examples illustrating how rambling sentences can be improved:

NO: The night was foggy, but the road was clear; the moon was shining, and we all had the spirit of adventure in our heart and a song of the open road on our lips, so we took the turn that took our car up the winding mountain road.

YES: The night was foggy, but the road was clear. The moon was shining. All of us had the spirit of adventure in our heart and a song of the open road on our lips. So we took our car up that winding mountain road.

NO: Everyone knows someone like that, a person who has no concern for others, who will pretend to be a friend, but only because she profits from the relationship, and she never really gives of herself, she just takes, and one cannot call her a friend in any sense of the word.

YES: Everyone knows someone like that, a person who has no concern for others. She will pretend to be a friend, but only because she profits from the relationship. She never really gives of herself, but she just takes, and one cannot call her a friend in any sense of the word.

Although rambling sentences are typically grammatically correct, they present a problem to the reader. They interfere with the reader's comprehension. A good rule of thumb to follow in writing sentences is if it runs for more than two typewritten lines, you probably want to rewrite it. You could be "rambling."

Another important aspect in writing sentences centers on **voice**. **Voice** is the feature of the verb that indicates whether the subject of the sentence acts or is acted on. Two types of voice are used in writing—**active voice** and **passive voice**. In **active voice**, the subject does the action expressed by the verb. Whereas, in **passive voice**, the subject receives the action of the verb. Active voice is preferable in writing because it is emphatic and direct. However, passive voice is essential when the action of the verb is more important than the person doing the action, when the person doing the action is unknown, or when the writer wants to emphasize the receiver of the action and not the doer. The following are examples of passive and active voice:

PASSIVE: The garbage can was hit by the Ford Explorer.
ACTIVE: The Ford Explorer hit the garbage can.
PASSIVE: The witnesses were questioned by the investigator.
ACTIVE: The investigator questioned the witnesses.

Using appropriate word choices, a variety of sentence types, and active or passive voice can help make your sentences more effective. By learning these basic writing premises, you are now ready to combine them into logical paragraphs.

Paragraphs

The sentence and the paragraph are the two most fundamental units of communication. Paragraphs also have several common characteristics, which help them to focus on and to develop their subjects more fully. No rule of thumb exists with regard to length of paragraphs. Nonetheless, you should avoid writing a single sentence as a full paragraph. You will find that a minimum of three sentences are essential to developing a topic to some degree. Also, since most paragraphs are organized around a central idea, all sentences in that paragraph must relate to this idea.

Topic Sentences

The sentence that tells the reader what the paragraph is about is called the **topic sentence**. Topic sentence placement is usually set as the first sentence in the paragraph. However, not all topic sentences come first. Often it is found at the end or near the middle of the paragraph. As a writer, you should decide where you want to place your topic sentence to be placed. If you write it at the beginning of the paragraph, the topic sentence can capture the readers' attention or interest and tell them what to expect next. Most magazine and newspaper articles use this placement of the topic sentence for the very purpose of getting attention. If you place the topic sentence at the end of the paragraph, you can reinforce or emphasize details that were discussed in the paragraph.

A topic sentence guides and influences readers. Nonetheless, the writer should find it equally important as well. The topic sentence gives you, the writer, a focus. By referring back to the topic sentence, you should be able to keep your work organized and consistent. Remember that your writing should be coherent and composed of logically arranged thoughts.

Expanding your topic sentence into a paragraph involves the use of detailed information. Remember that your topic sentence is a statement that the remainder of your sentences must clearly and completely support. The following methods can be used to develop a topic sentence.

1.   **Facts.** Used to substantiate historical and scientific writing.
2.   **Examples.** Helps to clarify a statement by offering the reader evidence.
3.   **Argument.** Used in editorials, philosophical writing, and literary criticism to support a theory.
4.   **Anecdote.** Often found in narrative writing. Used to entertain the reader while clarifying a point. (An **anecdote** is a short account of an incident, usually personal.)
5.   **Definition**. Gives the writer an explanation through definition of a concept or term.
6.   **Comparison and Contrast**. Essential qualities of two people or theories can be highlighted through this mechanism.
7.   **Analogy.** Can be used to bring out the essential qualities of a subject. (An **analogy** is explaining something by comparing it point by point with something else.)
8.   **Cause and Effect**. Usually involves the use of data or general observation to explain a theory or subject.

Transitions

Arranging sentences logically will not ensure a coherent paragraph. Using linking expressions or phrases is crucial for smooth transitions between ideas and subjects. As discussed earlier in Chapter 5, **Conjunctive Adverbs** are useful for transitioning from paragraph to paragraph. Pronouns are also helpful for referring to a previous sentence without repetition. The following examples demonstrate various methods for linking or connecting your text.

1.   **To elaborate on an idea already discussed:**

again	furthermore	moreover
also	in addition	similarly
too	for example	and

Examples:
a.   I intend to vote for Mayor Bryant in the upcoming election. He is a diligent worker with a good personality. **Moreover**, he has experience.
b.   We feel it would be best to change the date of the dance. Many members said they could not attend. **Also,** there is a reunion that night.

2.   **To qualify, limit, or contradict a statement:**

but	yet	although

however   on the other hand   nevertheless

Examples:
a. After I located the suspect, I thought I could get him to confess. I had to simply ask the right questions. **However**, I didn't anticipate his speech difficulty, and a speech pathologist had to be called to assist me.
b. Officer Smith thought she had secured the crime scene. All the necessary precautions had been taken. **Yet** for some unknown reason, the evidence became tainted.

3. **To show a time or place arrangement of an idea:**
    at the present time   second   meanwhile
    at the same time   finally   eventually
    at this point   first   further

Examples:
a. After going over the testimony several times, I decided to ask my supervisor for help. After we had discussed it fully, I looked the testimony over one more time. **Finally**, I began to see the cracks I was searching for.
b. It was a hectic day. First, I was late for work. Then, a car pulled into traffic in front of me, and I was forced to go into the ditch to avoid it. When I finally reached home, it began to rain. **At this point**, I was about to cry.

4. **To conclude a paragraph effectively:**
    as a result   for these reasons
    as can be seen   hence
    consequently   therefore

Examples:
a. We were cautioned not to move if we heard voices. Suddenly something fell. **As a result**, no one moved an inch.
b. The weatherman has forecast a blizzard for tomorrow. He expects the accumulation to be heavy. **Therefore,** I decided to stock up on food items at the grocery store today.

You may also use pronouns as transitional words as well as a repetition of key words or ideas appearing in the preceding paragraph or line. Remember that the aim in your writing should be to enable the reader to connect paragraphs and ideas in his or her mind. Deciding to use a transition is a matter of common sense. The more you write, the easier it will become.

Consistency

In writing, consistency is equally as important as unity. If you change point of view or tone abruptly, you will confuse your reader. **Point of view** is the way in which something is viewed or considered; it is the writer's standpoint or the attitude the writer has toward the subject. **Tone** is the manner of speaking that indicates a certain attitude. Tone can be informal, formal, or dramatic, as determined by the writer's word choice and phrasing.

Example (Point of View)
NO: From his vantage point, Sgt. Jones could see the men enter the house. They broke the lock on the front door and went in that way. After that, he lost sight of them. **His partner saw everything from the top of the stairs**.

YES: From his vantage point, Sgt. Jones could see the men enter the house. They broke the lock on the front door and went in that way. **Although Sgt. Jones lost sight of them at this point, his partner was inside and saw everything.**

Example (Tone)
NO: At a special press conference at the White House today, the president offered reporters details of his new economic policy. Hoping to lower Medicaid funding, he proposed a series of tax cuts that will be made over the next three years. Many economists believe **it's about time the president did something**.

YES: At a special press conference at the White House today, the president offered reporters details of his new economic policy. Hoping to lower Medicaid funding, he proposed a series of tax cuts that will be made over the next three years. Many economists believe **it is a good time for the president to implement his new plan**.

Reports in Law Enforcement

The most frequently utilized form of written communication in law enforcement is the offense/incident report. Supplemental reports are the second most utilized form of intradepartmental communication. Virtually every department has its own unique or personalized form for reporting an offense or incident. Yet, while the form may be unique to that organization, the format is essentially the same. Every offense/incident report or supplemental report begins with field notes taken by the officer/investigator.

Note taking

Every officer is issued a variety of new equipment but none is more important than the pen and the field notebook. Good field notes are vital to the preparation of a thorough and inclusive report. Notebooks should be reserved for information that relates directly to an officer's investigations. Informational material of a personal nature should never be entered into an officer's field notebook since this notebook may be subpoenaed as evidence in a case or possibly examined by a defense attorney on the witness stand. Since investigations and court cases may take several months or years to resolve, officers should catalog their notebooks in chronological order. Notebooks should be maintained for a minimum of three years. This cataloging should include the officer's name, rank, departmental telephone number, and dates of inclusion.

The content of the notes should serve as an outline or brief synopsis of the event. These notes should contain personal observations, statements made by the victim, witness(es), and suspect(s). Descriptions of important persons, places, or things as well as any other relevant information should also be included. Information that may be construed as opinion rather than fact should be omitted. An officer should remember that this notebook is not a private or secure journal but a written account of investigations that may be confiscated by the agency or subpoenaed into court for examination.

Offense/Incident Reports

The form itself is self-explanatory; it is merely a matter of filling in the appropriate blanks or checking the appropriate blocks. The narrative is the integral component of any sound offense report. An appropriate narrative adheres to the three "C's." Offense reports must be **clear, concise,** and **complete**. In order to insure this adherence to the three "C's," the following questions should be answered: **who, what, when, where, why,** and **how**.

Who?
1. Who is the complainant?
2. Who is the victim?
3. Who is the suspect?
4. Who are the witnesses?

What?
1. What type of offense has occurred?
2. What type of action has occurred or is occurring (in the case of a domestic disorder or neighbor dispute, etc.)?
3. What was the relationship, if any, between the victim and the suspect(s)?

When?
1. When did this offense take place or when was the crime discovered?
2. When did you (the officer) arrive?
3. When did the suspect flee the scene or leave the area (if known)?

Where?
1. Where was the offense committed (specific address)?
2. Where are the victims, witnesses, and suspect(s) now?

Why?
1. Why was the offense committed?
2. Why were the victim and suspect(s) in this location?
3. Why did the suspect choose this victim and this time to commit this offense?

How?
1. How was the crime/offense committed?
2. How did the suspect flee the area (on foot, in a vehicle—description or license plate number, direction of travel)?
3. How many victims, witnesses, and suspects were involved in the crime or offense?

The first sentence of the first paragraph should set the tone for the report: "On October 6, 1998, at 14:00 hours, I, Officer M. W. Jackson, responded to 4853 Lucerne Road in reference to a larceny complaint." The second and subsequent sentences are composed in a manner as to support the initial or opening statement: "Upon my arrival, I spoke with the complainant, Ms. Melissa Hemby …." In these two sentences, the date and time of occurrence, location, type of offense, responding officer, and complainant have been identified.

On most occasions, reports should be written in first person singular—i.e., I arrived at the scene …. However, upon investigations involving multiple officers, reports must denote which officer initiated what action. For example, "While Officer Cravener searched the bedroom for weapons, I, Officer Jackson, detained the suspects in the living room."

Furthermore, every effort should be made to insure that reports are readable—both in terms of legibility and grammatically. Reports that contain insufficient evidence waste investigators' time pursuing facts which had been previously stated to the responding officer but which were omitted from the preliminary offense report. Further, poorly written reports serve as an impediment not only to investigators but to prosecutors as well. Reports that are poorly written force prosecutors to nolle prosequi or plea bargain otherwise sound cases. However, well-written reports allow prosecutors the latitude to prosecute suspects to the fullest extent of the law. They also place suspects in a position of jeopardy regarding certain statutes of the legal code.

Supplemental Reports

Supplemental reports are primarily designed to add to the existing information provided in the preliminary offense reports, to record victim and witness statements. Furthermore, supplemental reports may be utilized to record suspect statements with the intent to impeach the suspect's credibility or to compromise the suspect's integrity. These reports also provide supervisors with the pending status of a case and allow them to manage case logs. Supplemental offense reports are also used to denote the gathering, processing, and disposition of physical evidence. Supplemental reports need to adhere to the same rules of grammar, punctuation, and style as offense/incident reports.

Memoranda

Communication within departments and within agencies occurs through the use of memoranda. **Memoranda** serve to inform an individual or individuals concerning a particular event or occurrence, to make an official record, or to request action or a service. A memorandum is an inappropriate means of communication with the public since they are always reserved as "in-house" communication devices.

Memoranda take two forms: intradepartmental and interdepartmental. **Intradepartmental** memoranda are documents that are generated and circulated within a department. **Interdepartmental** memoranda are documents that are generated and circulated between two or more departments. These memoranda may take the formal or informal approach, depending on their purpose and the level of communication involved. For instance, a memo from contemporaries who may differ in rank may take an informal tone. However, in the situation where a subordinate addresses a superior officer and they are not contemporaries, a formal tone is adopted.

Memoranda always adhere to the same format with a heading that includes date, to, from, and subject. Memoranda may be more loosely constructed than offense/incident reports and supplemental reports. However, proper grammar and punctuation are essential to effective communication.

Formal Communication within the Agency: General Orders

Communication serves as the framework around which a criminal justice organization is formed. Thousands of pieces of information are processed daily in the course of normal operations. These pieces of information are formal and informal in scope, and they determine the nature of the department as reflected by the personality or leadership style of the chief law enforcement officer.

Agencies respond to a number of requests. These requests may be from the public or from governmental officials elected by the public to represent its best interests. The police represent that segment of the population responsible for enforcing the law and maintaining public order; however, the manner in which the police attempt to meet these mandates is a matter of constant interpretation. In order to create and maintain a viable law enforcement agency certain criteria must be established.

Criminal justice agencies, particularly those directly associated with the detection and suppression of crime as well as the arrest and detention of criminals, are founded upon a set of general orders. General orders supply the skeletal structure for the operation of the department. Divisions and bureaus are created with specific responsibilities and duties delineated for their function and operation. The number of personnel assigned to each unit, the rank of these individuals, and the rules specific to the operation of the unit are enumerated in these General Orders as well as the procedure for implementing changes or modifications as approved by the chief, his/her appointed designee, or the general staff. In essence, the General Orders serve as the blueprint for the structure of the organization.

Communication in this form is almost always formal. General Orders are always in a written form so as to establish a guideline for the operation of the department and to serve as constant reference in the case of confusion or controversy, very similar to the concept of case law or the judicial use of *stare decisis*. A great deal of thought and preparation goes into the creation of the General Order manual and much like a constitutional amendment, changes are usually very slow and very difficult to implement. The chief and general staff usually approve modifications or amendments before they are presented to the elected board of representatives for approval and inclusion into a governmental charter. Included within this formal blueprint is usually a manual consisting of Standard Operating Procedures (SOP) or Operational Directives.

Standard Operating Procedures (SOP)/Operational Directives

The SOP manual is a formal set of written directives on how to handle most situations confronting law enforcement officials. This manual is created in order to ensure a consistent and efficient approach to most situations and to reduce the possibility of litigation in the event of an "unfortunate" outcome in the resolution of a difficult situation. SOP manuals include items ranging from those as mundane as the proper uniform of the day and how it is to be worn to matters as complex as the proper procedure for searching an individual and the use of force in affecting an arrest.

This manual is more detailed in scope and more flexible in nature than General Orders. In fact, changes are easier to adopt and merely require the approval of the chief or the joint approval of the chief and appropriate legal counsel (frequently the state or city attorney) in matters relating to interpreting or implementing policies affected by federal, state, or local legislation. Informal modifications are frequently implemented by first line supervisors (sergeants) in order to facilitate a smoother operation of the unit. These modifications are generally at the discretion of the shift supervisor (lieutenant) and implemented or conveyed to the unit by the sergeant(s).

While these adaptations generally go unquestioned or unnoticed, instances do occur in which these unapproved changes create an organizational or legal problem. The gap created by the disparity between formal and informal modifications creates prosecution problems as well as civil litigation problems.

In recent years, through an increased desire to receive accreditation from the Commission on Accreditation for Law Enforcement Agencies, Standard Operating Procedures have been replaced by Operational Directives. These Operational Directives are much more specific and detailed. This change allows little or no latitude for informal adaptation on the shift or unit level. Operational Directives serve as the rules or laws with which the organization's everyday operation must comply.

Law enforcement organizations seek accreditation because it establishes a level of professionalism that is difficult to challenge in a court of law surrounding matters of litigation. In other words, governments save money. Governmental agencies face tremendous insurance costs in three areas—the first is law enforcement; the second is fire suppression; and the third is emergency medical services. Accreditation assists agencies in moderating these insurance costs or in mitigating the amount of damages awarded in a civil action.

Summary

Written communication serves as the backbone for criminal justice agencies. Thousands of pieces of information are processed daily in the course of normal operations. Some is formal in nature, and other is informal.

General Orders supply the skeletal structure for the operation of criminal justice agencies. Communication in this form is almost always formal in scope. General Orders are always written so that they establish guidelines for the operation of the department and serve as a constant reference in the case of confusion or controversy.

Standard Operating Procedures (SOP) are included within the formal blueprint of the General Orders. The SOP manual is created in order to insure consistent and efficient approaches to most situations and to reduce the possibility of litigation in the event of an "unfortunate" outcome in the resolution of a difficult situation. In recent years, SOP manuals have been replaced by Operational Directives. These directives are much more specific and detailed.

No discussion of written communication within criminal justice agencies would be complete without addressing the issues of reports such as offense/incident and supplemental reports. Writing reports involves more than merely placing words on a page. Knowing how to select the appropriate words and how to compose sentences and paragraphs is vital to the success of the communication.

The sentence and the paragraph are the two most fundamental units of written communication. Paragraphs have to be fully developed using a topic sentence to guide and influence readers. Transitional words or phrases must also be utilized in developing a coherent paragraph.

The most frequent type of report in law enforcement is the offense/incident report. Supplemental reports are the second most utilized form of intradepartmental communication. Every offense/incident report or supplemental report begins with field notes taken by the officer/investigator. Good field notes are vital to the preparation of a thorough and inclusive report.

The content of field notes should serve as an outline or brief synopsis of the incident. These notes should contain personal observations, statements made by the victim, witness(es), and suspect(s). Descriptions of important persons, places, or things as well as any other relevant information should also be included.

The offense/incident report should be clear, concise, and complete. The questions of who, what, when, where, why, and how should be answered. The first paragraph should set the tone for report. Every effort should be made to insure that reports are readable—both in terms of legibility and grammatically.

Supplemental reports may be utilized to record suspect statements with the intent to impeach the suspect's credibility or to compromise the suspect's integrity. These reports also provide supervisors with the pending status of a case and allow them to manage case logs. Supplemental offense reports are also used to denote the gathering, processing, and disposition of physical evidence.

Communication that occurs within departments and within agencies occur through the use of memoranda. Memoranda serve to inform an individual or individuals concerning a particular event or occurrence, to make an official record, or to request action or a service. A memorandum is an inappropriate means of communication with the public since they are always reserved as "in-house" communication devices.

Key Terms

Standard Operating Procedures	General Orders
Redundancy	Sentence
Wordiness	Rambling Sentence
Voice	Active Voice
Passive Voice	Topic Sentence
Anecdote	Analogy
Transition	Point of View
Tone	Offense/Incident Report
Supplemental Report	Memoranda
Interdepartmental Memoranda	Intradepartmental Memoranda

Discussion Questions

1. The following topics can be developed into paragraphs. Choose two and write a topic sentence for each. From these two, expand one of your topic sentences into a well-developed paragraph.
    1. A hero
    2. The quality of your training
    3. Your most memorable day on the job
    4. Your favorite supervisor
    5. Your most embarrassing moment
2. In the following sentences, change the voice when necessary. Also note the reason for the change.
    1. The brakes were not completely fixed by the garage repairman.
    2. The car crashed into the large oak tree during the rainstorm.
    3. The driver was absolutely lost.
    4. The recruits are learning the necessity of basic writing skills.
3. Explain why you believe accreditation is important to a law enforcement agency. In your explanation, describe how Operational Directives can help this type of agency achieve accreditation.
4. Analyze the effect word selection has on the development of solid sentences and paragraphs.
5. Analyze the following statement and decide whether or not you support the statements. If you support the statements, state your reasons. If you disagree with the statements, explain your position. "I have been a police officer for 17 years. I have never read a report after I completed it. I don't need to. I know what I said, and that's enough for me. I can always explain it later if I have to."
6. Create an incident report involving a purse snatching. The victim's name is Mary Leaves. Develop your own details and prepare this report in the appropriate format. Be sure to answer the questions who, what, when, where, why, and how.

CHAPTER 7

LAW ENFORCEMENT REPORTING: DEPARTMENTAL RECORDS AND THE COURT SYSTEM

Learning Objectives:

1. To understand the need for security of departmental records in criminal justice agencies.

2. To understand the procedures involved in criminal and civil actions.

3. To identify the roles of various personnel involved in criminal and civil actions.

4. To become familiar with the criminal justice professionals' role in criminal and civil actions.

5. To realize the importance of relaying credible testimony through the use of verbal and nonverbal communication.

6. To appreciate the importance of pretrial preparation.

. . . "It's not always possible to forecast which cases are going to turn out to be big, and in any event it's easy for sloppiness to become a habit across the board. Given the public view of police these days, jaundiced by the interminably rebroadcast Rodney King video and the embarrassing testimony of Mark Fuhrman, when you get to court with a skimpy report, the perception by the skeptical jurors is that you made things up in your testimony to cover you [sic] . . .. Officers do still walk into court with some perceived credibility. Whether they lose it or keep it depends on the officers and their preparation. Preparation starts with your report. When it is too brief, you lose things like excited utterances and a description of the scene—things that can be important to the prosecution."

Street Survival Newsline No. 356 (1999, March 21)

Law enforcement agencies are extremely protective of their records. For a number of reasons, law enforcement agencies prefer to have security surrounding the information they gather in order to protect and preserve the confidentiality of their records. Initially, agencies are concerned about compromising ongoing investigations. Secondarily, agencies are concerned about compromising undercover investigations and jeopardizing undercover officers. A third concern would be that some investigations might not lead to criminal prosecution. Therefore, individuals who might be the target of these investigations would have their reputations damaged if this information was made public knowledge.

Citizens do have a right to certain information gathered by law enforcement agencies under the Freedom of Information Act. However, agencies do retain the right to censor sensitive material and to restrict access in some instances to those individuals directly involved or mentioned in their records. For example, individuals involved in a traffic accident are entitled to receive a copy of the accident report for their insurance companies or attorneys. Defendants are entitled to certain information involving their defense but this information is generally released by the Commonwealth/State Attorney rather than the law enforcement agency.

The most frequent inquiry concerning law enforcement agency records comes from the media, particularly in high profile cases. Television reporters and newspaper reporters are relentless in their pursuit of information. In an effort to boost ratings or beat deadlines or the competition, these individuals will go to great lengths to secure confidential information. A major concern of all law enforcement agencies is that in reporters' zeal to report the news, an investigation will be compromised and a suspect will evade prosecution or fail to receive appropriate punishment due to premature influencing of the community.

The Courtroom Setting

The success of any criminal investigation is ultimately related to the adjudication of the case in a court of law. The investigating officer, therefore, plays a major role in determining the outcome.

The quality and effectiveness of the officer's presentation is of paramount importance in the judicial process. Every officer, whether uniformed or otherwise, should become skilled at testifying on the witness stand. Several steps can be taken to help officers become proficient in the courtroom, beginning with the following:

1. An officer should have a working knowledge of the **rules of evidence**. Possessing an understanding of these guidelines can help an officer work more efficiently at gathering evidence in the field and also help him/her to gain a grasp of courtroom procedures and the functions associated with the prosecution and the defense.

2. An investigator should understand the **rules of admissibility** and the relevance of evidence collected. Only relevant testimony will be allowed into evidence. The judge or defense counsel may object to any testimony that fails to follow the rules of admissibility.

3. An officer/investigator should understand his/her role in the courtroom, and he/she must understand the functions of all other parties in this process. Specifically, the officer/investigator should understand the functions of the judge and the jury in relationship to his/her role as witness.

The Participants in the Criminal Courtroom Drama

Any criminal trial process primarily involves several parties or actors: the **judge**, the **jury**, the **prosecutor**, the **defense attorney**, the **witnesses**, and the **defendant**. Each of these individuals has a specific role in the courtroom setting.

Judge. The **judge** is routinely referred to as "the trier of law" (unless a jury trial is waived, at which time the judge becomes "the trier of fact"). He/She sits as an impartial party whose responsibility is to determine that the trial is conducted in an orderly and lawful manner. Issues that arise concerning the admissibility of evidence or testimony are solely the responsibility of the judge. The judge also resolves any disputes concerning points of law.

After all testimony has been completed, the judge performs a vital phase of the trial process by charging (instructing) the jury. The significance of this action cannot be over-emphasized since many cases have been overturned upon appeal as a result of disputes surrounding instructions to the jury.

Jury. The role of the **jury** is at the crux of the American Criminal Justice System. The jury is referred to as the "Trier of Fact." The jury was historically created with the intent to afford the accused a fair and unbiased trial by a jury of peers. Some question the role of the jury in modern times. However, no other element is more fundamental to the process of justice.

Most juries are selected through a process known as **voir dire.** Potential jury members are screened and selected predicated upon their responses to a series of questions posed to them by both the prosecution and the defense attorneys. In an attempt to form a favorable or at least balanced jury, the prosecution and defense are allowed a series of strikes (or removal) of potential jurors who are deemed to be unsuitable (unsympathetic or damaging to one side or the other).

Acting as a member of a jury is not an easy task. As human beings, we are influenced by details outside the written rules and regulations to which a jury is subjected. Therefore, a jury does not make its determination of guilt or innocence based solely on the presentation of evidence or the testimony delivered in a trial. Nonetheless, juries are charged with the responsibility of determining guilt or innocence, and in **bifurcated trials**, determine punishment that may include life imprisonment or death.

Attorneys. All attorneys have a responsibility or obligation to their clients. In the case of the **prosecution**, this obligation or responsibility is to represent the citizens of the state or commonwealth. **Defense attorneys** represent the interests of their clients. These clients may be referred by the court (pro bono or indigent) or may seek the assistance of legal counsel on their own. In either case, defense attorneys have the responsibility for representing their clients to the fullest extent of their abilities or capabilities.

Prosecuting attorneys, also referred to as state attorneys or commonwealth attorneys, are charged with the responsibility of vigorously investigating and prosecuting those individuals accused of a crime. Mere suspicion and accusation are not sufficient for a criminal conviction. Therefore, prosecutors must prove that defendants are guilty of a crime beyond a reasonable doubt.

Defense attorneys, on the other hand, seek to create or reveal a reasonable doubt in the minds of the jurors or the judge as to the guilt of their clients. The issue of reasonable doubt may be examined or explored by defense attorneys through a variety of means. These means include but are not limited to the following:

1. highlighting the absence of evidence either directly or indirectly linking their client to the crime,
2. discrediting or minimizing the importance of physical evidence, or
3. discrediting or impugning the testimony or integrity of prosecution witnesses.

Witness. The role of any witness in a courtroom setting is to present firsthand knowledge of facts to the jury for consideration. From this statement, you should be able to ascertain that "personal conclusions" are not relevant and may not be offered as part of the testimony. Only information that the witness has observed or gathered through the use of the five senses (sight, smell, sound, taste, touch) is admissible. Attempting to restate what someone else told you is inadmissible because it is **hearsay**. Some exceptions to the hearsay rule do exist; however, as a rule of thumb, hearsay testimony is almost always inadmissible in court.

Defendant. This individual comes before the court accused of a crime. Defendants are presumed innocent until proven guilty and need not offer testimony in their defense. Furthermore, the fact that defendants fail to testify cannot be brought to the attention of the jurors in an attempt to infer guilt by silence.

The Participants in the Civil Courtroom Drama

Much like the criminal courtroom, civil actions involve several actors/players: the **judge**, the **jury**, the **plaintiff**, the **defendant**, their respective **attorneys**, and **witnesses**. In this setting, financial compensation, punitive sanctions, or a redress of grievances is the goal rather than incarceration. Therefore, the judge may grant a wider latitude to attorneys in their respective representation and defense of clients. However, the role of the judge in the civil courtroom is quite similar to that of the criminal counterpart, and little variation occurs in this setting.

Not all civil cases are presented before a jury. In many instances, a judge serves as the final authority. In those situations where a jury is requested or impaneled, the responsibility of the jurors is the same as that of the jury in a criminal trial.

Civil cases are initiated by individuals or a corporation who have suffered some injury or wrong. The initiators of a civil lawsuit are called **plaintiffs**. The persons or corporate entities that are being accused of the wrongdoing or injurious behavior are referred to in civil cases as **defendants**. The standard of proof in a civil case is much less than that required in a criminal prosecution. The plaintiff need merely prove guilt based upon a **preponderance of the evidence**. In other words, the slightest hint of guilt or injury is adequate to sustain a finding for the plaintiff. The defendant must show a lack or absence of responsibility or guilt in order to avoid an award being given to the plaintiff. However, if the defendant can show that the plaintiff was in some small way responsible for the wrongdoing or injury, then this mitigates the responsibility of the defendant and may allow them to eliminate or minimize a finding of guilt.

Attorneys for the plaintiff and the defendant both attempt to gain a strategic advantage by gathering as much information as possible about the evidence to be presented and the testimony to be given by potential witnesses. This information may be gathered via two routes: **depositions** and **discovery**. **Depositions** are sworn testimony given by witnesses in pretrial preparation. Attorneys for each side are permitted to ask questions of potential witnesses to ascertain the relative strength or weakness of their respective clients' position. The same care should be given to testimony related in depositions as to that given in trials since this information may be used at a later date to discredit or impugn the witness.

Much like a courtroom setting, the deposition is an adversarial setting. The defendant (the accused), the defense attorney, the prosecutor or state attorney, and witnesses are present. However, no judge is present. A deposition is a process whereby witnesses are questioned in an attempt to discern what information or facts they possess surrounding a particular occurrence. Witnesses are placed under oath to tell the truth regarding facts of the case just as they are in a courtroom setting, and penalties of perjury apply. **Perjury** is lying under oath and punishable by fine and imprisonment depending upon the finding of the judge. A court reporter (a neutral party) is hired to record the verbatim testimony of each witness including questions of attorneys, responses of witnesses, and objections raised by either party. This written record (transcript) is first reviewed by the witness who may clarify any statements he or she feels the court reporter did not appropriately record. The witness is then required to sign the transcript under oath stating that the transcript is a true and correct statement of facts as he or she knows them. The transcript may then be examined by the prosecutor, the defense, and the judge for rulings on inappropriate questions or unresponsive witnesses.

Depositions are a means of gathering facts and information, which may be used to compromise or discredit witnesses later at trial. The scope of the questions is not necessarily limited to the particular case at hand. However, most attorneys will attempt to limit the breadth of the questions so that they pertain specifically to the matter in question. Therefore, officers should not rely upon notes or offense reports in depositions because they can become part of the record as attachments to the transcript and may be used later to hinder or damage prosecution.

Discovery is a term given to describe a pretrial procedure by which the plaintiff or defendant gains information held by the other. Discovery is usually conducted in an attempt to probe the other party's position for possible weaknesses or areas that may be attacked in an effort to gain a legal advantage. Discovery may take the form of **interrogatories** propounded to either party, **motions** to suppress or produce key evidence or records, and meetings with investigators and expert witnesses.

The Grand Jury

In many jurisdictions prior to a criminal trial, a grand jury is convened. Unlike the courtroom setting, the grand jury is not an adversarial proceeding. Comprised of citizens from the community, the grand jury as a general rule may range in number from 6 to 12 individuals, depending upon governmental statute. The setting is less formal than that of the courtroom, and this lack of formality allows testifying officers to use their notes without fear of having them examined by the defense.

In a grand jury setting, only members of the grand jury, the individual testifying, and in some states, the prosecuting attorney is present. The officer may use his notes or the actual offense report itself. In the instance of a lengthy case, the case folder may be utilized as well as hearsay evidence. The grand jury is impaneled merely to determine whether sufficient evidence exists to bring an accused to trial.

The Criminal Trial

Criminal trials and their civil counterparts follow the same procedural guidelines with minor modifications previously identified. Seldom do police officers/investigators play a major role in civil cases; therefore, we will examine the criminal trial process and their role therein.

A criminal trial has several distinct parts. Initially, the court is called to order by a deputy usually referred to as a **bailiff**. After following a series of procedural steps, the jury is sworn in, and the trial begins with the opening statements of the prosecution and the defense. In the opening remarks, the prosecutor will outline the manner in which he/she intends to prove the state's case. The prosecutor is not allowed to present evidence nor question witnesses but merely to establish the means by which he/she intends to prove the guilt of the defendant. Defense attorneys may waive opening remarks or may choose to highlight the weaknesses in the state's case.

After opening remarks, the prosecution calls its first witness to the stand and the trial is underway. When the prosecution questions witnesses it calls to testify on the behalf of the state, this procedure is referred to as **direct examination**. Following questioning by the prosecutor, defense attorneys have an opportunity to ask further questions of prosecution witnesses or to clarify answers to their previous responses. This procedure is referred to as **cross-examination** since the witnesses were called on behalf of the prosecution. In the event that the defense manages to raise an issue during cross-examination that may require further clarification, the prosecution has an opportunity to conduct a **redirect examination** after the defense attorney is finished. Likewise, the defense has the opportunity to conduct **re-cross-examination** following any redirect examination of the prosecution. The judge serves as a final arbitrator with respect to ending the questioning of a witness.

After both parties have presented all evidence and witnesses, each attorney may make a closing argument. The prosecution summarizes the evidence against the defendant to the jury and entreats them to weigh all aspects of the testimony presented and to return a finding of guilt. The defense, however, takes this opportunity to highlight all the weaknesses in the prosecution's case by enumerating the lack of physical evidence or the confusion of witnesses. The defense attorneys request that the jury return a finding of not guilty since the prosecution has failed to prove its case beyond a reasonable doubt.

Following the closing arguments, the judge instructs the jury as to their responsibility and the points of law applicable to the case. Specifically, the jury is instructed to carefully weigh the testimony of witnesses and the evidence presented. Also, the judge details the aspects of the law that concerns the degree of proof necessary to sustain a finding of guilt and the law concerning punishment for such a finding.

The Investigator/Police Officer's Role in The Trial Process

From the moment the investigator/police officer enters the courtroom, he/she is under scrutiny from all involved. The manner of dress, body language, voice, and vocabulary all play an integral part in establishing their credibility and professionalism. Seasoned officers establish a routine in order to insure that they are perceived as open and honest. This routine includes the following preparations.

1. **Appropriate dress.** Whether in uniform or civilian attire, the witness should be neatly groomed. If not in uniform, the officer should wear dark, conservative clothing that gives the impression that he/she is a professional. Clothes should be clean and pressed, shoes shined, and hair neatly trimmed. Excessive jewelry, makeup, and perfume/cologne should be avoided.

2. **Speech patterns.** Speak clearly and with sufficient volume so as to be heard by the judge, jury, attorneys, and court reporter. Avoid the use of jargon or slang unless specifically directed by the prosecution to include those terms. Also, attempt to limit the number of fillers ("ah," "um," "er," "like," "you know") you use in your testimony since these have the ability to make you appear unsure.

3. **Body language.** Nothing enhances credibility more than the appropriate body language. A posture that exudes confidence clearly indicates to the jury or the judge that the testifying officer is sure of the facts and/or details of the case. Fidgeting or crossing and uncrossing your legs are indications that you are unsure of your testimony or are uncomfortable with questions asked by either the prosecution or defense attorneys. Therefore, testifying officers should sit in an erect manner and face the jury and/or the judge so as to ensure proper eye contact. Hands should be kept in your lap or on the arms of the chair. One caveat to remember is that a witness should always be natural. Your credibility is always enhanced when you do not attempt to "act" or to use theatrics.

4. **Preparing to Testify.** While previous court testimony or experience is the best teacher, several tips that may enhance your testimony in the interim are as follows:

   a. **Always review your field notes and reports prior to testifying in court.** This review should be thorough so that you refer to your notes as little as possible. In other words, testimony delivered from memory is generally deemed more credible by the jury or the judge. The officer/witness must rely on an accurate memory and an alert prosecutor. While cases often take weeks or months, or in some cases even years, to go to trial, officers are expected to remember the most minute details of an investigation. In order to facilitate an officer's memory, notes or reports must be reviewed prior to the courtroom appearance. Officers who take their notebooks or copies of offense/incident reports to court subject these documents to seizure by the defense. Furthermore, they give the impression that they are not fully aware of the facts of the case and need a memory boost or prop to aid their recollection of the facts. This creates a doubt in the mind of the judge, jury, or defense attorney as to how accurately an officer recalls the events of that particular investigation.

In the event that an officer is unable to recount the events of an investigation without notes or an offense report, the officer must realize that the notebook or offense report may be examined by the defense attorney. Examination of the notebook by the defense attorney should be restricted or limited to those notes or accounts of the incident before the court. However, defense attorneys may try to examine other areas of the officer's notebook in an attempt to discredit the officer's integrity or thoroughness by revealing errors or inappropriate remarks noted only for the officer's information involving other matters. If a defense attorney attempts to examine the officer's notebook beyond the scope of the case before the court, the prosecutor should strenuously object. Two ways to avoid this scrutiny are to (1) not take the notebook on the witness stand, or (2) ensure that only the portion of the notebook pertaining to the case before the court is available for examination. Two ways to ensure that only the portion of the notebook pertaining to the case at hand is available for review by the defense attorney is to staple together the pages not associated with this case (as in the case of a spiral bound notebook), or to remove those pages associated with this case from your notebook (as in the case of a loose-leaf notebook).

b.   **If possible, always try to meet with the prosecuting attorney prior to the case in order to clear up any areas that may be confusing.** Prior to testifying, an officer should review his or her notes and the offense/incident report in a meeting with the prosecutor to clear up any areas of confusion or ambiguity and to become acquainted with the questions the prosecutor intends to ask. Furthermore, it may be helpful to have the prosecutor play devil's advocate and anticipate what questions the defense attorney may ask upon cross-examination.

c.   **When you arrive in court, an important rule of thumb is to always <u>listen</u> to the question before answering.** Never anticipate the question or assume that you know the direction in which the attorney is attempting to proceed. The testifying officer should wait for the question to be delivered in its entirety before framing a response. In the event you are asked multiple questions or questions which are combined, you should ask the attorney to rephrase the questions so you may answer them individually.

d.   **Only answer those questions that are asked.** Do not attempt to embellish or add to your answer unless requested to do so. Also, do not guess or speculate.

e.   **If you do not know the answer to an attorney's question, do not be afraid to say, "I do not know."** Nothing damages a witness's credibility more than getting caught up in the speculation trap (or the guessing game). As a testifying officer, you are not a court-recognized expert witness, but oftentimes attorneys will attempt to place you in that precarious position in an effort to undermine your credibility.

f.   **Do not argue with the attorneys or lose your temper.** When you do so, you are perceived as antagonistic or arrogant rather than a professional. Criminal justice professionals present the facts of the case in a detached, impartial manner. When you allow yourself to become angry or to argue with other courtroom officials, you lose your objectivity and damage your credibility.

The Officer's Appearance in Court

The courtroom is a somber and ominous environment. Initially, officers have a sense of foreboding regarding their performance in court. Officers should never become complacent about appearing in court, but as the years pass, officers have a tendency to become more relaxed since their appearances have been regular and they have come to understand how the system operates and what is expected of them.

Court cases (hearings) are scheduled for the convenience of the judge and the attorneys. Law enforcement officers are seldom consulted with regard to scheduling their individual court appearances. Therefore, officers frequently spend a great deal of time in the courtroom waiting for their testimony to be heard. Law enforcement officials who have worked long hours or late hours often succumb to their fatigue and fall asleep in court. While this may not be particularly obtrusive to the workings of the court, it does present a poor first impression to a judge or jury. Prosecutors who have established a sound working relationship with the judge and defense attorneys may assist these individuals by attempting to schedule their cases as early in the day as possible. This early scheduling not only ensures that officers will be fresh during direct and cross-examination, but enables the officer to feel as though he or she has some impact in scheduling.

Having referred to initial first impressions, the appearance of the officer makes a statement about credibility. Officers who are appropriately and neatly attired lend a nonverbal credence to their statements. Judges and juries associate truthfulness and competence with individuals who are neatly dressed and who speak clearly and confidently. Some prosecutors require officers to wear their uniforms when appearing in court; others prefer that the officers dress in business attire (jacket and tie). Irrespective of the dress, common courtesy and respect should apply in all situations. Matters before the court are of a serious nature and, therefore, joking or jocularity is inappropriate.

Testifying

When an officer is called to the witness stand to testify, he or she will be placed under oath by a court clerk or other official and will then be asked to take a seat in the witness box by either the judge or the clerk. As a sign of respect, the officer should wait to be seated until he or she is told to do so. The officer should adhere to the rules of nonverbal communication—avoid fidgeting, wildly gesturing, looking around the courtroom, or failing to make eye contact with the appropriate individual—as these are interpreted as signs of deception or ineptitude. A confident voice is clear and respectful and under no circumstances cocky or arrogant. Questions should be answered with "Yes" or "No" unless asked to explain or expand upon the response by the prosecution or the defense.

The first questions an officer are asked will be directed toward personal information such as the officer's name, rank, current assignment, and then the questions will begin to focus more on the incident and the officer's involvement. The role of the officer is to testify to accounts that he or she has witnessed or facts that he or she has gathered, and not to attempt to aid the prosecution or to hinder the defense. The role of the prosecutor is to ensure that all pertinent information is solicited from the testifying officer and that any contradictory or confusing statement that has been made by the defense attorney is rebutted. The role of the prosecutor is to prosecute, and the role of the defense attorney is to defend his or her client.

Prosecutor: *Would you state your full name for the record, please?*

Officer: Officer M. W. Jackson.

Prosecutor: *What is your current assignment?*

Officer: I am a patrol officer for the X City Police Department.

Prosecutor: Officer Jackson, were you on duty the day of April 9, 1997, at 4:00 p.m.?

Officer: Yes, sir.

Prosecutor: *Did you have an occasion to respond to 4853 Lucerne Road?*

Officer: Yes, sir, I did.

Prosecutor: *And, Officer, upon your arrival, what did you discover?*

Officer:	Upon my arrival, I spoke with the complainant, Ms. Melissa Hemby, in reference to a larceny. Ms. Hemby directed me to a shed behind her house where I discovered a lock had been broken off the hasp and the door was open. I looked inside and noticed that the shed was empty. I had been informed that a riding lawn mower was stored in the shed between uses. Further examination revealed a wallet, which was located inside the shed. I looked inside the wallet and found a driver's license with the name and address of Harry P. Smith (the defendant), 1616 Mockingbird Lane.
Prosecutor:	*Officer, did you determine a value for the missing lawn mower?*
Officer:	Yes, sir, I was advised by the victim that the mower was valued at $1,500.
Prosecutor:	*Officer, did anyone have permission to take the lawnmower?*
Officer:	No, sir, according to the victim, no one had permission to take the riding lawn mower.
Prosecutor:	*Officer, was anything else located at the scene?*
Officer:	Yes, sir, I dusted the door for fingerprints and located one print on the hasp. I recovered this print and returned it to the identification bureau for comparison in the event that a suspect was developed.
Prosecutor:	*What were the results of the fingerprint analysis?*
Officer:	A fingerprint match was discovered by AFIS, and a subsequent analysis by a fingerprint technician revealed that the print recovered from the scene matched a fingerprint belonging to Mr. Harry P. Smith.
Prosecutor:	*Officer, did you have an occasion to speak with the defendant, Mr. Smith as a result of this fingerprint match?*
Officer:	Yes, sir, I did.
Prosecutor:	*Officer, what if anything did you learn from your conversation with the defendant?*
Officer:	Mr. Smith stated that he did not know the victim nor did he know anything about a missing riding lawn mower and he had never been to 4853 Lucerne Road nor did he know where it was located.
Prosecutor:	*Officer, what if anything did you do at this time?*
Officer:	I advised Mr. Smith that he was under arrest and read him his Miranda rights.

During testimony, the investigating officer should never feel compelled to alter facts or to make statements that could damage or hinder his/her credibility. Officers should realize that pressure could be exerted by ambitious or overly aggressive prosecutors or by the victim's grieving family. Yet under no circumstances should an officer succumb to pressure in an effort to appease or satisfy others. A successful career in criminal justice is predicated upon an officer's integrity in court.

After the prosecution and defense have exhausted their questions, the witness must wait to be excused by the court. On occasion defense attorneys will seek to "trip up" the witness by asking one last question. The witness should remember to remain alert until he or she has left the courtroom. The judge will dismiss or excuse the witness when all questions have been asked and answered. When exiting the courtroom, the witness should proceed directly to the doors and into the hallway without exhibiting any signs of emotion (no smiling, glaring, etc.). Also, the witness should refrain from speaking to any individual as he or she exits the courtroom.

Summary

Testifying in court is a necessary aspect of law enforcement. This particular part of law enforcement is not generally regarded as the most pleasurable; however, it should not be viewed as a burden. The interests of the community and the department are best served by truthful, accurate testimony. This type of testimony may best be achieved by being prepared, appropriately dressed, and well mannered. Investigation, arrest, and prosecution are vital links in the process of criminal justice.

A final note with respect to the decision of the judge or jury—criminal justice professionals must realize that they have fulfilled their responsibility by thoroughly investigating the case and accurately testifying as to those facts in court. The determination of guilt or innocence (the verdict) rests with the judge or the jury, and predicting the outcome is hazardous at best. Therefore, law enforcement officials must not gauge their success or failure predicated upon the decision of the judge or jury. Satisfaction should be derived from knowing that the case was thoroughly investigated and that the facts were accurately stated in court. Therefore, irrespective of the verdict, criminal justice professionals should refrain from expressing joy or disappointment with the subsequent finding of guilt or innocence.

Key Terms

Rules of Evidence	Rules of Admissibility
Judge	Jury
Prosecutor	Defense Attorney
Witnesses	Defendant
Voir Dire	Bifurcated Trials
Hearsay	Plaintiff
Preponderance of the Evidence	Deposition
Discovery	Perjury
Interrogatories	Motions
Grand Jury	Bailiff
Direct Examination	Cross-Examination

Redirect Examination   Re-Cross-Examination

Discussion Questions
1. Who are the principle actors in a criminal or civil action?
2. What roles do the prosecution and defense play in criminal procedures?
3. What is the process of voir dire?
4. How are depositions and discovery utilized in the trial process?
5. Of what significance is the grand jury?
6. What preparations are necessary in order for the testifying officer to make the best possible impression on the witness stand?
7. List at least three mistakes witnesses make that impugn their credibility.
8. Should officers conceal their feelings at the outcome (verdict) of a trial? Why or why not?
9. Given what you have learned in this chapter, do you feel it would be appropriate for a testifying officer to shake the hand of the prosecuting attorney on his/her way out of the courtroom following his/her testimony? Why or why not?
10. If not directly questioned about an event, should an officer leave out facts or information during his/her testimony that may assist the defense?
11. **Ethical Issue:** Should an officer become personally involved with the family of a victim? Why or why not?
12. **Ethical Issue:** If the investigator truly believes that the defendant is guilty, should he/she embellish or enhance facts which may not be strong enough to stand on their own in order to point the finger of guilt at the defendant?
13. **Ethical Issue:** Are there any conditions under which an investigator should commit perjury? Explain your answer.

Additional Topics for Investigation
1. Visit a court proceeding and observe the testimony of various witnesses. List the strengths and weaknesses of each individual's testimony and determine whether or not you believe them. What made an impression on you? What made you believe in their truthfulness? Write a brief summary of your findings and present them to the class. Focus on the factors involved in your decision-making processes concerning the veracity of the witnesses.
2. Observe police officers or investigators as they testify in a court setting. Pinpoint any weaknesses you observed. Did one officer testify "better" than another? Why? Do police officers make better witnesses? Why or why not?
3. Interview one prosecuting and one defense attorney. Ask what defines a good witness. Ask them, in their opinions, what differentiates a good witness from a poor witness. What areas do they seek to exploit or take advantage of in a witness's testimony?

CHAPTER 8

INTERVIEWING AND INTERROGATING: WITNESSES AND SUSPECTS[1]

Learning Objectives:

1.   To distinguish between interviews and interrogations.

2.   To understand the three basic purposes for an interview.

3.   To identify techniques for more effective interview questioning.

4.   To identify the steps involved in interrogations.

5.   To recognize the three areas for gathering information in preparation for an interview.

6.   To understand the importance of selecting an appropriate setting for interviews and interrogations.

7.   To compare and contrast open and closed questions.

8.   To determine which situations are conducive to eliciting more information.

9.   To be aware of the legal requirements necessary to acquire admissible statements.

10.   To recognize ploys used by suspects in trying to divert the investigator's attention.

11.   To recognize and understand patterns used by investigators in order to solicit information.

12.   To identify methods for effectively terminating an interview or interrogation.

In 1966, when the United States Supreme Court issued its finding in the *Miranda* case, no one expected the long-term ramifications of the Court's mandate. Most criminal justice professionals saw this edict as a means of providing structure for conducting investigations and interrogations—a way to ensure fair treatment for everyone. Unfortunately, over the decades since the Supreme Court delivered its charges, the tide has turned and more emphasis has been placed on the formal application of Miranda rather than on the search for the truth.

Harold J. Rothwax, a New York State Supreme Court Judge and a lecturer at the Columbia Law School, has called the criminal justice system a sporting event. By this comment, Judge Rothwax means that we give the defendant a sporting chance to evade society's punishments. What he is referring to is Miranda. The use of Miranda in its formal sense gives the defendant, much like a fox during a hunt, a fair chance to escape. Judge Rothwax calls Miranda the triumph of formalism. He goes on to state that "In my judgment, Miranda should be repudiated. It is bad constitutional law; it is ill-conceived policy; and most grievous. It has created a jurisprudence of formalism.[2]"

Recently the necessity of Miranda was brought into question by Congress in a case in which the Petitioner, Charles Thomas Dickerson, indicted for bank robbery, conspiracy to commit bank robbery, and using a firearm in the course of committing a crime of violence alleged that he had not received "his Miranda warnings before being interrogated." The District Court where Dickerson filed his petition granted his motion to suppress the confession. The Government took an interlocutory appeal to the United States Court of Appeals for the Fourth Circuit. That Court, in a divided vote, reversed the district court's ruling, concluding that Petitioner had not received Miranda warnings before making his statement. "But it went on to hold that §3501, which in effect makes the admissibility of statements such as Dickerson's turn solely on whether they were made voluntarily, was satisfied in this case. It then concluded that the decision in Miranda was not a constitutional holding and that therefore Congress could by statute have the final say on the question of admissibility. 166 F.3d 667 (1999).

On June 26, 2000, Chief Justice Rehnquist delivered the opinion of the Supreme Court in Charles Thomas Dickerson vs. The United States of America on Writ of Certiorari to the United States Court of Appeals for the Fourth Circuit as follows: "In *Miranda v. Arizona,* 384 U.S. 436 (1966), we held that certain warnings must be given before a suspect's statement made during custodial interrogation could be admitted in evidence. In the wake of that decision, Congress enacted 18 U.S.C. § 3501 which in essence laid down a rule that the admissibility of such statements should turn only on whether or not they were voluntarily made. We hold that *Miranda,* being a constitutional decision of this court, may not be in effect overruled by an Act of Congress, and we decline to overrule *Miranda* ourselves. We therefore hold that *Miranda* and its progeny *in this Court govern the admissibility of statements made during custodial interrogation in both state and federal courts.*

…

In sum, we conclude that <u>Miranda</u> announced a constitutional rule that Congress may not supersede legislatively. Following the rule of stare decisis, we decline to overrule <u>Miranda</u> ourselves. The judgment of the Court of Appeals is therefore <u>Reversed.</u>[3]"

At the very core of effective law enforcement is the ability to initiate and to sustain a conversation with people. Whether the intent is to gather information or to elicit a confession, good communication skills are essential.

Criminal justice professionals, by their very nature, are outgoing, gregarious individuals–in other words, people who like to talk. Speak with a police officer for five minutes and then realize how much information has been gathered by the officer in this brief time span. This process is a natural occurrence, not intrusive or offensive. Were you comfortable? Did you feel at ease with the officer? Congratulations! You have just been the unwitting subject of a police interview.

The Interview Process

Before you begin your study of interviewing and interrogation, you need to understand the difference between these two processes. An **interview** is conducted when a person who is not a suspect is questioned to determine whether the person possesses information that is of value to the investigator's cause. The definition for **interrogation** is essentially the same as that of an interview, **except** that the person being interviewed is a suspect in the case.

Interviewing

Interviewing may best be described as a conversation with a purpose. In a situation such as this, a speaker or interviewer is attempting to solicit information that may or may not be detrimental to the individual being questioned. Interviewing is more than a list of questions; it is an opportunity to establish a rapport.

Three basic purposes exist for an interview:

1. **Securing information**. The success of this type of interview is based on the interviewer's ability to solicit information with proper questions and to listen effectively.
2. **Giving information**. In this type of interview, the interviewer is the one providing information. Success here is determined by the interviewer's ability to choose and articulate the right information.
3. **Influencing behavior**. In these situations, the interviewer is attempting to persuade the interviewee to change behavior or to make a decision. The success of this type of interview is dependent upon the interviewer's ability to engender trust and credibility and to use persuasive tactics.

Successful interviewers develop a plan. This plan entails putting the interviewee at ease and allowing that individual to talk. This conversation frequently occurs in a relatively private setting. Good interviewers minimize distractions and select questions carefully. They know how to ask questions and when to ask questions. Good interviewers take brief notes and maintain control of the interview at all times. They do not overwhelm their subjects. Above everything else, good interviewers are good listeners. They always try to conclude an interview on a positive note in order to maintain a connection with the interviewee.

Becoming a good interviewer takes practice, but you also can follow several suggestions to help you develop and perfect your technique.

- ➤ **Carefully prepare**. The key to a successful interview involves preparation.
- ➤ **Maintain control**. A good interviewer maintains control at all times of both him/herself and the direction that the interview is taking. No matter how upsetting a crime is, you must be able to act sympathetic and nonjudgmental.
- ➤ **Listen**. An effective interviewer must also be a good listener. You need to be able to read both the verbal and nonverbal messages that your witness is delivering in order to know the appropriate direction for your attack.
- ➤ **Be alert and patient**. An effective interviewer is not pushy but is flexible in his or her attack. Maintain mental alertness and be patient.
- ➤ **Be a good actor**. An effective interviewer is a good listener but he or she is also a good actor. You should be self-confident and maintain a professional image at all times.

Scenario: A market owner observes a purse-snatching incident through the window of his store. He is reluctant to become involved. An officer arrives at the scene to take a report from the victim and in the process, interviews any persons he believes may have witnessed the incident. After taking the victim's statement, he goes into the market to interview the owner.

OFFICER: Good morning, sir, how are you today?

OWNER: I'm fine. How are you, Officer?

OFFICER: Fine, thanks. My name is Officer Jackson. I'm here investigating a purse snatching which occurred approximately 10 minutes ago. I was wondering if you heard or saw anything.

OWNER: I'm not sure. Where did it occur?

OFFICER: It occurred across the street from your store.

OWNER: What happened?

OFFICER:	According to the victim, she was walking down the street across from the front of your store when someone ran up behind her, grabbed her purse, and fled.
OWNER:	What did the purse-snatcher look like?
OFFICER:	She described him as a young white male, approximately 15-18 years old, with blonde hair, and wearing a black leather jacket.
OWNER:	No, I'm sorry. I didn't see anyone like that around here this morning.
OFFICER:	Have you seen anyone that looks like this person hanging around your store before today?
OWNER:	No, not around my store.
OFFICER:	Have you seen anyone hanging around the area that looks like this person?
OWNER:	Yeah, now that you mention it. I've seen a blonde kid in this area early in the morning over by the produce lot. There's a bunch of guys that hang around over there hoping to get a day job from the produce shippers.
OFFICER:	Would you happen to know which produce shipper he might have worked for?
OWNER:	Try Johnson's Apples; they're always looking for extra help to load and unload the trucks. As a matter of fact, I think I saw a blonde kid over there last week. Had a gold cross earring in his right ear.
OFFICER:	Thank you. I really appreciate your help. I'm sorry, I don't think I got your name when I introduced myself.
OWNER:	Oh, I'm sorry, my name is Travis Cravener.
OFFICER:	Mr. Cravener, if you see the young man you described in the area again or if you remember anything else, would you please call me? Here is my name and department telephone number. I really appreciate your taking the time to speak with me. Also, if there's anything I can do for you, be sure and give me a call. Thanks again.

As evidenced by the foregoing scenario, interviewing is a process of acquiring information through carefully worded questions. Good interviewers have a keen intuitive sense. They are able to elicit information and expand upon prior information by being sensitive to the needs of the interviewee. They have a high emotional quotient—they are empathetic to the interviewee, placing themselves in the interviewee's position—understanding that people are often reluctant to provide information or to get involved because they are afraid of the consequences that may follow.

Interviewers always try to conclude an interview by offering an opportunity for future assistance, thus establishing a *quid pro quo* (one hand washes the other) relationship. The interviewee then feels as if he is assisting the officer in the investigation and developing a friend at the police department—an invaluable contact for future reference.

Interrogating

Interrogating is confrontational by nature. While interviewing attempts to solicit information through the use of congenial or persuasive means, interrogating is a process by which the suspect is carefully maneuvered into a position of no retreat. The goal of interrogation is to solicit or acquire information that is generally not in the legal best interests of the individual being interviewed.

Interrogating involves a variety of psychological manipulations in order to facilitate a confession from a suspect. Most interrogations begin with an interview. As the focus becomes narrower or more specific, though, the interview transitions from a pleasant conversation to an accusation. Once the officer has initiated the interrogation process, however, no opportunity exists for a return to the pleasantness of the interview technique. Interrogations are structured, exacting and lengthy, usually commanding a minimum of four hours time and perhaps longer depending upon the skill of the interrogator and the resistance of the suspect. The interrogation may then follow a process which might include a number of steps, some of which are direct confrontation, theme development, eliminating denials, overcoming objections, gaining the suspect's attention, and finally, the confession.

1. **Direct confrontation**. The interviewee (suspect) is told that he is suspected of being involved in a crime. The officer presents the suspect with a synopsis of what occurred and then presents some evidence to support the scenario (evidence which may or may not be factual). The officer then observes the suspect.

2. **Theme development**. The interviewee (suspect) is provided with some justification or excuse for having committed the crime. An example would be a shooting incident involving the suspect and a friend who had slept with the suspect's wife. The officer might say, "If he had slept with my wife, I might have shot him myself." This type of statement gives the suspect an opportunity for an explanation for the crime and serves as a transition from the previous confrontation.

3. **Eliminating denials**. The interviewer (officer) is attempting to eliminate or narrow the opportunity for evasion. The officer uses facts of the case to support the involvement of the suspect in the crime.

4.   **Overcoming objections**. The interviewer (officer) proposes a reason why the suspect did not commit the crime. In this regard, the officer is attempting to allow the suspect to realize that no other explanation exists that fits the facts of the case. The suspect begins to realize that the evidence cannot be explained away.

5.   **Gaining the suspect's attention**. The interviewer (officer) attempts to project a sincere attitude in an effort to gain the suspect's trust. In this way, the suspect would feel compelled to confess to the crime in order to absolve him/herself of the psychological burden of guilt. The success of this technique is measured by the suspect's silence and acceptance of comfort.

6.   **Confession**. In this instance, the suspect finally surrenders to the officer and admits involvement in the crime. At this point, the officer must provide the suspect with comfort through a variety of physical and emotional techniques. Officers encourage the suspect to put his/her story in writing as a means of alleviating feelings of guilt. Officers must be particularly supportive at this time in order to convey a sense of absolution of guilt and to insure compliance on the part of the suspect.[4]

Officers involved in interrogations should always seek to calm a suspect prior to the conclusion of an interrogation segment. This debriefing is performed in order to reduce the propensity of the suspect for personal harm in the wake of a confession.

By developing proper interrogation techniques, officers facilitate the resolution of crimes and provide guilty suspects an opportunity for psychological relief or forgiveness. An element to be considered in this psychological manipulation, however, is the appropriateness of the setting.

Preparing for an Interview/Interrogation

When preparing for an interview, you must gather information or data from three areas: Case Information, Background Information, and Personal Information.

Case Information. To be successful as an interviewer, you must have the answers to several questions that you will ask. In this manner, you are prepared to recognize deception on the part of the interviewee early on, and you can confront him or her and attempt to have him or her believe you have all the answers.

Obtain case information by
* Reviewing a copy of the incident report and making note of the date and time of occurrence.
* Reviewing any and all photographs of the scene.
* Reviewing the information obtained from other interviews.
* Identifying key information that is known about the case that can be used to verify the suspect's truthfulness.

Background Information. Obtain background information for this incident by reviewing the following:
* **Prior arrests**. You should know what the suspect's prior involvement has been. In particular, pay close attention to notes of past techniques used by the suspect

and/or his or her associates. People tend to maintain the same habits. Therefore, this knowledge could be used against them.

- **Arresting officers**. If possible, you should interview officers who arrested the suspect on prior occasions. They could possess useful information.
- **Prior interviews.** Obtain copies of any previous interviews conducted with the suspect. Examine video or audiotapes for mannerisms and defenses that the suspect used.

Personal Information. Obtaining information of a personal nature about the suspect may give you some insight into which techniques will be most effective in questioning him or her. In particular, you will need to

- know age, date of birth, where the suspect was born, where he or she has lived, and the conditions under which he or she has lived.
- identify the suspect's likes and dislikes. Use this information in your interview.
- identify the suspect's marital status, the number of children he or she has, the children's names, if possible, and the suspect's parental information.

The Setting

The appropriate setting for an interview and interrogation may vary with the intent of the investigator. However, privacy is an essential element regardless of the setting. Prior to the initiation of any formal investigation, the officer will develop a plan or theme for acquiring information. In the development process of this theme is the issue of the appropriate setting. The appropriate setting may be divided into two broad categories: informal and formal.

Interviewing in the informal setting. Interviews of this nature may run the gamut from the casual conversation to the point at which the officer initiates an accusatory phase also referred to as a "narrowing of the focus." When a police officer narrows the focus of an interview to one suspect or begins to accuse one individual of a crime, a transition to the interrogation aspect occurs. However, prior to this transition, plenty of settings exist in which to gather information. The simplest and most effective technique may be the "street corner" conversation. With the renewed interest in "beat police officers" or community policing, the art of conversation is more important than ever. This simple technique allows police officers to network or become friendly with the citizens in their assigned areas of patrol.

Street corner conversations are designed primarily to build a rapport with the citizens and to become more familiar with the individuals and their respective positions in the community. Officers begin to develop a schematic or diagram of informal and formal social relationships among individuals and their families as well as individuals and their associates. The significance of this background work is that it places officers in a position to gather information more easily. People have a tendency to be more open, more candid with their friends than with a formal symbol of authority. Furthermore, these same people are more willing to take a stand or speak out against deviant or criminal elements in their neighborhoods if they have confidence in "their" police officers.

While not a formal setting, the tone or complexion of the conversation changes when an individual is asked to have a seat in a police cruiser. This setting provides the officer with a little more control of the situation and tends to reduce outside distractions. Officers may be more focused in the intent of their interview. In fact, this type of interview may be more goal directed in attempting to elicit specific information concerning a crime. By merely inviting the individual into the police cruiser, the officer has subtly increased the amount of psychological pressure.

By the same token, when an officer enters an individual's residence for the purpose of interviewing a witness, the psychological pressure becomes less because the officer is in the domain of the individual. Officers frequently interview citizens in their home in an attempt to establish rapport, gather information, or in some instances to initiate the previously mentioned "narrowing of the focus." Since most individuals are comfortable in their homes, if the interview becomes too specific or borders on accusation, these individuals are provided with a variety of distractions that eases the psychological pressure.

Another informal interview setting is the place of employment or business. Most individuals are relatively comfortable in their place of employment since they are generally surrounded with acquaintances, friends, or familiar objects. This provides them with a sense of psychological comfort. However, the arrival of a police officer may disrupt this comfort. Police officers frequently enter businesses to converse with the owners or managers about a broad array or variety of topics. Yet when the officer arrives to speak with a specific individual or with a specific intent, the workplace may become anxiety filled. The mere presence of the officer will certainly arouse curiosity and generate gossip among the workers. The individual being questioned loses his or her anonymity among colleagues and becomes the center of attention. This unwanted attention frequently induces a defensive response, which may serve as a barrier to the communication process. However, the officer may overcome this barrier by merely asking a few questions and establishing a later date and time to continue the line of inquiry. This date for further interviewing or questioning may be scheduled in a more formal setting which is usually associated with the individual coming to the police department to speak with the officer.

Interviewing in the formal setting. The officer who conducts interviews at the police department enjoys almost complete control of the situation. He is familiar with the physical surroundings and the official operations of the organization. The individual who comes to the police department, however, is almost always ill at ease or anxious. The symbols of authority associated with law enforcement adorn the walls of the facility; tremendous numbers of uniformed and non-uniformed police officers are milling about; and in the background is the omnipresent police radio. These accouterments set the stage for the officer and the individual's exchange.

In a formal setting, the officer attempts to isolate the individual being interviewed and to remove all of or to minimize the amount of distractions. This usually occurs by placing the individual in an interview room that is generally sparsely furnished and usually devoid of items that will serve to draw the focus away from the officer. The casual tone of questioning often is abandoned in favor of a more direct or pointed line of inquiry—in other words, specific answers to specific questions.

This type of interviewing is not to be confused with interrogation since the officer has not crossed the line from conversation to confrontation. Pointed questions or direct questions need not be confrontational yet may still remain specific in nature. There may come a time where the officer may be compelled to change the focus of the interview to an interrogation. If the mood or tone of the interview changes from the interview to interrogation, or if the officer's questions are structured in a such a manner as to narrow the focus of the investigation to this particular individual as a suspect, then legal issues concerning individual rights (<u>Miranda</u> decision) arise.

While interviews may be conducted in a variety of settings, most of which lend themselves to the informal, interrogations are almost always formal by nature. The interrogation does not lend itself to an informal setting. How could it? Interrogations are confrontational by definition. They imply an accusation, and the individual being accused is the one who is present before the officer.

Interview/Interrogation Questions

A **question** is a request, either direct or implied, for an interviewee to think about a particular subject. Interview questions should be kept simple so that you encourage the interviewee to answer. Remember that interview questions are the key to obtaining the interviewee's knowledge, feelings, or information about a particular incident. If you keep the interview as conversational in tone as possible, you will ensure that the interviewee provides responses to your questions. After all, holding a conversation requires a certain amount of give-and-take during the interview. An important point to remember is to ask questions—not to make statements. Statements do not require answers and the interviewee will not provide you with information.

Types of Questions

Two main types of questions are generally asked during investigative interviews: **closed questions** and **open questions**. **Closed questions** typically require a simple "yes" or "no" response or some undeniable fact such as the interviewee's address, telephone number, etc. This type of question is usually asked in the beginning stage of an interview in order to put the interviewee at ease. Closed questions are useful when you want to maintain maximum control over the interview, or when you want to save time because they limit the interviewee's response. You may also use this type of questioning with reluctant witnesses/interviewees who are not expected to give detailed explanations. Closed questions limit the ability to establish a rapport between the interviewer and the interviewee.

Open questions cannot be answered with "yes" or "no." These types of questions require the interviewee to think clearly and to reveal the greatest amount of information. These types of questions also cause the most distress in the interviewee. Open questions can help you:

- Discover the interviewee's needs, attitudes, values, priorities, and aspirations.
- Build rapport.
- Encourage the interviewee to express feelings in a nonthreatening environment.
- Determine the interviewee's frame of reference.

Open questions come in a variety of types, each with its own characteristics and purpose. The types of open questions are reflective, directive, pointed, indirect, self-appraisal, diversion, and leading.

1. **Reflective Questions**. These types of questions use the interviewee's comments as a means of handling objections the interviewee has to responding to an initial

question. "Let me see if I've got this straight . . ." or, "What I'm hearing you say is that you do not want to comment because you don't want our conversation to get back to . . . ; is that correct?" You can then assure the interviewee that your conversation is confidential, that any statements he or she makes will not get back to whomever, and then repeat the question that triggered the objection by the interviewee.

2.   **Directive Questions**. Directive questions help the interviewee understand the advantages of cooperation. These types of questions are designed to help the interviewee see the common ground he or she shares with the investigator. "You do want to get to the bottom of this, don't you?" "I know you would like your side of the story to be written in my report, right?"

3.   **Pointed Questions**. Pointed questions are specific in nature. They are complex, detailed, and persuasive. The interviewer asks exactly what is desired so that the interviewee understands that you believe they are ready, willing, and able to answer your questions. Pointed questions must be thoughtfully developed and not necessarily accusatory or offensive in nature.

4.   **Indirect Questions**. Indirect questions are often used at the beginning of an interview or at some point where you require a change of pace in the course of your discussion. This type of question helps interviewees express opinions, suggestions, feelings, etc. Through the use of indirect questions, interviewers can grow to understand the interviewee's thoughts or needs.

5.   **Self-Appraisal Questions**. This type of question is used to stimulate conversation between the interviewer and the interviewee. The interviewer uses this type of question to identify with the interviewee. An investigator can develop hypotheses about an incident through the use of self-appraisal questions. As a general rule, deceptive or evasive interviewees find it almost impossible to be consistent in answering self-appraisal questions.

6.   **Diversion Questions**. Diversion questions have two purposes: (1) to distract the interviewee's thoughts from the issue; and (2) to build rapport between the investigator and the interviewee. Diversion questions are particularly useful when attempting to distract highly emotional interviewees. For example, if you are interviewing a witness to a homicide, you might notice that the witness is extremely agitated and shaken by his or her experience. The witness requires time to realize that the danger is over. You might use diversion questions unrelated to the homicide to reassure her or him that all is well. You could ask, "What type of work do you do?" or "Have you lived in this area for very long?" As the witness begins to calm down, he or she will be able to focus on what was seen or heard during the homicide.

7.   **Leading Questions**. Leading questions can be used to build rapport and to communicate understanding and acceptance to the interviewee. When using leading questions containing implicit messages, an interviewer can maintain moderate emotional tension in the interview. When poorly used, however, leading questions can elicit unreliable, invalid responses. Nonetheless, leading questions used to build rapport can stimulate dialogue and encourage cooperation.[5]

Principles of Effective Question Development

The following guidelines will help you to develop effective questioning strategies:

> **Use closed questions when appropriate.**
> **Use open questions when appropriate.**
> **Keep questions simple.**
> **Avoid third-degree type questions.**
> **Ask leading questions where appropriate (i.e., assisting the interviewee in saving face).**
> **Ask tough questions.**
> **Ask self-appraisal questions.**

In developing your questions, consider that people often do things that we would consider "dumb," "stupid," "dangerous," or "foolish." Once you acknowledge that people do, in fact, commit crimes we cannot possibly begin to understand, then you can see how important the process of questioning witnesses, suspects, and victims really is. You must be brave enough to ask questions that would be considered rude or intrusive in polite society. You should also pursue unanswered questions by repeating those questions the interviewee has failed to answer. You should not demand an answer to your question or point out to the interviewee that he or she failed to answer your question, but try rewording the question. Many interviewees try to provoke an interrogator, even if they are not suspects but merely witnesses or victims.

Legal Issues

As a general rule, the laws surrounding admissions or confessions do not apply in the interview situation since interviews are generally construed to be a conversation. The tone of the conversation may vary depending upon the type of information the officer is attempting to gather, but unless and until the investigator narrows the focus of the investigation to one individual, Escobedo (378 U.S. 478, 1964), Miranda, and subsequent court cases do not come into play.

In the mid-60s, the Supreme Court set the tone for the use of confessions and admissions by introducing Escobedo and Miranda into police parlance. In 1960, Danny Escobedo was arrested for murder. He was interrogated by investigators who stated that they had an "air-tight" case and he should confess. Escobedo requested an attorney and was advised that he could not simply walk out. Meanwhile his attorney, who was present at the police station, was advised that his client was being interrogated and could not be disturbed. Eventually confessing, Escobedo was convicted and appealed his case to the United States Supreme Court. The Court stated that suspects are entitled to counsel during police interrogations in order to protect their rights, and counsel should be provided when requested.

Miranda went a step further in 1966 when the Court stated that defendants must be advised of their rights prior to questioning by police because of the inherent coercive nature involved in police interrogations. Ernesto Miranda was arrested for kidnapping and rape in Phoenix, Arizona. He subsequently signed a confession after a lengthy police interrogation. Miranda appealed this conviction and the United States Supreme Court set forth the guidelines for the issuance of the infamous "Miranda Warning" and "Waiver of Rights."

While these cases did not serve as a barrier to acquiring confessions, they did serve to provide some structure in which police conducted interrogations. In an effort to acquire statements of guilt, police officers became more sophisticated in their questioning techniques. The introduction of deception, trickery, and psychological manipulation allowed investigators to resolve their cases.

Attorneys responding to this new approach to obtaining confessions began to question the tactics of police officers with regard to interrogation. Voluntariness of the confession was no longer the focal point of the confession but whether or not police officers should be allowed to use trickery, deceit, and psychological manipulation in interrogating their clients.

Trickery, deception, and psychological manipulation do not necessarily render a voluntary confession inadmissible. However, in Lynumn v. Illinois, the Court ruled that a suspect's free choice was impaired by going beyond the evidence connecting her to a crime and introducing a completely extrinsic consideration in the form of an empty but plausible threat. In Spano v. New York, another extrinsic factor was examined when coercion was used to lead the suspect to believe that failure to confess would result in adverse consequences for others.

On an individual basis, these factors may become confusing and burdensome for the court to resolve. Therefore, in an effort to establish clarity and a reasonable alternative, in Arizona v. Fulminante, the Supreme Court used a totality of circumstances test to determine that a confession made to an informant in exchange for the promise of protection from other prison inmates was involuntary because it was coerced by a credible threat of physical violence.

Some courts will not accept confessions induced by either direct or implied promises. The United States Supreme Court and courts of local jurisdiction will allow police officers some gamesmanship when it comes to interrogating suspects. Nevertheless, no court will allow an admission of guilt if it is coerced by a government official. Latitude in this area will be determined by the local court of jurisdiction. Therefore, the officer must become acquainted with the practices of the local jurists and their rulings concerning the admissibility of evidence concerning confessions. However, the issuing of a Miranda warning need not serve as an impediment or a major hurdle in the process of acquiring a confession. The Miranda warning may be issued in such a way that it need not deter the suspect from speaking with the criminal justice professional.

> **Sample Interrogation Scenario**: At 1:50 a.m. district officers were advised of a robbery, which occurred at the local 7-11. The suspect was described as a white male in a dark jacket who had brandished a knife at the clerk and taken the cash from the register. The suspect had fled from the store on foot and was stopped by responding units two blocks from the 7-11 at 2:00 a.m. The officers conducted a pat-down search of the suspect and found a knife. The clerk was brought to the location of the suspect and made a positive identification. The suspect was arrested and booked. The next day, prior to an arraignment hearing, the suspect was questioned by investigators concerning this incident.
>
> **Investigator**: Good morning, Mr. Jackson.

Suspect: Mornin'

Investigator: How are you feeling this morning?

Suspect: Okay. How 'bout you?

Investigator: Fine, thanks. Can I get you some coffee?

Suspect: Yeah, black is good.

Investigator: I'm glad you could come down to the department
this morning. I just want to clear up a few things
since the last time we spoke. Is that okay with you?

Suspect: Yeah, okay.

Investigator: Now before we get started I need to inform you of
your Miranda Rights. This is just a formality so we
can clear up those few things. Okay?

Suspect: Okay

Investigator: You have the right to remain silent. Anything you say can and will
be used against you in a court of law. You have the right to talk to
an attorney and to have an attorney present while you are being
questioned. If you desire an attorney and cannot afford one, an
attorney will be appointed for you before any questioning begins.
If you answer questions now without an attorney present, you still
have the right to stop answering questions at any time. Do you
understand these rights as I have explained them to you? If so,
please place your initials by the "yes" box.[6]

Suspect: Yeah. Okay.

Investigator: Good. Please put your initials here.

[Suspect places initial where indicated.]

Investigator: Do you wish to waive these rights? [In other words,
do you want to talk to me?] If so, please sign on the
line and place the date and time.

[Suspect places initials where indicated.]

Suspect: Yeah. Okay.

Investigator: Good. Now that we have that out of the way, let's talk. Mr. Jackson, I need to just clear up a few things. According to my notes, the last time we spoke you stated you were on your way back from the 7-11 when the police stopped you. And you told the officer that you had gone to the 7-11 in order to buy a pack of cigarettes. Is that correct?

Suspect: Yeah, that's right.

Investigator: Well, Mr. Jackson, you didn't have any cigarettes at home? So you came out in the rain in order to get a pack of cigarettes?

Suspect: Yeah, that's right. Do you smoke?

Investigator: No, I don't.

Suspect: When you need a cigarette, you need a cigarette. I didn't have any butts or anything in the ashtray.

Investigator: I guess I understand. Now, according to what you told the officers, you didn't see anyone at all run past you?

Suspect: No, I didn't see nobody.

Investigator: Well, Mr. Jackson, how is it then when the officer searched you, you had a knife in your jacket pocket?

Suspect: It's a dangerous neighborhood and I carry the knife for protection.

Investigator: After you were arrested and taken to booking, why did you ask the officer for a cigarette? And why were there no cigarettes listed on the booking property intake slip?

Suspect: I must have lost them.

Investigator: Mr. Jackson, can I call you Bob?

Suspect: (Nods in the affirmative.)

Investigator: Bob, isn't it true that you went to the 7-11 with the idea of robbing the place?

Suspect:	No. I just went for some cigarettes.
Investigator:	Bob, what happened to the cigarettes between the time you left the 7-11 and the two blocks in which the officer stopped you?
Suspect:	I don't know.
Investigator:	Bob, let's look at this from my position. Suppose you were me. What would you think about what you just told me?
Suspect:	I don't know. I'd guess you would think I was lying.
Investigator:	Bob, I'm not trying to say that you're lying. I just want us to get to the truth here together. I know you're under a lot of pressure. Why don't we take a break and you can have a cigarette, okay?
Suspect:	No, I quit about two years ago. I'll just have another cup of coffee.

While this scenario is certainly a brief and simple example of the interrogation process, the elements essential to acquiring an inculpatory statement are present. The investigator has endeavored to establish a rapport and level of trust with the suspect in an effort to find the truth. The Miranda warning was presented in a lawful manner but in such a way that it did not present a major obstacle or hurdle to the interrogative process. While some deception or trickery may have been utilized, the suspect was not placed in an environment that could be construed as coercive when viewed through the Supreme Court's edict—totality of the circumstances.

Terminating the Interview/Interrogation

Just because you seem to be at the conclusion of the interview, you should not assume that there is no more information forthcoming from the interviewee. You should continue to assume that more information is available, and you should ask questions such as, "What else is there that you can tell me about what happened?" or "What else should I know about this incident?"

At some point, however, you will determine that the interview has reached its concluding or termination point. At this time, you can end the interview in one of the following ways:

1. Tell the interviewee you may contact him or her sometime in the future for a follow-up interview.
2. Make an appointment with the interviewee for a second interview and give yourself time to prepare further.
3. Lead into a confrontation with the interviewee by announcing that you believe there are inconsistencies in his or her story and that these inconsistencies must be addressed.
4. Attempt to gain a confession or admission of guilt.

Summary

Several keys are associated with becoming a good interviewer or a good interrogator. Chief among these is patience, patience, patience. The art of conversation takes time to learn and develop. The art and science of interrogation is no less demanding in its utilization of time. Good interviewers and interrogators are good listeners. They are empathetic and sometimes sympathetic to the people they are speaking with. However, any interview is a conversation with a purpose, and every interrogation is confrontational.

By developing good interview and interrogation techniques, criminal justice professionals facilitate the resolution of crimes and provide guilty suspects an opportunity for psychological relief or forgiveness. In addition to devising effective questioning methods, criminal justice professionals should prepare for interviews by obtaining case, background, and personal information. Reviewing copies of previous incident reports, speaking with prior arresting officers, and obtaining information of a personal nature concerning a witness are important in the development of a case.

Interview questions are the key to obtaining the interviewee's knowledge, feelings, or information about a particular incident. If you keep the interview as conversational in tone as possible, you will ensure that the interviewee provides responses to your questions. Both closed and open questions should be a part of any interview setting.

At the conclusion of an interview, remember that the interviewee probably has additional information to convey. You should continue to assume, therefore, that more information is available and you should ask questions such as, "What else is there that you can tell me about what happened?" or "What else should I know about this incident?"

You should attempt to end your interview by either asking for a possible follow-up interview, scheduling a second interview to give yourself further preparation time, and/or leading into a confrontation with the witness to attempt to elicit a confession or admission of guilt.

Key Terms

Interview	Interrogation
Quid pro quo	Question
Closed questions	Open questions
Pointed questions	Reflective questions
Directive questions	Indirect questions
Self-appraisal questions	Diversion questions
Leading questions	Escobedo v. Illinois
Miranda v. Arizona	Lynumn v. Illinois
Spano v. New York	Arizona v. Fulminante

Discussion Questions

1. Compare and contrast settings that are appropriate for conducting an interview versus settings that are appropriate for interrogations.
2. Are some settings more conducive to soliciting information than others?
3. Can the setting in which an interview or interrogation is conducted be manipulated to aid the investigator?
4. What are the legal guidelines concerning interrogations?

5.   Does coercion, trickery, or deception nullify the admissibility of a confession? Why or why not?

6.   As a probation and parole officer, you routinely conduct interviews with your clients. During the course of such an interview, a client inadvertently slips and admits to having information concerning a highly publicized ongoing homicide investigation. At this point, does the probation and parole officer have a legal obligation to stop the client from speaking any further concerning this matter? Why or why not?

7.   A corrections officer inadvertently overhears two inmates bragging about their past crimes. One of the inmates states that he has committed a murder that was pinned on another individual. Not only was the other person arrested but was convicted of the crime and is currently in another state penitentiary. Should the corrections officer make his or her presence known and stop the inmate from speaking any further about the crime? What should the corrections officer do with the information he or she has already obtained?

8.   A security officer in a local department store was advised by the clerk that a shoplifter had removed a watch from the jewelry counter. The security officer detained the suspect and escorted him to the rear of the store where a small security office is located. At this point, the security officer asks the suspect, "Did you steal the watch?" What are the legal implications or restrictions placed upon the security officer in this situation?

9.   **Ethical Issue:** Should an officer be obligated to question a suspect when the physical evidence clearly points to the suspect's guilt? Why or why not?

10.   **Ethical Issue:** During the interrogation process, should an officer be allowed to lie to the suspect in an effort to elicit a response or open another avenue of questioning? Why or why not?

11.   **Ethical Issue:** Should an officer be concerned with trying to provide the suspect some psychological relief or support after a confession, particularly if the crime was heinous in nature? Why or why not?

Notes

1. Most material developed through personal experience of author Grubb (retired police officer with the Roanoke City Police Department, Roanoke, VA).

2. Rothwax, H. *Guilty: The Collapse of Criminal Justice.* NY: Random House, 1996. p. 82.

3. Chief Justice Rhenquist Opinion of the Court. *Charles Thomas Dickerson, Petitioner v. United States* on Writ of Certiorari to the United States Court of Appeals for the Fourth Circuit, No. 99-5525.June 26, 2000. Washington, DC: Supreme Court of the United States.

4. Interviewing and Interrogation Seminar. Federal Bureau of Investigation, Indiana, PA, October 1997.

5. Ibid.

6. Grubb, R. E. (Sgt.), Roanoke City Police Department, Roanoke, VA, 1985.

CHAPTER 9

TECHNOLOGICAL COMMUNICATION: NOT JUST SURFING THE INTERNET

Learning Objectives:

1.   To identify and explain the organizational intranet and its uses.

2.   To become familiar with the uses of the Mobile Data Terminal.

3.   To know the strengths and weaknesses of electronic mail (e-mail).

4.   To identify and explain specialized databases such as AFIS and CODIS.

5.   To explain the uses and benefits of technology in the courtroom.

6.   To become familiar with new technologies in law enforcement and corrections.

7.   To identify and explain the Internet and its uses.

8.   To become familiar with bulletin boards and listservs and their uses.

9.   To identify uses of electronic journals.

10.   To examine the potential benefits of departmental web pages.

11.   To identify and explain the concept, "cybercrime."

12.   To explain the migration of "traditional" crimes from the physical to the online world.

13.   To list the reasons criminals are migrating online.

14.   To explain the three challenges of crimes involving computers.

15.   To list and explain the three ways computers are being used for criminal behavior.

> *"There was a time when Andy Sipowicz, hero of 'NYPD Blue,' made the perfect cop. He's tough, street-smart and knows how to squeeze a perp till he squeals. But old-school Andy lacks a skill that may soon be a prerequisite for 21st-century detective work: knowing how to glean secrets from a suspect's hard drive. In an age when computers hold the key to everything from terrorist plots to accounting scandals, nearly every crime can potentially leave 'digital evidence.'"[1]*

Technology has influenced the means by which communication occurs, and criminal justice agencies, like most other professions, have also experienced a metamorphosis in the manner, the speed, and the mechanisms by which they communicate. While some organizations have greatly expanded their use of computer technology, still other criminal justice agencies are on the verge of discovering the potential this tool offers. With the rapid advance in technology and the declining cost of hardware, many law enforcement agencies have employed the use of computers. However, technology in criminal justice agencies has not been limited solely to the utilization of computers. Advances in audio and visual technology have also provided these agencies with a wide array of options.

Additionally, due to the increase in use of computers and the Internet, criminals have begun to exploit these technologies to commit crimes and to harm the safety, security, and privacy of everyone.[2] Titled "**cybercrime**," this lucrative new venue for criminals is causing a migration of "traditional" crimes from the physical to the online world as well as spawning a new set of criminal activity that targets computer networks themselves. Criminal justice agencies are facing technical, legal, and operational challenges in their battle with cybercrime. According to Michael Chertoff, Assistant Attorney General, Criminal Justice Division, United States Department of Justice, in his speech before the Subcommittee on Crime, U.S. House of Representatives, on June 12, 2001, "… it is clear to me that cybercrime is an extremely serious threat, and that its complexity and constant evolution present a tremendous challenge to law enforcement." This chapter will focus on some of these issues and the mechanisms by which agencies are addressing them.

The Intranet (Organizational Network)

One of the most significant advances in criminal justice technology centers upon the use of organizational networks often referred to in the private sector as **intranets**. An **intranet** is a group of connected computers that exchange information and share equipment within a specific organization. Prior to the advent of network typologies, criminal justice agencies relied upon clerks, secretaries, or office personnel to retrieve information or data from extensive file cabinets and records centers. This method of maintaining and retrieving data was extremely time consuming, labor intensive, and costly.

In the corrections area, the use of intranets offers options that facilitate the manner in which inmates are admitted to the institution, tracked during their incarceration, and their release date established. Again, prior to the implementation of intranets, inmate files were stored in a secured records facility and retrieval involved lengthy and arduous procedures. From a terminal (computer) offering access to the organizational network, records can be reviewed by authorized correctional personnel in order to confirm identities, to determine the appropriate classification and assignment of inmates, to track inmates' disciplinary problems, to review credit for "good time," as well as any other administrative functions.

Mobile Data Terminals (MDT)

The establishment of an organizational intranet allows authorized personnel to access information from a variety of locations. Officers in patrol cars have access to database information via the use of a **Mobile Data Terminal (MDT)**. The **Mobile Data Terminal** is a screen and keyboard that connects the patrol car to the central computer and allows the officer to stay in contact with the dispatch center. The use of the MDT not only enhances the officer's ability to access information but also eliminates the need to use the police radio. Furthermore, the use of the MDT provides an additional measure of security because the communication cannot be accessed by the general public, unlike radio communication, which is frequently monitored by civilians who possess police scanners.

MDTs allow officers to be dispatched on calls for service without the utilization of the police radio. When a call is received, the MDT makes a noise—either a beep or a buzz. This sound notifies the officer that an incoming call will be received on the terminal. As the call is received, the officer reviews the nature of the call and the address and strikes a "function" key, which notifies dispatch that the call has been received and that the unit is en route. When the officer arrives at the designated address, another "function" key is struck which notifies dispatch that the officer is on the scene and out of service. In some of the more advanced MDT units, a follow-up tone will notify the dispatcher that the unit is still out of service and may require assistance. This innovation was designed to ensure that dispatchers checked on the safety of officers who have been marked out of service for a specified period of time.

Once the unit has handled the call, the officer returns to the unit and prepares an initial offense report. At one point, offense/incident reports had to be prepared by hand. However, with the development of appropriate software, reports may be generated by utilizing the MDT keyboard to type and send them to a supervisor for review. One caveat, nonetheless, even though you prepare your reports using the MDT, you still need to adhere to the rules of report writing discussed in earlier chapters.

Once the report is completed and forwarded to the appropriate supervisor, the officer again strikes a function key on the MDT which notifies the dispatcher that the unit has cleared from that address and is in service or able to receive a call.

Another vital aspect of the MDT is the ability of the officer to retrieve information while in the field. Frequently officers see suspicious vehicles and want to know to whom the vehicle is registered. By utilizing the MDT, an officer may access the State Division of Motor Vehicle (DMV) records and determine the owner of the vehicle. Additionally, officers may verify the license status of a driver by accessing the DMV records to determine if the driver has a valid operator's license or if their privilege to drive has been suspended or revoked.

Officers frequently come in contact with a wide variety of individuals during the course of their patrol activities and will routinely run what is referred to as a "wants and warrants check." The MDT allows them to ascertain the status of these individuals locally, state wide, and nationally. Officers can obtain information from the Federal Bureau of Investigation's National Crime Information Center (NCIC) through a link from their MDT. They also have the capability of retrieving data from their state system such as Virginia's VCIN (Virginia Crime Information Network).

Department or Bureau Terminals

Much like their MDT counterparts, these terminals (computers) allow authorized personnel access to a variety of information. The only significant difference is that these terminals are located on the desks of officers or supervisors or in a central location that is easily accessible. Generally these terminals are used to prepare supplemental offense reports that have been discussed elsewhere in this text. However, these terminals may be used to transcribe the notes from victim, witness, or suspect statements. Additionally, these terminals may take the place of typewriters in general office communication.

Department or bureau terminals may have expanded capability or access to information unavailable to their MDT counterparts. Access to sensitive information, however, may be limited to certain individuals by issuing passwords for specific levels. An example of sensitive information may be a list of informants or suspected drug dealers that would be contained within the narcotics or vice bureau. An administrative example of sensitive information would be the salary structure for the department.

Typically, networked computers (terminals) require users to "log on" by typing in a user name and a password. This user name and password are considered to be of an extremely sensitive nature and, therefore, should be kept confidential. Only select administrative personnel should have access to user names and passwords.

Electronic Mail (e-mail)

E-mail, or electronic mail, is a means by which a message, a bulletin, or other information may be distributed to an individual or a group of individuals from a single source. E-mail is the electronic equivalent of the U.S. Postal Service. However, unlike the postal service and the confidentiality assumed in the delivery of a letter, e-mail can and is frequently monitored by other individuals. These individuals may be supervisors or "hackers." Either way, anytime e-mail is sent, be aware of the fact that it is not generally secure.

E-mail may be a particularly effective means of disseminating information that must be brought to the attention of a large group of people immediately, such as changes in the warrant status of current offenders, changes in the current status of search warrants, or any modifications to departmental policy.[3] Additionally, e-mail may be utilized to handle the more mundane aspects of organizational operation such as the date of change from summer to fall uniforms, shopping vehicles for maintenance, or extra duty assignments. E-mail could also be utilized to submit routine information like the number of officers on sick leave, number of officers on vacation, or the number of officers on special assignment.

If e-mail is adopted as the official channel of intradepartmental or interdepartmental communication, then it holds the same authority and status as any written document containing the same information. The same rules of composition and grammar that are used to create a written document also apply to e-mail.

Specialized Criminal Justice Databases

Two important databases that exist for use of criminal justice professionals are the **Automated Fingerprint Identification System (AFIS)** and the **Combined DNA Index System (CODIS)**. AFIS is utilized at the national and state level. At the national level, AFIS is maintained by the Federal Bureau of Investigation. At the state level, however, AFIS is maintained by regional centers within the state that allow smaller local law enforcement agencies access to this unique type of technology.

AFIS is a database where images of fingerprints are digitally scanned, stored, and retrieved. Stored images may be compared against suspect prints retrieved from crime scenes in a matter of minutes, as opposed to the days and weeks needed to sort through standardized fingerprint cards currently utilized by fingerprint examiners across the nation. As a matter of fact, hundreds of thousands of prints may be searched by AFIS within a matter of an hour. AFIS provides a list of possible matches, which are then confirmed by the fingerprint examiner. These possible matches are predicated on a standard of over 200 points of possible comparison. AFIS technology is said to be 98-100% accurate. However, AFIS technology is not a panacea. Some limitations exist with this technology, in particular, the breadth of the fingerprint database. In other words, if a suspect's print is not located in the database, then no positive match will be recorded or achieved.[4]

A recent development in fingerprint technology involves the use of the **live scan fingerprinting process** where law enforcement officers are permitted to print and compare a suspect's fingerprints without inking the fingertips. The suspect's hand is placed on a glass plate, which is digitally scanned and sent via telephone lines to an AFIS computer center for immediate comparison. The Los Angeles County authorities today operate the largest live scan system in the world. They have 97 live scan stations serving 48 police agencies. This system also allows correctional officers to immediately determine the warrant status and arrest history of inmates. The value of this new technology is in the prevention of prematurely releasing offenders who have been arrested and who have attempted to conceal their identities to avoid incarceration. Furthermore, magistrates or judges now have information which may assist them in determining bond status—whether or not to grant bond or the amount of bond which should be posted in order to insure the appearance of the defendant.

CODIS is a national DNA database which allows state and local law enforcement agencies to link serial crimes—most prominently, violent sexual offenders—and to identify suspects by matching DNA from crime scenes with the DNA of convicted sex offenders. This database is being developed and maintained by the Federal Bureau of Investigation (FBI). Currently, 90% of the states have passed legislation requiring convicted sex offenders to provide DNA samples for the national database.

Principally, two types of DNA tests exist: **PCR** and **RFLP**. Prior to the use of **PCR (polymerase chain reaction), RFLP (restriction fragment link polymorphism)** was used as the primary means in **DNA (deoxyribonucleic acid)** testing. In **RFLP**, genetic material is extracted from the sample and mixed with enzymes to cut the DNA into fragments. The fragments are put into a special gel and exposed to an electrical charge to sort the fragments by size. After they are exposed to electricity, genetic tracers are used to lock onto specific fragments of the DNA. These tracers reveal a pattern. This evidence sample pattern is then compared with the sample from the victim and from the suspect.

PCR (polymerase chain reaction), on the other hand, produces billions of DNA strips that can be reproduced rapidly in a test tube. The amplified DNA is then analyzed and the evidence sample is compared with that of the victim and the suspect. The PCR technique has been used to assist pathologists in identifying the remains of soldiers killed in war, to assist the FBI in identifying suspects of the Word Trade Center bombings, and to free individuals wrongly convicted of rape and murder.

Recently, many major metropolitan departments, such as Dallas, Texas, and Seattle, Washington, have formulated Cold Case Squads. These Cold Case Squads review case folders or file folders of unsolved homicides or other violent crimes. AFIS and CODIS are part of the computer technology that has assisted these Cold Case Squads in resolving these past crimes.

Technology in the Courtroom

Nothing is more dramatic than the positive identification of the suspect by an eyewitness in the courtroom. However, this type of identification is frequently exploited and dismissed by defense attorneys. Research has shown that unfortunately the human memory is fallible, and positive eyewitness identification is not always an asset. Historically, suspects have been identified through a variety of means including in larger metropolitan departments the "sketch artist." Victims or witnesses would come to police headquarters and provide an artist with details from which a sketch or composite would be created. In some instances, these sketches or composites were remarkably accurate. Unfortunately, in some instances, these sketches or composites were remarkably inaccurate.

Since sketch artists are few in number and not readily available, several attempts were made to create a library of different facial characteristics. Generically, these attempts were marketed as "Ident a Kits." Initially, these Ident a Kits provided investigators with a means of developing a visual representation of a suspect without having any particular expertise or specialized training in sketching. Ident a Kits are transparencies that overlay each other in order to develop a facial reconstruction of a suspect.[5] The investigator begins with a facial shape such as round, oval, or square, and from this point proceeds to the shape of the eyes. Then the shape of the nose and the mouth, the hairline and its relationship to the ears are developed until ultimately a visual representation of the suspect is created.

An improvement on the Ident a Kit resulted from the creation of computer-aided identification software. These software programs typically store more than 100,000 different facial features or images. By using key commands or a computer mouse, a facial reproduction may be electronically composed, stored, and printed within a matter of moments. Furthermore, this image may be distributed very rapidly to local, state, or national authorities that may assist in the apprehension or detention of a suspect. A valuable aspect of the computer-aided identification system is that, if necessary, it may be reproduced in court and provide the jurors or judge with a visual representation of how the technology assisted in developing and questioning the defendant.

The computer-aided identification system is not the only tool of technology available to the prosecutor in the courtroom. The axiom, "a picture is worth a thousand words," is never more true than in a courtroom setting when the prosecutor is trying to describe a crime scene and the relationship that may exist between pieces of evidence. **AutoSketch** and **CompuScene** are two examples of computer software that aid an evidence technician in diagramming a crime scene. Crime scenes presented in court are the result of a scaled final product prepared by a law enforcement evidence technician. Upon arrival at the crime scene, an evidence technician prepares a rough draft of the scene, which includes the position of the victim, any evidence, and the layout or design of the area. These technicians formulate a sketch by utilizing a variety of methods, but three of the most prominent are the **grid, triangulation,** or **cross-projection**. These methods allow technicians to accurately draw the crime scene and to insure the relationship between pieces of evidence is factual. Once this diagram is completed, then a scaled drawing is constructed by the technician for display in court. AutoSketch and CompuScene allow these technicians to more efficiently and effectively create diagrams of the crime scene.

Other design technologies similar to AutoSketch and CompuScene are utilized in the recreation of crime scenes and traffic accidents. However, the use of these technologies for court purposes has been limited. Generally, these technologies have found more success in civil proceedings than in criminal trials.

Furthermore, with the declining cost and increasing availability of video equipment, video camera recording of crime scenes has become more prolific. A distinct advantage to camcording crime scenes is the addition of color and the clarity with which the scene may be presented. Jurors and judges are impressed with being able to view the entirety of a crime scene and the relationship that exists between the evidence and its relative position in a specific location. Camcording could eliminate the necessity of transporting the judge and/or jury to the actual crime scene, thereby saving time and money for the local jurisdiction. An important factor to consider given today's high cost of prosecution.

Video cameras are also being used in law enforcement vehicles to monitor the officer's safety and to serve as a visual confirmation of the officer's observations and the suspect's actions. In many instances, defendants who are charged with driving under the influence plead guilty once they or their attorneys have viewed the officer's videotape of the traffic stop. In other cases, suspects have been found guilty by a judge or jury as a result of having viewed the videotape. In extreme cases where officers are injured or killed, in addition to serving as evidence in the trial of the suspect, these videotapes serve as a graphic training reminder for new officers and seasoned veterans to remain vigilant.

Video cameras do have some drawbacks, however. Some judges will not allow videotaped crime scenes to be used in their courtroom. Therefore, local agencies must always insure that rough sketches and finished to-scale diagrams are present for court. Furthermore, during the videotaping process, the camera should not be started and stopped. In other words, no gaps should exist in the taping for these voids serve as points of attack for the defense or areas about which the jury may speculate.

New Technologies in Law Enforcement

Just as Video cameras are utilized in patrol cars to intensify an officer's testimony, other government agencies are experimenting with the use of new technology to enhance training and performance for their new personnel. In particular, trainers at McKenna Range, an urban-combat training facility at Fort Benning, Georgia, have installed Simulcast AAR (after-action review) software. Simulcast AAR records and replays live video from the 70 Video cameras positioned throughout the training facility. The software records every movement in MPEG-1 or MPEG-2 video files for immediate computer playback. As the soldiers complete their maneuvers, they leave the field and immediately are able to review their battle tactics and strategy on a computer. Instructors are able to move to a particular moment and camera with the click of a mouse, thereby helping participants to identify mistakes and to learn corrective measures. In the past, instructors had to observe these large-scale training simulations and record what happened during the action. A feat near impossible since no one can observe and record the actions of a large-scale simulation without failing to note some miscues. Since implementing this program, however, better communication and fewer war-game casualties have resulted.[6] This program can be adapted for any large group of persons who work together as a team, and it definitely has implications for use in law enforcement training academies.

Some law enforcement training academies use a technology similar to Simulcast AAR in their firearms training. A standard firearms training technology has been **FATS (firearms training system)**. This type of technology places police officers in a variety of scenarios, which forces them to make "shoot/don't shoot" decisions, and thereby strengthens their decision-making skills. Additionally this type of training limits the possible liability of the officer and the agency with respect to an excessive force civil lawsuit.

New Technologies in Corrections

Booking suspects in the docket has historically involved fingerprinting and photographing. Photographs were taken in black and white with the standard 35 mm camera. While this provided a visual representation of the suspect, these pictures were not always the best quality. Differences in skin tone, light facial hair, or facial scars were not always discernible. In an effort to enhance the visual quality of these photographs, color film was introduced. Now, with the availability of digital cameras and the adjoining software, photographs of suspects have taken a huge leap forward. Digital cameras allow a suspect to be photographed from at least three different angles and for this information to be stored in the local computer database. Those facial anomalies that were previously undetectable may now be enhanced in order to provide a better photograph or description of the subject. Furthermore, these photographs may be altered by means of new software to reflect the addition or removal of mustaches, beards, toupees, glasses, etc. Since these photographs may be stored in a computer, the accompanying disks may be reused at a fraction of the cost spent to purchase, develop, and store traditional film.

In addition to the digital camera, certain metropolitan departments are using the previously mentioned live scan fingerprint process. These two new technologies not only improve the processing of incoming suspects, but they also reduce the possibility that violent or repeat offenders will be released or lost in the system.

Rural counties in West Virginia are currently experimenting with an innovative approach to arraigning suspects. This new approach involves **synchronous** transmission of information. Synchronous transmission of data or information is "real time" transmission or reception of video images and audio. A suspect in the local jail is taken to an interview room that contains a microphone, television camera, and a monitor. The suspect is able to hear as well as to see the local magistrate or judge, who advises him/her of the charge and the determination of bail. Local law enforcement agencies are pleased with this adaptation of existing technology because it eliminates the need to transport prisoners over long distances and reduces the probability of an escape attempt. Deputies may be reassigned to other duties or placed in the field rather than used for transport details.

The Internet: Criminal Justice's Newest Weapon

On college campuses, in homes, and in private industry across the country, the Internet has exploded. Businesses advertise, students and family fraternize, and professors and teachers educate using this superhighway system. Moreover, law enforcement professionals around the world are now using the World Wide Web as a means of tracking and capturing criminals, communicating between agencies, isolating and identifying problem areas, and establishing a link with the outside world which was previously possible only through personal contact.

What is the Internet?

The **Internet** is a worldwide computer network that is comprised of thousands of networks connected together. As discussed earlier under the topic of Intranets, a network is a group of connected computers that exchange information and share equipment (i.e., printers, etc.). The Internet, the largest computer system in the world, is often called the Information Superhighway, Cyberspace, or the World Wide Web.

Originally, the Internet was utilized by the government, the military, and faculty at institutions of higher learning as a research tool. In the late 1980s and early 1990s, use of the Internet grew astronomically to include college students, businesses, and the average family.

Today, millions of locations can be accessed from a personal computer equipped with a modem and access to an Internet service. Computer crime specialists use the Internet to exchange techniques and information; forensics experts are exchanging data with their counterparts; and crime prevention specialists, dispatchers, officer survival experts, and other law enforcement specialists are recognizing the benefits of "surfing" the Word Wide Web.

Commercial Service Provider

In order to begin your journey in cyberspace, you must first have the appropriate equipment and access to the Internet. You need specific equipment such as a computer, a **modem (exchanges information between your computer and the Internet)**, a telephone line or **ISDN line (Integrated Services Digital Network is a special telephone line specifically designed for the transmission of computer data at very high speeds)**, and then you must acquire a **service provider (a company that gives you access to the Internet for a fee)** and their concomitant program for accessing the Internet.

The easiest, most cost effective means of accessing the World Wide Web is through a commercial service provider. You have probably heard of America On-Line, CompuServe, or Microsoft Network. Any one of those services could provide you and your agency with access to the Internet. Most commercial services provide the software you will need to use the Internet, but you must have your own computer, modem, and telephone service. A dedicated telephone line would be the optimum set-up since you do not want to restrict community access to your law enforcement agency because someone was using the Internet and tied up the phone line.

As far as cost of service goes, Internet providers charge a monthly fee for online time. Most services, however, offer unlimited access per month for a set fee. An important factor to consider in selecting a commercial service provider is the telephone number for connection to your service provider. If that telephone number is out of your area code or is considered long distance by your telephone company, you will be charged for the number of minutes you spend surfing the net since that is long distance phone time. You want to utilize a service provider within your local telephone area.

Bulletin Boards

A bulletin board system (BBS) is often called a "chat" room where people with similar interests meet online to discuss issues of importance. Bulletin boards exist for political activists, hobbyists of all types, collectors, and law enforcement officers, to name a few. Anyone who has access to the Internet can become part of a bulletin board system. Bulletin boards frequently have ongoing discussions concerning noteworthy events, and anyone can set up their own BBS. For this reason, many bulletin boards are transitory. In some cases, this temporary status is a benefit because many unscrupulous people use BBS as a means of defrauding credit card consumers, and pedophiles and other deviants use them to spread illicit information online.

A BBS allows individuals to leave messages on the Internet that may be read and answered by anyone who has access to that bulletin board. In a more sophisticated BBS, individuals may conduct an online discussion where one individual leads the discussion and others reply and interact. Many law enforcement agencies maintain bulletin board systems as public relations tools. Some examples of bulletin board systems of interest to law enforcement professionals are

> **Topcops of IRC**
> **Streetcops IRC Network**
> **WBS Doorway—Law Enforcement**

ListServs

Requiring only an e-mail connection, listservs are one of the most cost effective means for networking among criminal justice professionals worldwide. Individuals join a listserv by e-mail. Most often, you are required to e-mail the listserv address and state your desire to subscribe to that service. The listserv will respond by e-mail to your request and advise you that you are now a subscriber. Shortly thereafter, you will begin to receive e-mail from the listserv.

As a member of a listserv, you have several options. You may read the current information and message traffic between other subscribers and make no response–in which case you are referred to as a "lurker." However, if you so desire, you may comment upon new items or items discussed by other listserv members and become an active participant in the discussion group.

Some listservs are moderated by a list owner who reviews each message and decides whether or not to send it to the subscribers. The list owner can also edit messages before sending them. Examples of listservs that may be of interest to the criminal justice professional would be as follows:

A. **BJS, The Bureau of Justice Statistics**. Provides information on crimes and victims, drugs and crime, criminal offenders, and special topics. To subscribe to the listserv, visit the web address for the Bureau of Justice Statistics, <www.ojp.usdog.gov/bjs>.

B. **Justice Information Center**. A service of the National Criminal Justice Reference Service. This site is one of the most extensive sources of information on criminal and juvenile justice in the world. A collection of clearinghouses supporting bureaus of the United States Department of Justice Office of Justice Programs, the National Institute of Justice, and several other government agencies. To subscribe to the listserv for the Justice Information Center, see their web page at <www.ncjrs.org/>.

A listserv that receives a great deal of attention in the police community is POLICE-L. Membership in this listserv, however, requires that the subscriber send proof of either active or retired law enforcement status.

Examples of other listservs available for membership, depending on your area(s) of interest and specialization, are described as follows:

1. **CJTREAT**. This listserv is dedicated to treatment issues within criminal justice prison systems. All aspects of treatment behind prison walls, including medical, mental, health, substance abuse counseling, recreational therapy, education and schools, halfway houses, parole and probation programs, behavior modification, and any other treatment provided for criminal justice offenders. All interested parties may subscribe to this list by sending e-mail to
       <majordomo@lists.downcity.net>
   and place the following command in the body of your e-mail message:
       subscribe cjtreat

2. **CJUST-L**. Hosted by the City University of New York's John Jay College of Criminal Justice, this listserv has a subscribership of approximately 1200. This is a high-volume list with various subscribers, including students. With the exception of POLICE-L (a closed list for only current law enforcement officers), CJUST-L is the world's largest discussion list dedicated to justice issues. To subscribe, send e-mail to
       <listserv@listserv.cuny.edu>
   stating simply in the body of your e-mail message
       "subscribe CJUST-L YourFirstName YourLastName"

3.   **CORREX**. This listserv is the United State's National Institution of Corrections' public forum for the discussion of corrections issues and practices and for the exchange of views and information. It is also intended to facilitate communication between the institute and field practitioners, policy makers, researchers, etc. To subscribe, send e-mail to

   <correx-request@www.nicic.org>

   Leave the subject line blank and include the word "subscribe" in the body of your message.

4.   **JUSTINFO**. Sponsored by the United States Department of Justice, Office of Justice Programs, this electronic newsletter service provides the latest criminal justice news and information. To subscribe, send your e-mail message to

   <listproc@ncjrs.org>

   and state in the body of the message

   subscribe justinfo YourFirstName YourLastName

5.   **PRISON-L**. Yale University hosts this discussion list on prison issues and topics. To subscribe, send e-mail to

   <listproc@lists.yale.edu>

   and state in the body of the message

   SUBSCRIBE PRISON-L YourFirstName YourLastName

6.   **UNIVPD-L**. A discussion list for sworn law enforcement officers, its purpose is to provide a forum for law enforcement officers to discuss issues of campus safety, crime prevention, and law enforcement as they relate to university and college environments.

Electronic Journals

   Criminal justice administrators will find a variety of information on a plethora of topics located on the Internet. The most useful tool for gathering and examining information on topics of current interest may well be electronic journals. These journals are generally published by leading authorities in the field or in academia. Some examples of available electronic journals are as follows:

1.   Journal of Criminal Justice and Popular Culture <www.albany.edu/scj/jcjpc> "Is a scholarly record of research and opinion on the intersection of crime, criminal justice, and popular culture."

2.   American Journal of Criminal Justice <www.louisville.edu/journal/ajcj/> Is "a multidisciplinary journal devoted to the study of criminal and deviant behavior, the social and political response to crime, and other phenomena related to crime and social justice."

3.   Law Enforcement Internet Intelligence Report <www.lawintelrpt.com/> "A monthly newsletter that provides law enforcement with a digest of the best relevant information for law enforcement on the Internet."

4.   Police and Science Management <www.henrystewart.co.uk/journals/PSaM/>

"The major new journal on best practice and latest thinking and research in police science and management ...."

Law Enforcement and the Internet

As evidenced by the introductory scenario that occurred in State College, Pennsylvania, the Internet has practical applications for small- to medium-sized police departments. In a town that is predominantly populated by college students, law enforcement officers are constantly required to investigate offenses involving students in off-campus disputes and altercations. Oftentimes, students are uncooperative, not desirous of providing information which they feel may not be in their best interests. However, as most college professors who utilize E-mail in their classrooms have discovered, students are more likely to express honest opinions when there is no required one-on-one confrontation. Having the ability to provide information without fear of identification or conflict, students come forward more readily. State College Police depended on this anonymity to help them identify their perpetrators. Crime Line and Tips programs have utilized this approach (anonymity) in the past, but the addition of this technology adds a new twist to an old program.

According to Ken Reeves, a Microsoft Corporate manager,[7] more than 2,000 police agencies have gone on-line. As an example, in northern California, Placer County residents can file complaints, commendations, and crime reports on the sheriff department's Internet site; in Roanoke County, Virginia, citizens can click on a map to find out about the latest crimes in their communities; and in Seattle, Washington, the Internet was credited for helping to capture a bank robber who was hiding in Guatemala.

The Internet is a powerful, versatile law enforcement tool because it offers instant communication and it crosses jurisdictional barriers. Citizens are able to report crimes, ask questions, and obtain information, all instantaneously. Law enforcement officials are also able to receive information, post pictures of wanted criminals, and communicate with local citizens.

Many web sites have been developed which are linked to federal agencies and state police departments. One of the best-known sites is CopNet [www.copnet.org]. CopNet touts itself as a "free community service without affiliation to any police agency, government body, or special interest group of any kind unless clearly stated." CopNet maintains links to international agencies, crime prevention, search and rescue, electronic crime, events, firearms, forensics, list servers, missing, most wanted, seminars, security agencies, traffic, training, fitness, and standards, and other sites of interest to the police world. The Federal Bureau of Investigation, the United States Department of Justice, and the International Association of Chiefs of Police also maintain Internet sites for public access.

You need only search the web for police sites, and a myriad become available for you to view–just one click away. In addition to the information mentioned previously, these sites carry information on training, where to get training, how much an officer can expect to be paid, physical standards for officers, job vacancies, etc. Training academies that specialize in law enforcement preparation use the Internet as an advertising forum for their programs as well.

According to Cmdr. Dave Pettinari of the Pueblo County, Colorado, Sheriff's Department, criminals will use cyberspace increasingly to commit thefts and to escape punishment. Moreover, without a law enforcement presence on the Internet, criminals have the distinct advantage. The public's concern for the increase in crime demands that law enforcement develop new, more efficient ways to communicate criminal justice information. One of the ways to meet this demand is for law enforcement agencies to develop and utilize a web site so that they have a visible presence in the cybercommunity.

As evidenced by the information presented beforehand, access to the Internet provides law enforcement agencies with another tool to serve their communities more effectively. Unfortunately, many police departments do not understand how this system can benefit them and have yet to make use of the Information Superhighway.

Cybercrime

As mentioned in the introduction to this chapter, Cybercrime is of increasing concern to criminal justice agencies. Crimes such as threats, child pornography, fraud, gambling, extortion, and theft of intellectual property are migrating to the online world. Other crimes such as hacking, releasing viruses, and shutting down computers by flooding them with unwanted information ("denial of service" attacks) are on the rise leading to an entirely new set of criminal activity.

Computer crime also has global connotations. Criminal Justice agencies in the United States, and in other nations as well, are seeing computers being used for criminal behavior in three ways:

> · "First, a computer can be the target of an offense. When this occurs, a computer's confidentiality, integrity, or availability is attacked. That is services or information are being stolen, or victim computers are being damaged. The denial of service attacks that were experienced by numerous Internet sites earlier this year and the recent proliferation of the "I Love You" virus and its variants are but a few examples of this type of computer crime.

> · Second, a computer can be used as a tool for committing criminal behavior. This category includes those crimes that we in law enforcement have been fighting in the physical world but now are seeing with increasing frequency on the Internet. These crimes include child pornography, fraud, intellectual property violations, and the sale of illegal substances and goods online.

> · Third, a computer can be incidental to an offense, but still significant for our purposes as law enforcement officials. For example, pedophiles might store child pornography and drug traffickers and other criminals may store business contact information on their computers."[8]

The reasons that criminals are moving from the physical to the online world is four-fold:
1. They can reach more victims quickly;
2. They can collaborate with other criminals;
3. They can disguise their identities; and
4. They can use the global nature of the Internet to remain anonymous.[9]

Because of the ease with which criminals can access technology and use computers for criminal behavior, law enforcement agencies are facing challenges in their battle with cybercrime on three fronts: technical, legal, and operational.

Technical challenges are those that hinder law enforcement's ability to find and prosecute criminals operating online. Examples of these challenges are when a hacker disrupts air traffic control at a local airport, when a child pornographer sends computer files over the Internet, when a cyberstalker sends a threatening e-mail to a school or a local church, or when credit card numbers are stolen from a company engaged in e-commerce. Because in these instances investigators have to locate the source of the communication, law enforcement officials must trace the "electronic trail" leading from the victim back to the perpetrator. This task can be very difficult, though, if the perpetrator attempts to hide his/her identity, if technology hinders the investigation, or if the investigator requires international cooperation.

Cybercriminals who are experienced or more "sophisticated" know how to conceal their fingerprints in cyberspace. They often weave their communications through service providers in a number of different countries to hide their tracks. In addition, they might use other services available in some countries, which increase their anonymity. Pre-paid calling cards are one example of a technology that makes identifying criminals more difficult.[10]

The second type of challenge faced by criminal justice professionals is in the legal arena. If the law enforcement community is to deter and punish cybercriminals, a worldwide legal structure supporting detection and successful prosecution of these offenders is necessary. Because of the pace at which technological advances occur, the legal tools and laws defining computer offenses often lag behind. The absence of these standards create legal challenges for criminal justice agencies. Another problem arises when some countries have not yet adopted computer crime statutes. As J. K. Robinson stated in his presentation to the International Computer Crime Conference, (May 29-31, 2000), "at a time when the number of crimes carried out through the use of computer technology is increasing at an alarming rate, it is especially important that law enforcement officials around the world demonstrate that such crimes will be punished swiftly and with an appropriate degree of severity."

The third significant challenge facing criminal justice agencies around the world is that of **operational challenges**. Because of the complexity of technologies surrounding computer-related crime, jurisdictions must have individuals who are dedicated to high-tech crime and who have a firm understanding of computers and telecommunications.[11] The United States Department of Justice has a cybercrime program known as the Criminal Division's Computer Crime and Intellectual Property Section (CCIPS). This cornerstone of cybercrime detection and prevention was founded in 1991 and, as of May 2000, has grown from five attorneys to twenty attorneys.[12]

As part of the investigative side of cybercrime, the National Infrastructure Protection Center (NIPC) was created in 1998 to coordinate the FBI's investigation of computer crimes. As of this year (2000), approximately 100 investigators, computer scientists, and analysts are working on computer crime in the NIPC. Also, the FBI has almost 200 agents located in the FBI field offices throughout the United States who are assigned to investigate computer crime.[13]

In conclusion, cybercrime and the appearance of cybercriminals have given a new threat to individuals, businesses, and governments around the world. Criminal justice agencies worldwide must heed the advice of J. K. Robinson: "Given the quickly evolving nature of computer technology, … continue to increase … computer forensic capabilities, which are so essential in computer crime investigations. Twenty years ago, a new police officer was given a gun, a flashlight, and a notepad. When that officer retired, the three items would be returned to the police department, and the only intervening equipment expenses would have been replacement bullets, batteries, and note paper. Today, keeping pace with computer criminals means that law enforcement experts in this field must be properly equipped with the latest hardware and software."[14]

Summary

Criminal justice professionals in both law enforcement and corrections have long been enamored with technology and its potential application. This fascination has traditionally been limited to specialized weaponry or equipment used in subduing aggressive violators. Tasers and stun guns are two examples of this technology. However, as the sophistication of criminals and criminal behavior has increased, so has the technology with which to detect and apprehend these individuals. AFIS and CODIS, two specialized and independent databases, represent tremendous advances in crime fighting capability. In conjunction with the organizational intranet and the Internet, they provide access to essential information regarding fingerprinting and DNA testing.

The organizational intranet and Internet serve as two primary means of communication to disseminate information among law enforcement agencies and to help stem the tide of criminal activity. Furthermore, these two communication tools assist corrections personnel in maintaining a complete and accurate record of incarcerated individuals and in insuring that the guilty pay the fullest measure of their debt to society.

Other criminal justice technology such as MDTs, live scan fingerprinting process, and synchronous transmission not only increase the effectiveness of law enforcement and corrections, but they also help to insure that the public is provided with the best and most cost effective means available for maintaining a safe community.

The migration of "traditional" crimes from the physical to the online world is increasing. Cybercrime has become more lucrative to the criminal because of the ability to disguise identities, to reach more victims quickly, and to collaborate with other criminals. As computer technology advances with the identification of fingerprints and DNA, so too does the identification of cybercriminals become ever important. Agencies are constantly searching for officers with new skills in computer investigation and telecommunications. Additionally, governments need to develop global legal structures that will support detection and successful prosecution of offenders. To keep pace with the cybercriminal of today, criminal justice agencies must be properly equipped with cutting-edge software and hardware, and also be confident of laws and statutes governing prosecution of cybercrimes.

Key Terms

Cybercrime	"Denial of Service" attacks
Intranet	Mobile Data Terminal (MDT)
Automated Fingerprint Identification System (AFIS)	Live Scan Fingerprint Process
Combined DNA Index System (CODIS)	Polymerase Chain Reaction (PCR)

Restriction Fragment Link Polymorphism (RFLP) Deoxyribonucleic Acid (DNA)
Firearms Training System (FATS) Synchronous Transmission
Internet Modem
Integrated Services Digital Network (ISDN)

Discussion Questions

1. Compare and contrast an organizational intranet and the Internet.
2. Evaluate the effectiveness of the Mobile Data Terminal (MDT).
3. Are MDT transmissions superior to police radio transmissions? Why or why not?
4. How do specialized databases such as AFIS and CODIS aid in law enforcement?
5. Compare and contrast the value of CompuScene and AutoSketch and the traditional methods of grid triangulation and cross-projection.
6. Compare and contrast the use of videotaping a crime scene and the traditional method of sketching.
7. List the advantages and disadvantages of installing video cameras in law enforcement vehicles. Explain each statement.
8. List the advantages and disadvantages of having a departmental web page.
9. What are some uses for criminal justice bulletin boards or listservs? How are they useful?
10. Suggest ways in which technology may enhance the effectiveness and efficiency of law enforcement and correctional agencies.
11. **Ethical Issue:** Should individuals who have paid their debt to society still have a DNA record stored in CODIS? Why or why not?
12. **Ethical Issue:** Is videotaping an individual suspected of a crime an invasion of privacy?
13. **Ethical Issue:** Who should be responsible for retrieving, reviewing, and storing videotapes from law enforcement vehicles?
14. **Ethical Issue:** If an officer is accused of wrongdoing, which may be captured on the patrol car videotape, should it be used in an internal affairs investigation?
15. **Ethical Issue:** If an officer is accused of wrongdoing and it is captured on videotape that is used by internal affairs for departmental disciplinary procedures, could the same videotape be used in a criminal prosecution?
16. **Ethical Issue:** Should individuals be punished who use the computer and the Internet to enter networks and databases to which they have no authorization? Keep in mind that most young "crackers" enter these sites for the challenge rather than to tamper with or remove information.
17. **Ethical Issue:** Most of us know that it is wrong to break into our neighbors' houses and steal things or damage their property. Is there a correlation between this behavior and computer hacking and virus dissemination? Why or why not?

REASONS TO HAVE A LAW ENFORCEMENT HOME PAGE

1	Establish a presence
2	Network with other agencies, individuals, etc.
3	Make information readily available for community and others
4	Serve citizens more effectively and efficiently
5	Heighten public interest in law enforcement issues
6	Release time-sensitive materials
7	Answer frequently asked questions
8	Stay in contact with employees
9	Create a 24-hour service
10	Make updating and changing information quick and easy
11	Solicit feedback from customers and community
12	Test-market new services (i.e., Citizen Police Academy)
13	Reach the media

WAYS IN WHICH LAW ENFORCEMENT IS USING THE INTERNET

1	Exchanging information with other departments/agencies on police procedures and technical matters
2	Exchanging information with the public—getting the public's opinion on service, the public's perspective on the use of force, etc.
3	Sharing criminal and safety information with the public (i.e., missing persons reports, crime alerts [fraud, robbers, rapists], requests for help from the public—solving crimes, etc.
4	Communicating with experts
5	Keeping in touch with officers from other departments/agencies met through conferences, training courses, and investigations
6	Exchanging intelligence across jurisdictional lines

Notes

1. McGinn, D., "Brave New Job Hunt," *Newsweek.* September 23,2002, pp. 54-57.

2. Chertoff, M. (Assistant Attorney General, Criminal Division, U.S. Department of Justice), Statement before the Subcommittee on Crime, Committee on the Judiciary, U.S. House of Representatives, June 12, 2001. <http://www.cybercrime.gov/cybercrime61201_MChertoff.htm> March 10, 2002.

3. Lyman, M. D., *Criminal Investigation* (2nd ed). Upper Saddle River, NJ: Prentice Hall, 1999, p. 178.

4. Berg, Bruce L., Horgan, John, J., *Criminal Investigation* (3rd ed). NY: Glencoe McGraw-Hill, 1998.

5. Swanson, C. R., Chamelin, N. C., and Territo, L., *Criminal Investigation* (6th ed). New York: Mc-Graw Hill, 1996.

6. *Seeing It All: After-Action Review on Video,* OnLine Learning News, Vol. 2, No. 4, April 1999. Lakewood Publications Inc. (Lakewood1@list.emailpub.com) April 27, 1999.

7. I.D. Link. <http://www.idlink.com/law.htm> January 25, 1997.

8. Robinson, J. K. (Assistant Attorney General for the Criminal Division at the United States Department of Justice). Presentation entitled "Internet as the Scene of Crime" at the International Computer Crime Conference, Oslo, Norway, May 29-31, 2000. <http://www.cybercrime.gov/roboslo.htm> March 10, 2002.

9. Chertoff, pp. 1-2.

10. Robinson, pp. 4-5.

11. Ibid, p. 6.

12. Ibid.

13. Ibid.

14. Ibid, p. 7.

CHAPTER 10

COMMUNICATION WITH SPECIAL GROUPS: THE ELDERLY, YOUTH, and CULTURALLY DIVERSE POPULATIONS

Learning Objectives:

1. Explain what makes the United States a pluralistic society.

2. Explain the shift in demographics related to ethnicity and age.

3. Explain what the "graying of America" refers to.

4. Identify communication issues associated with the disabled, the elderly, children and youth, and diverse cultures.

5. Explain the parameters for determining that an individual has a disability.

6. Discuss how the Americans with Disabilities Act has impacted law enforcement.

7. Identify and explain the types of disabilities.

8. Describe common issues for law enforcement in interacting with people with disabilities.

9. Identify law enforcement agencies' means for accommodating disabled individuals.

10. Define elderly.

11. Identify facts to consider when interviewing an elderly victim, and explain why the elderly are more vulnerable to crimes.

12. Identify factors to consider when interviewing a child victim of a crime.

13. Define gang.

14. Explain the concept of ethnocentrism as it relates to culture.

15. Compare and contrast the priorities of cultural values of Americans, Japanese, and Arabs.

175

On February 22, 1999, Jacob McDonald, 78, stopped his 1989 Oldsmobile in a "no on-street parking" zone in Newport News, Virginia's East End. The reason McDonald parked his vehicle in this area was because he needed to help his 95-year-old mother from the car, up the steps into her home. As he was pulling away from the curb, a police officer approached his car from the rear and stopped him. Mr. McDonald tried to explain his reason for parking in this zone, but unfortunately since he lost his voice box to cancer several years ago and requires a battery-operated speaking device to communicate he is sometimes difficult to understand. The officer told Mr. McDonald that he was getting a ticket. Mr. McDonald's summons lists his crime as being "improperly stopped on the roadway."

Mr. McDonald was, in fact, improperly stopped on the roadway. However, he was stopped there because his mother requires assistance climbing the steps to her home. Even though she is still preaching at a small East End church and remains quite spirited for her age, she has no other means of entering her home than by the steps from the street. As a matter of fact, her home has no driveway and sits by a street with no shoulder or parallel parking. The closest legal parking for access to her home is across the street. So, Mr. McDonald chose to put himself in danger of receiving a ticket rather than risk his mother's life in asking her cross the street. Just down the street from where Mr. McDonald received his ticket, lookouts for drug dealers constantly man the street corners. In fact, you can walk from the home of Mr. McDonald's mother down the street to the scenes of at least half a dozen murders.

This improper stopping citation was Mr. McDonald's first traffic ticket in more than a decade. Even though he lives on a fixed income, Mr. McDonald went to the traffic court clerk's office and paid the ticket. In actuality, he could hardly afford the $20 fine and $30 processing fee. "But his wife said he was ashamed of how poorly he talks now that cancer has cost him his voice box. He was afraid, she said, the judge wouldn't be able to understand his explanation of what happened any better than the officer did."

Jim Spencer, <u>The Daily Press</u>, Sunday, 3/14/99

Because America's society is a pluralistic one, communication issues develop involving generation gaps, frames of reference, changing values, and culture. Criminal justice professionals need to be aware of the manner in which age differences, racial or ethnic experiences, and changing values impact the communication style of each unique group of individuals.

America's demographics have shifted rapidly over the last quarter of a century, with the fastest growing segment of our population now being classified as elderly. Historians and gerontologists now refer to this phenomenon as the "Graying of America." Research indicates that by the year 2025, more than 25 percent of our population will be comprised of retired persons (Enter, 1991, p. 67).

According to demographers, another large population group is comprised of 12- to 19-year-olds. In fact, approximately 31 million children fall into this age range (10 percent of the total U.S. population), with predictions for the year 2010 reaching as high as 35 million teens. This population bulge is even greater than the peak of the baby boom. In many aspects, our youth are growing up uniquely privileged. They have not had to concern themselves with global war, the draft, or sustained economic poverty. They have access to cable and the Internet, which provides them with a tremendous amount of information. This increasingly sophisticated group plans to go to college and have unprecedented opportunities, especially girls. Yet, with all these benefits, teenagers still report being increasingly alone and alienated and unable to related to their parents, teachers, and sometimes peers. "The new teen wave is bigger; richer; better educated and healthier than any other in history. But there's a dark side ...."[1]

Historically, America has viewed itself as the "Great Melting Pot" where millions of immigrants in the late 19th and early 20th centuries were assimilated into one native culture. This concept, however, has been a misnomer since these immigrants have maintained their distinctive customs, beliefs, and values–their individual **culture**. A more realistic view is that America is a pluralistic society.

The dominant Anglo European culture in America has traditionally imposed its value structure upon immigrants as well as the native inhabitants of North America. With the arrival of the pilgrims at Plymouth Rock and the Puritans in Massachusetts Bay, Native Americans were subjected to the language and behavioral norms of these new inhabitants, even to the extreme of having the immigrants' religious beliefs imposed on them in a misguided attempt to "save their souls from eternal damnation." Even as much as the early American settlers tried to deny their original immigrant status, Americans do not originate from a common stock. America is in fact a cornucopia of cultures.

Some scholars[2] suggest that America may be more of a mosaic "in which all races and ethnic groups are displayed in a form that is attractive because of the very elements of which it is made". This mosaic allows each culture to maintain its unique identity and to be appreciated for the distinctiveness of that culture. Hence, the terms Mexican-American, Asian-American, and African-American are seen as an attempt to establish a foothold in two cultures.

However, some individuals reject this concept of a mosaic. Whoopi Goldberg, in a recent interview with Oprah Winfrey, made the comment that she refused to allow anyone to call her an African-American. Ms. Goldberg stated that she had never been to Africa, had no relatives in Africa, and doubted seriously if any person in Africa would be willing to claim her as a relative. She was born in the United States to parents who had also been born in the United States, and she did not see herself as anything other than an American. While her statement lends some support or credence to the belief that Americans have participated in the melting pot concept, this view is rather limited in its approach to multiculturalism.

Just as Ms. Goldberg had expressed her point of view, so too do millions of other Americans. Frequently, their points of view are limited to something known as ethnocentrism. **Ethnocentrism** is the belief that the dominant culture (whether it be American, European, Asian, etc.) is the <u>only</u> appropriate culture. Simply put, ethnocentrism is the refusal to adapt to a different culture even when immersed in that culture. Ethnocentrism may well be the result of arrogance, fear and/or ignorance. Many traditional Americans have adopted this limited view, which conflicts with those immigrant Americans who maintain their own ethnocentric views. This battleground is evident in the recent controversy over California Proposition 227, "the landmark citizens initiative to dismantle bilingual education ... [which states that] By fall, all students are supposed to be taught only in English (emphasis added)."[3]

Communicating With Diverse Groups

As mentioned in the introduction to this chapter, law enforcement professionals will be communicating with diverse groups of people-persons with disabilities, of varying ethnic and cultural backgrounds-both young and old, both male and female. Since the process of communication is imperfect, individuals must learn to be flexible and make adaptations to their frames of reference, prior opinions, and perceptions. Otherwise, communication will not take place.

The Disabled

Police officers, sheriff's deputies, and other law enforcement personnel have always interacted with persons with disabilities. "An individual is considered to have a disability if he or she has a physical or mental impairment that substantially limits one or more major life activities, has a record of such an impairment, or is regarded as having such an impairment."[4]
Since the implementation of the Americans with Disabilities Act (ADA)[5] on July 26, 1990, (PL 101-336, 42 U.S.C. §12101 *et seq*) law enforcement agencies have made efforts to comply with Title II of the ADA. Title II of the Americans with Disabilities Act "prohibits discrimination against people with disabilities in State and local governmental services, programs, and employment. Law enforcement agencies are covered because they are programs of State or local governments, regardless of whether they receive Federal grants or other Federal funds."[6] The ADA impacts virtually everything law enforcement officials do:

- Receiving citizen complaints;
- Interrogating witnesses;
- Arresting, booking, and holding suspects;
- Operating telephone emergency centers (911);
- Providing emergency medical services; and
- Enforcing laws.

Types of Disabilities

More than 43 million Americans have disabilities.[7] Among those are visual impairments, hearing impairments, orthopedic/mobility impairments, hidden disabilities, psychiatric disabilities, muscular or neurological limitation, and mental retardation.[8]

Visual impairments. Blindness or vision impairment can mean either a complete or partial loss of vision. For some persons, the edges or a part of the visual field might be obscured; or some persons might have no central vision but peripheral vision still exists. Sometimes a person's visual acuity may change under different light conditions. Many people who are blind use a guide dog or cane to ambulate.

Hearing impairments. Individuals may be deaf or hard of hearing. Not all people who are deaf or hard of hearing know or use sign language. Some individuals with hearing deficits may be difficult to understand (speech is not clear).

Orthopedic/mobility impairment. Many types of injuries, diseases, and conditions cause mobility impairments that can affect an individual. Some of these disabilities are acquired at birth while others stem from accidents or illnesses later in life. This type of disability can affect basic mobility, coordination and balance, strength and endurance, and other aspects of body function. Many people who have mobility impairments are required to use adaptive equipment of one kind or another such as canes, walkers, and wheelchairs. Prosthetic devices (artificial arms or legs) and body braces might also be used. "Some people with mobility impairments use service animals to assist them with carrying or retrieving items and opening doors in order to achieve greater independence."[9]

Invisible/Hidden disabilities. Many disabilities such as asthma, arthritis, heart disease, environmental illness, AIDS, chronic fatigue syndrome, attention deficit hyperactivity disorder (ADD), and mild mental retardation are not visible to an onlooker.

Psychiatric disabilities. Anxiety disorders, depression, bipolar disorders, schizophrenia, and other conditions are part of the diverse group of psychiatric disabilities. Many psychiatric patients take medications that cause excessive thirst, insomnia, or fatigue.

Muscular or Neurological limitations. Motor ability and speech may be impacted by muscular or neurological disabilities. Some involuntary or halting movement or limitation of movement in one or more than one appendage, some lisping, and/or indistinct speech or flatness of tone due to lack of fine motor control of the tongue or lips might be present in individuals with these type disabilities. The severity and functional effects of the disability vary from person to person. Some persons who have significant cerebral palsy or other muscular or neurological disabilities may communicate by writing, typing, or using a communication board of other electronic device.

Autism is one example of a neurological disorder that affects the functioning of the brain. "Autism is a complex developmental disability that typically appears during the first three years of life…. Autism and its associated behaviors have been estimated to occur in as many as 1 in 500 individuals."[10] Since autism interferes with the normal development of the brain in the areas of social interaction and communication skills, individuals with autism typically have difficulties in verbal and nonverbal communication, social interactions, and leisure or play activities.

Mental retardation. Many persons with mental retardation have average or superior abilities in some respects. Some persons with mental retardation, however, may not be able to think, reason, or remember.

Common Issues in Interacting with People with Disabilities

Law enforcement professionals may misconstrue actions taken by some individuals with disabilities as suspicious or illegal activity or uncooperative behavior.

<u>**Example:**</u> A police officer approaches a vehicle and asks the driver to step out of the car. The driver, who has a mobility disability, reaches behind the seat to retrieve her assistive

device for walking. This action appears suspicious to the officer.

Deaf individuals or those who have speech disabilities or mental retardation, or who are blind or visually impaired may not recognize or be able to respond to police directions. Those individuals may erroneously be perceived as uncooperative.

Example: An individual is seen running from an area in which a crime has been reported. The officer on the scene yells "STOP" or "FREEZE" to the individual. The individual, who is deaf and cannot hear the officer, continues to run. The officer mistakenly believes that this individual is a suspect who is fleeing the scene.

In addition, individuals with disabilities that cause them to have a staggering gait or slurred speech, either from their disability or medications used to treat them, may be perceived by law enforcement officers as being intoxicated. When, in fact, these individuals may have neurological disabilities, mental/emotional disturbances, or hypoglycemia causing the staggering gait and/or slurred speech.

Example: A police department receives a call from a local restaurant. The manager claims that a customer is causing a disturbance in the restaurant. When the responding officer arrives at the scene, she discovers a 30-year-old woman standing and grimacing. The woman has pulled the tablecloth from the table. At first glance, the officer believes the woman has had too much to drink and is behaving aggressively. In fact, the customer is having a seizure.

The foregoing examples indicate how easy it is to make assumptions based on individuals' nonverbal behaviors. In each of the above scenarios, the nonverbal behavior of disabled individuals was perceived by law enforcement professionals to be either threatening, uncooperative, or suspicious.

Law Enforcement Agencies and Accommodations for the Disabled

Law enforcement agencies must provide accommodations for persons with disabilities. "The ADA requires law enforcement agencies to make reasonable modifications to their policies, practices, and procedures that are necessary to ensure accessibility for individuals with disabilities, unless making such modifications would fundamentally alter the program or service involved."[11] Training, sensitivity, and awareness will help to ensure equitable treatment of individuals with disabilities as well as effective law enforcement. Law enforcement professionals should:

- be aware that the driver of a vehicle displaying visible signs that a person with a disability may be driving (designated license plate, hang tag, etc.) will or might reach for a mobility device;
- use hand signals or calling to people in a crowd to signal for a person to stop to get the attention of a deaf individual;

- speak clearly and slowly to ensure that an individual understands what is being said;
- use breathalyzers to obtain accurate results and to reduce the possibility of false arrest of individuals with mobility or neurological disabilities; and
- be trained to distinguish behaviors that pose a real risk or threat to health and safety from behaviors that do not when an individual is having a seizure or exhibiting signs of psychotic crisis and needs medical attention.

Transporting and holding persons with mobility disabilities. When a law enforcement officer arrests a person who uses a wheelchair, standard transport practices may be dangerous. The best approach to use in the transport process is to ask the individual what type of transportation he or she can use and how to lift or assist him or her in transferring into and out of the vehicle. The important point to remember is not to harm an individual or to cause damage to his or her wheelchair. Some individuals who use assistive devices such as crutches, braces, or manual wheelchairs might be safely transported in a patrol car. Transport of other individuals who use manual or power wheelchairs, however, might require departments to make minor modifications to existing cars or vans or to use life-equipped vans or buses.

In the case of an arrest of a mobility-impaired individual, law enforcement agencies must ensure that he/she has access to the toilet facilities and other amenities provided at the lock-up or jail. Structural changes can be undertaken to ensure officer safety and general security. For instance, grab bars in accessible restrooms can be secured so that they are not removable.

Communicating effectively with individuals with visual impairments. Law enforcement officers should identify themselves and state clearly and completely any directions or instructions to individuals with visual impairments. If a visually impaired or blind person needs to sign documentation, officers must read out loud in full any such documents. In addition, if fingerprints or photographs are required to be taken of the visually impaired individual, officers should describe the procedures in advance so that the individual will know what to expect. When a visually impaired individual is required to complete a form to report a crime, the simplest solution for law enforcement agencies is to have an officer or clerk assist the person in reading and filling out the form. For individuals with moderate vision disabilities, law enforcement agencies should have a copy of the form in large print to make it accessible to them.

Law enforcement agency responsibilities to deaf individuals. "State and local law enforcement agencies have a federal mandate to ensure adequate and appropriate communications with deaf and hard-of-hearing persons. Without effective communication in dealing with law enforcement personnel, serious violations of constitutional and civil rights can occur."[12] The needs of the deaf or hearing-impaired individual dictate the type of communication aid required, whether it be a sign language interpreter or other auxiliary aid (lip reading, telecommunications devices for the deaf, telephone handset amplifiers, assistive listening systems, and videotext displays). However, law enforcement professionals should generally not rely on family members to provide sign language interpreting except in some limited circumstances. Regardless of the type of assistance, and even if an interpreter is not required, police officers should take all steps to ensure effective communication. Writing information and making other accommodations in their usual practice will protect the rights of the hearing impaired individual. For example, in communication with a lip reading individual, an officer should face the individual directly and have the communication take place in a well-lighted area.

As further evidence of the need for effective communication with deaf or hearing-impaired individuals, courts[13] have suppressed evidence obtained from a deaf defendant where it was found that the Miranda warning was not adequately communicated to the defendant. "If a hearing impaired person is arrested, the arresting officer's Miranda warning should be communicated to the arrestee on a printed form approved for such use by the law enforcement agency where no qualified interpreter is immediately available and communication is otherwise inadequate. The form should also advise the arrestee that the law enforcement agency has an obligation under Federal law to offer an interpreter to the arrestee without cost and that the agency will defer interrogation pending the appearance of an interpreter."[14]

Communication with persons having mental retardation. When an individual who has mental retardation is arrested, the arresting officer must modify the procedure for giving Miranda warnings. Law enforcement personnel should use simple words and ask the individual to repeat each phrase of the warnings in her or his own words. The officer should also check for understanding by asking the individual such questions as "What is a lawyer?" "How might a lawyer help you?" or by asking the individual for an example of what he/she considers a right. In essence, using simple language or pictures and symbols, speaking slowly and clearly, and asking concrete questions are all ways to communicate with individuals who have mental retardation.

Individuals with neurological disabilities and communication difficulties. As mentioned previously in this chapter, persons with autism have communication difficulties because their disorder makes it hard for them to relate to the outside world. Some examples of the communication difficulties an autistic person might exhibit are as follows:

- may be nonverbal or may only repeat what is said to him/her
- may not respond to "STOP" command, may run or move away, may cover ears and look away constantly
- may appear argumentative, stubborn, or belligerent; may say NO in response to all questions; may ask "Why?" incessantly
- may have difficulty recognizing and repairing breakdowns in communication (for example, asking for clarification or responding to a request for clarification)
- may be poor listener; may not seem to care what you have to say; lack of eye contact may lead you to believe they aren't listening
- may have passive, monotone voice with unusual pronunciations (often sounding computer-like)
- may have difficulty judging personal space; may stand too close or too far away; may stare at the police officer; may continue to invade your "space;" may not differentiate private body parts
- may not recognize danger or hurt; may approach and talk to strangers; may possess weak help-seeking skills; may not be able to distinguish between minor and serious problems; may not know where/how to get help for problems; may not be able to give important information or be able to answer questions
- will have difficulty interpreting body language and social cues, such as defensive

posture and facial expressions; may not recognize jokes, teasing, and nonverbal/verbal emotional responses

Law enforcement professionals may unexpectedly encounter or be asked to find a person who has autism. The ability to recognize the behavioral symptoms and to know contact approaches is necessary to avoid situations of risk. In law enforcement situations with autistic individuals, officers should consider the following responses:

- Talk in direct, short phrases (for example, "stand up," "go to the car"),
- Allow for delayed responses to questions, directions, or commands.
- Talk calmly and/or repeat. Talking louder will NOT help understanding.
- Model calming body language (slow breathing, keep hands down).
- Use low gestures for attention (avoid rapid pointing or waving).
- Look and wait for responses and/or eye contact. Don't interpret limited or lack of eye contact as deceit or disrespect.
- Never lightly touch or pat on shoulders or near face.
- Avoid standing too near or behind.
- Avoid stopping the individual's repetitive behaviors unless self-injury or potential injury for others is present.
- Evaluate the person for injury. Individual may have high threshold to pain or may not indicate pain.
- Consider the use of "YES-NO" sign board, alphabet, simple phrase word board, or picture board.
- Avoid literal or slang expressions (i.e., "I'd give my eye teeth to know," "spread eagle," or "you think it's cool?")

If an individual is taken into custody for booking and arraignment and the arresting officer believes this person may have a neurological disorder such as autism, the primary rule is to "err on the side of caution." Because he/she is at extreme risk of abuse from the general prison/jail population, you should segregate him/her from it. As further steps, you should seek advice from the prosecutor's office or ask for evaluation from community health personnel.[15]

When dealing with persons with disabilities, law enforcement professionals must keep in mind certain responses and behaviors that are typical of this population, behaviors that can often result in grave legal situations for the disabled when the behaviors are not recognized in their full context. Persons with disabilities may exhibit or demonstrate the following:

- An inordinate desire to please authority figures
- The inability to move to abstract from concrete thought
- Watching for clues from interrogators
- The longing for friends
- Relate best with children or the elderly
- Bluffing greater competence than one possesses

- An all-too-pleasant facade
- Abhorrence for the term "mental retardation"
- Real memory gaps
- A quickness to take blame
- Impaired judgment
- An inability to understand rights, court proceedings, or the punishment
- Problems with receptive and expressive language
- Short attention span and uncontrolled impulses
- Unsteady gait and struggling speech
- Exhaustion and surrender of all defenses[16]

The Elderly

In defining what constitutes "elderly," gerontologists have determined a set of factors to be studied rather than focusing solely on age. These factors include

1. **Physical function**. Physical activity—are they still active and can they get around easily?
2. **Employment status**. Are they retired or still employed, either full- or part-time?
3. **Life activities**. Social activity—do they maintain a circle of friends and do they meet new people?
4. **Self-perception**. Do they define or refer to themselves as old? (Godwin, 1992.)

In dealing with an aged or geriatric individual, you must be especially sensitive to several potential needs. You must also remember to try to demonstrate your sensitivity in a way that will not appear to be condescending to the person. As a law enforcement professional, in dealing with older persons you may find some of the following techniques to be very useful.

- Carefully identify yourself to the person(s) to avoid confusion.
- When first addressing the person, use his or her title (Mr., Mrs., Ms. Miss, or rank) and last name. You may use the first name of the individual(s) later if requested by the person(s).
- Do NOT assume senility or lack of understanding.
- Watch for signs of a hearing deficiency.
- Speak directly if you need to be heard; do NOT shout.
- Allow extra time for responses.
- Ask the person what will make him/her comfortable.
- Maintain eye contact.

Remember, advanced age may only be one of many special circumstances you may have to consider. Other conditions about which you must be aware are physical and mental handicaps.

Communication Issues Associated with the Elderly

Hearing Impaired or Deaf Individuals. While dramatic in nature, the scenario presented at the beginning of this chapter is just one example of the difficulty associated in communicating with the elderly. Mr. McDonald's problem was one of a physiological nature due to the removal of larynx. The majority of persons receiving this type of surgery are male and have an average age of 62. These individuals must then communicate through writing, mouthing words, gesturing, and facial expressions. Some are fortunate enough to receive reconstructive surgery in order to reacquire minimal vocal skills or, as in Mr. McDonald's case, some use electronic assistance.

Communication involves sensory, motor, and cognitive skills. Hearing is the most important for comprehending verbal communication. "In 1980, 43% of people over 65 had hearing loss; by 2020, it is expected to rise to 54%."[17] While most individuals associate a loss of hearing with advanced age, research shows that a decrease in hearing ability begins around age 30 in males and age 37 in females.[18] Many people who suffer from a decline in hearing are either unaware of this decrease in their ability or choose to ignore the fact that they may require some sort of hearing device. The two most common types of hearing loss associated with aging are conductive and sensorineural. For individuals with either of these types of hearing impediments, the criminal justice professional must be patient and persistent. Vital to communicating with these persons is the use of visual cues. Therefore, the officer must make sure to speak slowly and clearly and include gestures (nonverbal) and lip movements to enhance the communication process.

In her new book, *Wake up, I'm Fat!*, Camryn Manheim described an incident in which she saw a group of Santa Cruz, California, police officers attempting to communicate with a man who had been hit by a car. She noticed that the man's eyes were wide open, but he seemed dazed. The police officers were shouting at him "WHAT—IS—YOUR—NAME?" but he was not giving them any information. Being a student of sign language, Ms. Manheim suspected that the man was possibly deaf so she knelt down beside the injured man and signed "Are you deaf?" His eyes lit up and he signed, "Yes" to her question.[19] Realizing that Ms. Manheim could serve as a conduit for information, the police officer asked her if she would accompany them to the local hospital and serve as an interpreter. This excerpt serves as an excellent example of law enforcement personnel who encountered a communication problem but were fortunate enough to have a bystander who was able to assist them. These officers had the foresight to use the means available to them to resolve a difficult situation.

Tips for the Communicating With the Hearing Impaired

Communication with a mentally or physically impaired person can be difficult and frustrating. Good communication skills, however, can prevent catastrophic reactions. The following information includes tips for communicating with the hearing impaired and the deaf.

- If the person wears a hearing aid and still has difficulty hearing, check to see if the hearing aid is in the person's ear, if it is turned on, adjusted, and has a working battery.
- Wait until you are directly in front of the person, you have the individual's attention and you are close enough to the person before you begin speaking.

- Be sure that the individual sees you approach; otherwise, your presence may startle the person.
- Face the hearing impaired person directly and be on the same level with him/her whenever possible.
- Do not eat, chew, or smoke while talking to the hearing impaired individual; your speech will be more difficult to understand.
- Keep your hands away from your face while talking.
- Recognize that hearing impaired individuals hear and understand less well when they are tired or ill.
- Reduce or eliminate background noise as much as possible when carrying on conversations.
- Speak in a normal fashion without shouting. See that the light is not shining in the eyes of the hearing impaired person.
- If the person has difficulty understanding something, find a different way of saying the same thing rather than repeating the original words over and over.
- Use simple, short sentences to make your conversation easier to understand.
- Write messages if necessary.
- Allow ample time to converse with a hearing impaired person. Being in a rush will compound everyone's stress and create barriers to having a meaningful conversation.

Tips for Communicating with the Deaf

Communicating with the deaf is similar to communicating with the hearing impaired. The following tips should be included in addition to those presented for communicating with hearing impaired individuals.

- Write a message if the person can read.
- Use a pictogram grid or other device with illustrations to facilitate communication.
- Be concise with your statements and questions.
- Utilize as many other methods of communication as possible to convey your message (i.e., body language).

Visually Impaired or Blind Individuals. Vision is also an essential element in the process of communication. As previously discussed, 93% of the communication process involves nonverbal cues. While a hearing deficit serves as a major impediment, imagine the difficulty associated in communicating with an individual who suffers both a hearing and a vision loss. Visual acuity decreases with age and is usually prevalent in individuals between 60 and 80. In order to facilitate communication with a visually impaired person, you should beware of the following:

1. if you are entering a room with someone who is visually impaired, describe the room layout, other people who are in the room, and what is happening.
2. if you are leaving the room, tell the person you are leaving. Let him/her know if

others will remain in the room or if he/she will be alone.

3. use whatever remaining vision the individual might possess.
4. allow the person to take your arm for guidance.
5. ask how you may help (i.e., increasing the light, reading the document, describing where things are, or in some other way).
6. call out the person's name before touching. Touching lets the person know that you are listening to him/her.
7. allow the person to touch you.
8. treat him/her like a sighted person as much as possible.
9. use the words "see" and "look" normally.
10. explain what you are doing as you are doing it (for example, looking for something or putting something away).
11. describe walks in routine places. Use sound and smell clues.
12. encourage familiarity and independence whenever possible.
13. leave things where they are unless the person asks you to move something.

Remember that legal blindness does not necessarily mean total blindness. Use large movements, wide gestures and contrasting colors to assist in your communications.

Cognitive Impairment. If hearing and vision are normal, then a third area of concern in the communication process is cognition. Cognition is the ability to process, store, retrieve, and express information. Some aspects of cognition and memory decline as a result of age and can be contributed to a gradual deterioration of the central nervous system. "There is an approximate 11% decrease in brain weight between the ages of 25 and 96 which is accompanied by a decrease in neuronal density."[20] Law enforcement and corrections officials need to be aware of the fact that there are little differences between the young and old concerning short-term memory. Significant differences appear, however, in long-term memory. The problems concerning long-term memory are associated more with encoding and retrieving information. Therefore, some tips for insuring more effective long-term memory recall include the following:

1. Speak slowly;
2. Give the individual plenty of time to comprehend what is being asked;
3. Give the individual plenty of time to respond;
4. Do not assume they do not understand the question; and
5. Be patient.

An additional cognitive problem in the elderly is aphasia, a total or partial loss of the power to use or understand words, often as a result of a stroke or other brain damage.

Expressive aphasics are able to understand what you say; receptive aphasics are not. Some victims may have a bit of both kinds of the impediment. For expressive aphasics, trying to speak is like having a word "on the tip of your tongue" and not being able to call it forth. Some suggestions for communicating with individuals who have aphasia are as follows:

1. Be patient and allow plenty of time to communicate with a person with aphasia.

2. Be honest with the individual. Let him/her know if you cannot quite understand what he/she is telling you.
3. Ask the person how best to communicate. What techniques or devices can be used to aid communication?
4. Allow the aphasic to try to complete his/her thoughts, to struggle with words. Avoid being too quick to guess what the person is trying to express.
5. Encourage the person to write the word he/she is trying to express and read it aloud.
6. Use gestures or pointing to objects if helpful in supplying words or adding meaning.
7. A pictogram grid can sometimes be used to great advantage. These devices are useful in "filling in" answers to requests such as "I need" or "I want." The person can merely point to the appropriate picture.
8. Use touch to aid in concentration, to establish another avenue of communication, and to offer reassurance and encouragement.

In the elderly, Alzheimer's Disease or related disorders may also present problems in the communication process. As members of the law enforcement community, you should be aware of strategies in aiding communication with persons with Alzheimer's Disease or other related disorders.

1. Always approach the person from the front, or within his/her line of vision—NO SURPRISE appearances.
2. Speak in a normal tone of voice and greet the person as you would anyone else.
3. Face the person as you talk to him/her.
4. Minimize hand movements that approach the other person.
5. Avoid a setting with a lot of sensory stimulation, like a big room where many people may be sitting or talking, a high-traffic area, or a very noisy place.
6. Maintain eye contact and smile. A frown will convey negative feelings.
7. Be respectful of the person's personal space and observant of his/her reaction as you move closer. Maintain a distance of 1 to 1 ½ feet initially.
8. If the individual is a pacer, walk with him/her, in step with him/her as you talk.
9. Use distractions if a situation looks like it may get out of hand.
10. Use a low-pitch, slow speaking voice which older adults hear best.
11. Ask only one question at a time. More than one question will increase confusion.
12. Repeat key words if the person does not understand the first time around.
13. Nod and smile only if what the person said is understood.

The Realities of Aging and Crime
"Everyone must face the realities of aging. Situations vary as do the ways people deal with growing older. Regardless of the circumstances, however, most older people say they worry about crime. Many fear becoming victims of crime. As a group, older people can be a powerful and active force. As individuals, they often can be vulnerable and may need help."[21] Older people can be vulnerable to violent crimes, property crimes, frauds, and scams, and elder abuse.

One of the main reasons that elderly individuals may be vulnerable is that they are isolated within the community. Communication with others, including law enforcement officials, may be infrequent. In response to the lack of communication between criminal justice agencies and the elderly, the American Association of Retired Persons, the International Association of Chiefs of Police, and the National Sheriffs' Association developed "Triad." The major purpose of Triad is to develop, expand, and implement effective crime prevention and education programs for older community members and to improve their quality of life. Through Triads, law enforcement officials and local citizens work to protect senior citizens against fraud, abuse, and neglect. Triad means

(1)   a three-way commitment among the chiefs of police in a county, the sheriff, and older and retired leaders,
(2)   an agreement to work together to reduce criminal victimization of the elderly, and
(3)   dedication to enhancing the delivery of law enforcement services to older persons.

At the core of Triad is an advisory council comprised of law enforcement members (county and municipal), older people of the community, and people who work with the elderly. The council acts as an advisory group for the area's law enforcement personnel on crime and security issues concerning the elderly. It discusses and recommends programs, increases communication, and recruits older volunteers to help with its objectives.

Triads can assist with strategies to increase crime reporting and provide assistance to victims (either through moral support, or access to personal services and counseling, or to act as a guide through the criminal justice system). In addition, Triads can offer crime prevention education addressing personal safety precautions for the elderly. As a communication mechanism for law enforcement and the elderly, Triads decrease isolationism for older persons and provide them with necessary information to help them maintain a secure environment.

In summary, interviewing elderly victims of crime requires law enforcement professionals to make adjustments to their typical communication processes. Officers should

1.   Identify language ability level of the victim;
2.   Identify emotional and physical capability of the victim to be interviewed;
3.   Communicate in a compassionate and nonjudgmental manner;
4.   Ensure that the victim is comfortable and understands the purpose of the interview (i.e., the officer needs to learn what happened to hurt/injure the victim);
5.   Adjust their language as needed to help the victim understand questions; and
6.   Identify special circumstances and assistance needed to interview a mentally challenged victim.

Children and Youth

Roughly 14.5 million American children—nearly one in five—experience poverty and as a result are more likely to suffer an array of problems regarding their health, emotional well-being, school readiness, and achievement-and their employability as adults. Child abuse and neglect are at epidemic levels in the United States. During 1997, an estimated 3,195,000 children were reported to authorities as abused and neglected. Children who are abused and neglected often experience problems down the road involving juvenile crime, poor academic performance, drug and alcohol abuse, domestic violence, and other social ills.[22]

As adults, we hope that children never have to face tragic outcomes. We want to protect them and keep them free from the pain and the horror of difficult situations. Unfortunately, we can't. Therefore, communicating with children requires law enforcement professionals to adopt strategies to help them feel safe and secure. Given what a child might have witnessed, he/she needs to know that violence is isolated and he/she will not be harmed. When tragic events occur, children may be afraid that the same will happen to them. Some young children may even think that it already did happen to them. We need to let them know that they are not at risk-if they are not.

The horrific high school massacres of the 1990s in Littleton, Colorado; Pearl, Mississippi; and Paducah, Kentucky, forced Americans to focus attention on the issues of children, guns, and crime. Even though the violent crime rate for juveniles actually declined in the 90s, the juvenile arrest rate increased.[23] In fact, between the years of 1979 and 1996, more than 75,000 American children and teens were killed and another 375,000 were wounded by firearms-a total figure that surpasses the number of deaths and casualties suffered by U.S. troops during the Vietnam War.[24]

During the 1990s, an increase in juvenile violence led many states to change their juvenile justice laws and to place more violent juvenile offenders on trial as adults. Because of tougher laws, violent juvenile crime arrests have fallen 25 percent since 1994.[25] However, the volume and visibility of crimes involving children, both as victims and as perpetrators, has remained unacceptably high. In 1997 alone, law enforcement agencies made about 2.8 million arrests of youths under the age of 18.[26]

In communicating with child victims of crime, law enforcement professionals should

1. Identify language ability level of the victim;
2. Identify the emotional and physical capability of the victim to be interviewed;
3. Communicate in a compassionate and nonjudgmental manner;
4. Ensure that the victim is comfortable and understands the purpose of the interview (i.e., the officers needs to learn what happened to hurt/injure the victim);
5. Adjust language as needed to help the victim understand questions; and
6. Identify special circumstances and assistance needed to interview a mentally challenged victim.

Definition of "Youth"

Each state uses its own definition for youth. Most states view youth as those individuals who have not yet reached the age of 18. Some states are currently examining the legal issues associated with lowering the age of responsibility/majority in order to stem the rising trend in violent juvenile crime.

Just as communicating with the elderly has its unique set of challenges so too does communicating with young people. While pre-schoolers and young children listen to and respect the advice of their parents and older adults, adolescents seem to rely more on their peers for advice and guidance. This shift in information providers creates a chasm between young people and their parents or caregivers. Communication at this stage of development is difficult, but not impossible. Adolescents are experiencing a tremendous amount of physical and psychological change which must be taken into account when attempting to converse. These changes frequently take the form of moodiness or rebellion. At the same time adolescents are trying to assert their independence, they are regressing to childhood behaviors when they are unsure of themselves or their decisions. Criminal justice professionals should keep in mind that the "attitude" they are receiving may not be the true nature of the young person but rather a manifestation of a stage of development. Therefore, communicating with youth requires just as much, if not more, patience than communicating with the elderly.

In order to effectively communicate with this age group, law enforcement and corrections officials must

1. sincerely and genuinely listen;
2. establish mutual trust and respect;
3. set limits;
4. avoid labeling and belittling comments;
5. avoid ordering and lecturing, filibustering;
6. avoid mixed messages;
7. respect the need for privacy;
8. brainstorm and problem solve;
9. demonstrate praise; and
10. show confidence in decisions or judgments.

Gangs

As we mentioned earlier, youth tend to look toward their peer group for advice and guidance. Wanting and needing to be part of a group or to belong is perhaps one of the foundations for **gang** membership. A **gang** is commonly defined as "any ongoing organization, association, or group of three or more persons, whether formal or informal, having as one of its primary activities the commission of one or more of the criminal acts ... which has a common name or common identifying sign or symbol, whose members individually or collectively engage in or have engaged in a pattern of criminal gang activity".[27]

Street gangs are not a recent development, having their roots in the United States in the early 1820s. Irish Americans in New York City established a deviant subculture that engaged in murder, robbery, and muggings. When the United States economy worsened in the early 1930s, gangs appeared all across the nation as the chasm between the rich and poor widened. In the 1950s gangs flourished and this deviant subculture was immortalized in the Broadway play, Westside Story. In the 1970s, gangs grew as a direct result of the increase in drug trafficking, and by the 1980s, gangs grew increasingly more violent and their economic base was expanded by dealing in weapons and drugs.

Today, street gangs differ from their predecessors in four critical ways:

1. They are larger.
2. They are more organizationally sophisticated.

3. They have full access to powerful weaponry.

4. They recruit children as young as seven and eight years old.[28]

In addition, street gangs are expanding their markets from the inner cities to the rural communities in an attempt to bolster shrinking profits from a decreasing base. Gangs have been reported in all fifty states with the typical member being a young male. However, a recent phenomenon has been the inclusion of females not just as associates, but also as full-fledged members. Furthermore, females have formed gangs of their own and typically exercise the same types of deviant behavior and violence associated with their male counterparts.

Gang Awareness. Every large urban school district is affected by street gang activity; however, youth gangs are not simply a large city or inner city problem. Nor are they a problem of particular race or culture. Gang membership crosses all ethnic, racial and geographic boundaries.

A youth/street gang may be small or large in membership, with subdivisions determined many times by location of the gang or ages of the members. (Sometimes smaller gangs will be called "sets," "cliques," "posse," or "crews".)

Identification. No single warning sign indicates that a child is behaving in a manner that potentially places the youth at risk of gang involvement.

Gang recruitment of youth: Recent research data has identified that the primary age for recruitment into street gangs is 11-15 years. This age group is where many gangs actively recruit new members at schools.

Youth gang involvement, however, may begin as early as elementary school. Children as young as 7-8 years are extremely vulnerable and may start acting out, adopting the style and language of a gang, acquiring the status of a "wannabee".

Early involvement signs: Indicators of a child/student possible early involvement with youth gangs are most often present. Changes in behavior or activities are early warning signs and may include the following:

- Failing, or poor, grades
- Being truant from school
- Affiliating more closely with peers than with family
- Changing friends (associating with gang members)
- Changing clothes, hair styles
- Using alcohol and/or drugs
- Developing attitude and behavior problems
- Glamorizing youth gang lifestyle

The following are physical indicators that may appear:

- **Graffiti** – Youth gang members will advertise their gang affiliations by writing gang graffiti on their schoolbooks, school bathrooms, school desks, and other school property. They will also write gang graffiti on walls of neighborhood properties adjacent to schools. Additionally, gang members will write gang graffiti at their personal residences. Gang graffiti will most certainly be found in the bedroom area of a youth gang member.

- **Youth gang clothing attire** – Clothing continues to be a gang membership indicator; however, variations of gang clothing are in vogue and currently in style with many school age youth who are not involved in gang activities. Gang members associate extremely baggy clothing, clothes of particular colors, styles, and certain athletic teams (specifically baseball caps) as being affiliated with and important to gang membership. Clothing preferences change over time.
- **Hand signs/signals** – Many gang members communicate their affiliation through hand signs. Youth practicing hand signals is an early warning sign of gang affiliation.
- **Gang style language** – Most street gangs adopt the use of a form of gang slang and many forms of gang slang exist. Although students who are not gang members may use some gang forms, an excessive amount of gang slang is an indicator of possible gang involvement.

Signs of actual gang membership: Once involved directly with a street gang, a youth/student's behavior may change gradually or suddenly. Most likely, it will follow a pattern or process. At school the youth will promote his affiliation and new status with the gang. The student will most likely become more disrespectful towards teachers and behavior problems involving defiant issues may increase.

Indicators of actual gang membership are as follows:

- **Monikers** – Gang members pride themselves in being given nicknames, or monikers, by the gang. The moniker may highlight a physical characteristic or some personal trait.
- **Attitude** – One of the main activities of gang members is the intimidation of other youth and/or adults. By promoting a defiant and arrogant attitude, gang members obtain a reputation for being tough and aggressive.
- **Tattoos** – The majority of youth gang members, after initiation or acceptance into the gang, are tattooed, indicating their allegiance and affiliation. These tattoos could be crude or elaborate. Most likely, the gang members' monikers and/or the gang's name will be involved in the tattoo.[29]

Communicating with Gang Members. Youth become involved in gangs for several reasons. (1) They may have a need for belonging to something special. Gang membership will provide the recognition, the identity, the attention, the support, and the acceptance of their peers. Many gang youth will join the gang to satisfy the need of belonging. (2) Gang membership may be a family tradition. A youth may join a gang because a brother, sister, parent, or relative has or had a gang affiliation. (3) The gang lifestyle may be seen as exciting, daring, and dangerous. The potential for violence has a certain level of attraction for many young people. (4) A youth may join a gang for physical protection from rival gang members. Some youth will feel they are targets for violence if they don't join a gang. Many of today's gang youth do not believe in themselves outside of their gang structure. They do not see themselves being successful in school or having employment opportunities in their communities.

The key to understanding gang behavior lies in properly identifying the gang's primary objectives and leadership structure. Generally, most youth gangs fall into one of three distinct categories: corporate, territorial, and scavenger.

Corporate Gangs focus their attention on making money. They have a clearly defined division of labor. Any activities that gang members participate in are almost exclusively for profit. Corporate gangs tend to have a well-entrenched vertical hierarchy and are likely to participate in group rather than individual violence. The vertical hierarchy of these gangs tends to limit their visibility to law enforcement. It also makes it exceedingly difficult to leave the gang if one wishes.

Territorial Gangs tend to focus on the possession of turf, and gang members are very quick to use violence to secure and protect what they see as theirs. These type gangs have a flatter hierarchal structure than Corporate Gangs, and this results in less control over individual members and a higher rate of gratuitous violence. Because Territorial Gangs are tied to their turf, they are easier to keep track of, contain, and leave if a member so desires to do.

Scavenger Gangs have very little organizational structure, and gang membership is motivated more by a need to belong to a group than anything else. The crimes committed by Scavenger Gangs tend to be impulsive and often senseless. No objectives and goals are established for the gang, and leadership is very fluid, often depending on who is the most violent that day. Members of Scavenger Gangs tend to be low achievers who are prone to violence and erratic behavior.

Communication with gang members by criminal justice officials is difficult in the best of situations, if not impossible. Since gangs are closed societies and gang membership breeds suspicion of outsiders, communication and effective dialogue is extremely unlikely. Gang members derive their identity from group acceptance and, therefore, do not seek outsider approval. In order to attempt to communicate with a gang member, the dialogue must be with the individual–not the gang member. Rapport must be established with the person, devoid of gang personality or identify, in a neutral site or location. If these criteria are met, then a personal relationship may become possible. However, once the individual returns to gang turf or is reunited with the gang, the old identity and mistrust return and the officer is once again an enemy.

The following tips are some general rules of thumb to help law enforcement officers gain and keep the trust of gang-affiliated youth. The guidelines are simple, but most be applied consistently.

✓ **Be reliable**. Most gang-affiliated youth have been let down numerous times.
✓ **Always look for the positive in the youth**.

✓ **Be real**. Do not be somebody you're not.

✓ **Absolutely do not make any promises that you cannot keep**.

✓ **Be a good role model**. Practice what you preach.

✓ **Avoid stereotyping**. All youth are not the same.

✓ **Be aware that every person has different experiences than you**.

✓ **Listen to the youth**. And he/she will listen to you.

✓ **Be very aware of your body language**. Remember, gangs do a lot of posturing and may feel threatened by sudden hand movements.

✓ **Strive to understand the gang member's language**. Do not be afraid to ask, "What does that word mean?"

✓ **Avoid taking things personally**.

✓ **Remember, you cannot help those who do not wish to be helped**.

Culturally Diverse Populations

Values, according to Thiederman, form the core of a culture. **Values** are social principles, goals, or standards accepted by persons in a culture; they establish what is proper and improper behavior as well as what is normal and abnormal. Values are learned by contacts with family members, teachers, and religious leaders.

People from varying cultures hold different viewpoints of and attitudes toward women, ethical standards, and work. Understanding differences in cultural values is essential for communicating with persons who come from different cultural backgrounds.

Some values held by people in the United States are not shared by people in other cultures. For example, equality, informality, individualism, directness, and attitude toward the future, time, and work are some of the U.S. values and assumptions. The following list contrasts the priorities of cultural values of Americans, Japanese, and Arabs. ("1" represents the most important value).[30]

Americans	Japanese	Arabs
1. Freedom	1. Belonging	1. Family security
2. Independence	2. Group harmony	2. Family harmony
3. Self-reliance	3. Collectiveness	3. Parental guidance
4. Equality	4. Age/Seniority	4. Age
5. Individualism	5. Group consensus	5. Authority
6. Competition	6. Cooperation	6. Compromise
7. Efficiency	7. Quality	7. Devotion
8. Time	8. Patience	8. Patience
9. Directness	9. Indirectness	9. Indirectness

10. Openness	10. Go-between	10. Hospitality

As can be seen from the foregoing table, vast differences are present in the value structure of these cultures.

In addition to value differences, many other behavioral areas differ from culture to culture. As law enforcement professionals, you need to be able to understand variances in greetings and body language between cultures. The following summary offers tips for communicating (verbally and nonverbally) with members of the diverse cultures that make up this country.

Japanese

Japan has a highly structured and traditional society. Great importance is placed on loyalty, politeness, personal responsibility, and on everyone working together for the good of the larger group. Education, ambition, hard work, patience, and determination are held in the highest regard.

Meeting and Greeting
⇨ A handshake is appropriate upon meeting. The Japanese handshake is limp and with little or no eye contact.
⇨ Some Japanese bow and shake hands.

Body Language
⇨ Nodding is very important. When listening to Japanese speak, especially in English, you should nod to show you are listening and understanding the speaker.
⇨ Silence is a natural and expected form of nonverbal communication. Do not feel a need to talk.
⇨ Do not stand close to a Japanese person. Avoid touching.
⇨ Prolonged eye contact is considered rude.
⇨ Never beckon with your forefinger. The Japanese extend their right arm out in front, bending the wrist down, waving fingers. Do not beckon older people at all.
⇨ Sit erect with both feet on the floor. Never sit with your ankle over your knee.
⇨ Never point at someone with four fingers spread out and thumb folded in.

Verbal Communication
⇨ Avoid using the number "four" if possible because it has connotations of death to the Japanese.
⇨ Do not expect a Japanese person to say "no." "Maybe" generally means **"no."**
⇨ The Japanese do not express opinions and desires openly. What they say and what they mean may be very different.

French

The French adhere to a strong and homogeneous set of values. They cherish their culture, history, language, and cuisine-which is considered to be an art.

Meeting and Greeting
⇨ Shake hands with everyone present when arriving and leaving. A handshake may be quick with a light grip.
⇨ Men may initiate handshakes with women.

Names and Titles
⇨ Use last names and appropriate titles until specifically invited to use first names.
⇨ Address people as Monsieur, Madame, or Mademoiselle without adding the surname. Madame is used for all adult women, married or single, over 18 years of age.

Body Language
⇨ Do not slap your open palm over a closed fist (this is considered a vulgar gesture).
⇨ The "okay" sign, made with the index finger and thumb, means "zero."
⇨ The French use the "thumbs up" sign to say "okay."

Italians
Cultural achievement is Italy's greatest source of pride. Inventiveness, imagination, intelligence, and education are prized. The family is the most important affiliation in Italy.

Meeting and Greeting
⇨ Shake hands with everyone present when introductions are made. Shake hands again when leaving.
⇨ Ladies should extend their hand first to men.

Names and Titles
⇨ Use last names and appropriate titles until specifically invited to use first names.
⇨ Females almost always use their maiden name in business and on legal documents.

Body Language
⇨ Maintain eye contact while talking, otherwise Italians might think you are hiding something.
⇨ Italians are known for using the most body language of all European nations.
⇨ Italians are open, curious and tolerant of others' uniqueness and manners.
⇨ They will tolerate lateness, inefficiency, and sincere mistakes but dislike arrogance and rudeness.

The Arab World
The so-called Arab World consists of about 20 countries stretching from Mauritania in the west to Oman in the east. Within that area is a diverse group of people bound together primarily by language and religion. While religion is a strong common denominator, adherence ranges from very strict and fundamentalist to very loose and liberal. The same spectrum applies

to gestures and body language.

Meeting and Greeting
⇨ Shaking hands is important. The grip may be less firm than Europeans and Americans use.
⇨ Arab males are considered a "touching society." Handshakes may be prolonged, elbows may be grasped, and two men may even hold hands while walking on the street.

Body Language
⇨ Avoid showing the sole of the shoe, or inadvertently point it at someone. The shoe soles are the lowest and dirtiest part of the body; and, therefore, it is rude to point them at someone.
⇨ The right hand prevails; eat with it, present gifts with it, touch with it. The left hand is generally regarded as the "unclean" hand and is used primarily for bodily hygiene.
⇨ Long direct eye contact among men is important. In fact, staring is not necessarily considered rude or impolite.
⇨ When two men converse, they will probably stand much closer than Westerners.
⇨ Gesturing "no" is often done by tilting the head backward and either raising the eyebrows, jutting out the chin, or making a clicking sound with the tongue.[31]

Learning basic differences in culture will assist law enforcement officials to better communicate with individuals who comprise our diverse country. No compendium exists that provides all the necessary details for communicating across cultural divides. However, recognizing and understanding that because of differing values and customs, individuals being interviewed, interrogated, or charged in criminal acts require modifications and adaptations to our "normal" communication processes.

Summary
This chapter focuses on those issues associated with communicating with special groups. These special groups include the disabled, elderly, youth, and culturally diverse populations. Each group presents its own unique set of problems and solutions. While similarities in communicating with these groups are present, a one-size-fits-all approach will not suffice. Specific techniques exist for overcoming communication barriers with each group, and criminal justice professionals must be aware of them.

Since the implementation of the Americans with Disabilities Act (ADA), on July 26, 1990, law enforcement agencies have made efforts to comply with Title II of this legislation. The ADA impacts virtually everything law enforcement officials do, whether enforcing the law, interrogating witnesses, arresting, booking, and holding suspects, or receiving complaints from citizens. Because over 43 million Americans have disabilities, you need to be aware of distinguishing characteristics of these individuals. Among the types of disabilities are visual impairments, hearing impairments, orthopedic/mobility impairments, hidden disabilities, psychiatric disabilities, muscular or neurological limitation, and mental retardation. Each disability brings its own set of actions and requires a different means of communication by law enforcement officers. For instance, nonverbal behavior of disabled individuals can imply threatening, uncooperative, or suspicious acts, and you must be aware of their pre-existing perceptions.

The elderly in this country comprise a large majority of the population. Since communication involves sensory, motor, and cognitive skills, law enforcement officers must use techniques to provide older citizens with additional time for responses. Advanced age is only one of many circumstances you may have to consider. Other conditions about which you must be aware are physical and mental handicaps.

The elderly fear becoming victims of crime. They are often vulnerable and may need help. One of the main reasons that elderly individuals may be vulnerable is that they are isolated within the community. Communication may be infrequent for them. Triads have been formed in communities to develop, expand, and implement effective crime prevention and education programs for older community members and to improve their quality of life. As a communication mechanism for the elderly and law enforcement, Triads decrease isolationism for older persons and provide them with necessary information to help them maintain a secure environment.

Communicating with children and youth also presents a unique set of challenges for the law enforcement community. The involvement of youth in gangs creates additional roadblocks to the communication process. Gangs are closed societies and gang membership breeds suspicion of outsiders. Gang members derive their identity from group acceptance and, therefore, do not seek outsider approval. General rules of thumb to help law enforcement officers gain and keep the trust of gang-affiliated youths involve such things as looking for the positive in the youth, not making promises that you cannot keep, being a good role model, avoiding stereotyping, listening to the youth, and avoiding taking things personally-among others presented in this chapter.

Cultural sensitivity is a major issue in the 21st century. Police departments that fail to plan for this contingency will find their officers in jeopardy, their departmental reputations in peril, and their municipal/city governments in litigation. Understanding that people from varying cultures hold different viewpoints of and attitudes toward women, ethical standards, and work will help you in the communication process. In addition, as law enforcement professionals, you need to be able to understand variances in greetings and body language between cultures. Learning basic differences in culture will assist law enforcement officials to better communicate with the diverse group of citizens who comprise our nation.

Key Terms

Culture	Ethnocentrism
Elderly	Youth
Gang	Racism
Disability	Autism
Americans with Disabilities Act	Cognition
Aphasia	Triad
Monikers	Corporate Gangs
Territorial Gangs	Scavenger Gangs
Values	Graying of America

Discussion Questions

1.   Does America live up to its promise of "all men are created equal?" Why or why not?
2.   Is America really a great melting pot? Why or why not?
3.   How did the Americans with Disabilities Act impact law enforcement, particularly in relation to victims of crime?
4.   Over 43 million Americans have disabilities. Identify the types and give a brief description of each.
5.   Give some examples of ways law enforcement professionals can effectively communicate with individuals with visual impairments.
6.   What can an officer do if he/she is attempting to communicate with an individual who has a neurological disability?
7.   Identify some responses and behaviors that are typical of the population of persons with disabilities.
8.   List some tips for communicating with the hearing impaired.
9.   What is aphasia and how can it impact communication?
10.   Why are the elderly so vulnerable to crimes?
11.   How can the formation and establishment of a Triad in a local community help law enforcement to protect senior citizens?
12.   What type of challenges do law enforcement professionals experience when attempting to communicate with young people?
13.   How do street gangs differ today from their predecessors?
14.   List indicators of a child/student's possible early involvement in youth gangs.
15.   Generally, most youth gangs fall into one of three distinct categories. Identify each category and compare and contrast them. How are they different? How are they similar?
16.   Compare and contrast the top five (5) priorities of cultural values of Americans, Japanese, and Arabs. Are they similar? Are they different? How?
17.   List some examples of body language differences between Japanese and Americans.
18.   **Ethical Issue:** As a responding officer to a violent crime, you find that your best source of information is an eyewitness with a cognitive disability (aphasia). You exhaust your patience waiting for the witness to give you the full story. He/she has difficulty finding the right words and has lengthy gaps in his/her speech. You do not wish to rely on this witness and begin to look for another individual who has less direct knowledge of the crime. Should you abandon your eyewitness?
19.   **Ethical Issue:** As a police officer you respond to a minor crime, the maximum penalty for this crime is less than a year in jail and a fine of $1,000. The suspect has a learning disability and does not fully comprehend the Miranda warnings. Do you let the suspect go with a warning, or do you arrest the suspect?
20.   **Ethical Issue:** While investigating a violent crime, your information leads you to a gang member as a suspect. You are sure the gang member is guilty of this crime and, upon questioning, discover the suspect has only a limited knowledge of English. Should you seek the services of an interpreter at this point or proceed with the Miranda warning and questioning?

Notes

1. Kantrowitz, Barbara and Wingert, Pat, *Newsweek,* 5/10/99, p. 36

2. Shusta, R. M., Levine, D. R., Harris, P. R., & Wong, H. Z., *Multicultural Law Enforcement: Strategies for Peacekeeping in a Diverse Society.* Englewood Cliffs, NJ: Prentice Hall, 1995.

3. Ritter, J., "English Only, Ready or Not," *USA Today,* July 31, 1999, p. 3A.

4. Commonly Asked Questions About the Americans with Disabilities Act and Law Enforcement (1996). United States Department of Justice: Civil Rights Division, Disability Rights Section.
<http://www.usdoj.gov/crt/ada/q&alaw.htm> September 1, 2002.

5. Americans with Disabilities Act; New information added August 5, 2002. Municipal Research & Services Center.
<http://www.mrsc.org/legaVada/adainfo.htm> September 15, 2002.

6. Commonly asked questions about the Americans with Disabilities Act and Law Enforcement (1996). United States Department of Justice: Civil Rights Division, Disability Rights Section.
<http://www.usdoj.gov/crt/ada/q&alaw.htm> September 1, 2002.

7. Americans with Disabilities Act: New information added August 5, 2002. Municipal Research & Services Center.
<http://www.mrsc.org/legal/ada/adainfo.htm> September 15, 2002

8. Federal Employment of People with Disabilities, (n.d.). United States Office of Personnel Management.
<http://www.opm.gov/disabilitv/mngr 4-09.asp> September 15, 2002.

9. Federal Employment of People with Disabilities, (n.d.). United States Office of Personnel Management.
<http://www.opm.gov/disability/mngr_4-09.asp> September 15, 2002.

10. Debbaudt, D. (2000, April 24). Avoiding Unfortunate Situations. <http://policeandautism.cjb.net/avoiding.html>
September 1, 2002.

11. Commonly Asked Questions About the Americans with Disabilities Act and Law Enforcement (1996). United States Department of Justice: Civil Rights Division, Disability Rights Section.
<http://www.usdoj.gov/crt/ada/q&a_law.htm> September 1, 2002.

12. Police and Law Enforcement Agency Responsibilities to Deaf Individuals, (n.d.) National Association for the Deaf Law Center. <http://www. advocacvinc.org/AC 15.htm> August 6, 2002.

13. *State of Maryland v. Barker, Md. Cir. Ct. Dec. 8, 1977; State of Oregon* v. *Mason, Or. Cir. Ct May 27, 1980.*

14. Police and Law Enforcement Agency Responsibilities to Deaf Individuals, (n.d.) National Association for the Deaf Law Center. <http://www.advocacyinc.org/AC15.htm> August 6, 2002.

15. Debbaudt, D., Ibid.

16. Ibid.

17. Lewis, C.B., *Aging: The Health Care Challenge*(2nd ed). Philadelphia, PA: F.A. Davis Co., 1990.

18. Carmichael, C.W., Botan, C.H., and Hawkins, R., *Human Communication and the Aging Process.* Prospect Heights, IL: Waveland Press, 1988.

19. Manheim, Camryn, *Wake Up. I'm Fat!.* NY: Broadway Books, 1999.

20. Oyer.H. J., and Oyer, E. J. (Eds.) *Aging and Communication.* Baltimore: University Park Press, 1976.

21. How Can Senior Citizens Protect Themselves Against Crime? Denton County Department of Information Services. <http://sheriff.dentoncounty.com/mam> September 22, 2002.

22. Public Opinion on Youth, Crime, and Race; A Guide for Advocates. Building Blocks for Youth Initiative.
<http://www.buildingblocksforyouth.org> September 22, 2002.

23. Public Opinion on Youth, Crime, and Race: A Guide for Advocates. Building Blocks for Youth Initiative.
<http://www.buildmgblocksforyouth.org> September 22, 2002.

24. Public Opinion on Youth, Crime, and Race: A Guide for Advocates. Building Blocks for Youth Initiative.
<http://www.buildmgblocksforyouth.org> September 22, 2002.

25. Key Facts on Youth, Crime, and Violence. Children's Defense Fund, April 29, 1999.
<http://www.childrensdefense.org/crime> September 22, 2002.

26. Estimated Number of Juvenile Arrests. Office of Juvenile Justice and Delinquency Prevention.
<http://www.ojjpd.ncjrs.org/ojstatbb/qaOO 1. html> September 22, 2002.

27. California Penal Code Section 186.22{f}

28. Introduction to Youth Gangs, (n.d.) EMT Group. <http://www.EMTGroup.com> September 23, 2002.

29. Sandoval, G. S. (Det., Retired). Office of the Chief of Police, Los Angeles, CA, School Police Department. <http://www.laspd.com/gangs.html> March 11, 2002.

30. Hofstede, G., *Cultures and Organizations.* London: McGraw-Hill Book Company, 1992.

31. Axtell, R. E., *Gestures: The Do's and Taboos of Body Language Around the World.* NY: John Wiley & Sons, Inc., 1998.

CHAPTER 11

COMMUNICATION: THE SMALL GROUP/TEAM PROCESS

Learning Objectives:

1. To identify the characteristics of effective small groups.

2. To compare and contrast groups and teams.

3. To explain how a group achieves cohesion.

4. To differentiate task roles and maintenance roles.

5. To identify negative roles and methods for eliminating them from groups.

6. To compare and contrast strengths and limitations of group communication.

7. To identify influences of cultural values on team and group communication.

"… The key to the bureau's new training is fostering teamwork.... They're learning how to be a team, because that's essential to law enforcement in the future. We not only have to be a team inside the FBI, but we have to team with law enforcement all over the world in order to succeed. Crime is global; terrorism is global. Gone is the day where any one country can do it all alone.[1]

-Cassandra Chandler, Assistant Director of Training for the FBI

When people work together, performing the same or similar tasks, they bond with each other and develop a sense of solidarity. Criminal justice agencies are no strangers to this phenomenon; in fact, police agencies tend to exhibit a strong solidarity. **Solidarity** refers to "consensus, integration, friendship, personal intimacy, emotional depth, moral commitment, and continuity in time."[2]

"Police culture recognizes that officers can only function successfully when they work with colleagues whom they trust."[3] Since law enforcement is fraught with opportunities for mistakes, officers operate as a team—each protecting the other so that no one is falsely accused of inappropriate decision-making.

Small Group Communication

All people have been involved in group activities at one time or another. For example, through involvement in volunteer programs, organizations, social and religious groups, or some type of committee, you have engaged in group work. Furthermore, as businesses and institutions move progressively toward the preference for work teams, rare will be the case where an individual does not possess a wealth of group experiences. The reliance on team efforts stems from the belief that teams often perform better than do individuals. Here we can apply the old adage, "the minds of many outweigh the mind of one." In essence, the diversity of ideas and creativity that flow from the group communication lead to greater results and increased satisfaction.

A group is defined "as three or more individuals who interact over time, depend on each other, and follow shared rules of conduct in order to reach a common goal."[4] An important facet of the definition involves the individuals' interdependence. They must recognize that they need each other and count on each other in order to generate group cohesion or a feeling of group identity. Cohesion will be discussed more fully later in this chapter under the heading of Effective Small Group Characteristics.

A team, on the other hand, is defined as "a special kind of group that is characterized by different and complementary resources of members and by a strong sense of collective identity."[5] Even though a team shares many characteristics of the group environment (i.e., interaction, interdependence, shared rules, and common goals), they differ from general groups in two ways. First of all, a team consists of individuals who bring specialized knowledge and skills to a common project. Groups, however, are comprised of individuals who make contributions to all aspects of the group work. Secondly, a greater sense of interdependence and identity occur in teams than in standard groups. In fact, teams view themselves more as a unit than do ordinary groups. Examples of specialized teams in law enforcement encompass the following: vice, narcotics, intelligence, special weapons and tactics (SWAT). These same examples are present in correctional institutions where intelligence and emergency response teams (ERT) are unique elements within that setting. In each of these instances, unit cohesion and interdependence are vital to the safety of the members and to the success of an operation.

Effective Small Group Characteristics

Research has demonstrated several key components that identify effective small groups:[6]

1. They generally have a good working environment;
2. They have an optimum number of members;
3. They show cohesiveness;
4. They are committed to the task;
5. They respect the rules;
6. They find ways to achieve consensus;
7. They are well prepared; and
8. They meet key role requirements.

The success of the group, however, depends on the members' commitment to the group and on their effective participation in group activities. Members must understand group features and use good communication skills, both verbally and nonverbally. Communication between and within groups is essential to the organization. In law enforcement, for example, vice and narcotics units need to work closely with the intelligence unit in order to obtain the latest information. An important aspect of the uniform division is to ensure that the intelligence unit is supplied with the most recent information concerning suspects they come in contact with in the field (i.e., names, aliases, scars, marks, tattoos, addresses, associates-so intelligence is aware of the fact that these individuals have been released from correctional institutions or are on parole or have moved to another section of the local jurisdiction). This exchange most frequently occurs through the use of a document known as an FI card (Field Intelligence or Field Information card) or Intelligence Reports (IRs).

Working Environment

The seating arrangement of the work environment can often enhance or inhibit the group process. A "too formal" seating approach is one likened to that used in board of directors meetings. This style indicates status and can develop into a boss-and-subordinate pattern that restricts group interaction. Just as the "too formal" approach creates problems, so too can an excessively informal seating arrangement. When individuals are allowed to sit wherever they choose, often subgroups will form and limit the effectiveness of the group.

The ideal arrangement for optimum group interaction is the circle. Each individual is allowed to see all group members so everyone appears to have equal status. Throughout the discourse of the group activity, some individuals may earn higher status as a result of having a more logical perspective, better information, or greater insight. An effective group, however, provides the climate for each member to potentially earn such status. In addition, each participant within the group should know each other by name or by the role each individual plays, or both.

Traditional police chiefs or sheriffs, though, have a tendency to adopt the "formal" seating arrangement (since law enforcement and corrections are patterned after a military format) where the head of the organization is seated at the head of the table and on his/her immediate right is seated the second in command. However, younger leaders have a tendency to adopt a style more conducive to equal participation without the trappings of rank structure.

Number of Members

Arguments abound as to the optimum number of members for a group. Most research, however, has shown that between five and seven members is the ideal size.[7] Problems arise within groups of three to four members due to an absence of specialization or the lack of participation of members. In groups with more than seven participants, those members who are hesitant to actively participate will be even less likely to contribute. In larger groups, where some members are active participants and others will not or cannot contribute, cohesiveness will not exist and decisions will seldom be a product of the group process.

Cohesion

"All for one and one for all-the motto of the Three Musketeers—is a perfect example of cohesion in a group setting. What do we mean by cohesion? **Cohesion** is the degree of members' closeness (sticking together), of members' esprit de corps (pulling for one another), and of group identity. The attractiveness of the group's purpose is one of the qualities that seems most important in developing cohesion. For example, the Fraternal Order of Police builds cohesiveness out of devotion to service or brotherhood. A decision-making group, however, depends on how important the task is to its members to develop cohesiveness.

Many groups engage in **team-building** strategies to assist in their development of cohesion. These activities are designed to help groups work better together. Examples might be comprised of such things as merely having the group meet at a location outside its normal setting to engage in tasks to recognize one another's strengths, to share in group processes, and to develop rituals. An important point to remember is that a one-meeting group will be unable to develop cohesiveness. Ongoing meetings are vital to group success.

In law enforcement or corrections, having a group meet outside of its normal business location without the formality of uniforms or rank may place members on a more level plane. The presence of a formal rank structure may inhibit creativity or participation due to a subordinate's reluctance to overshadow or disagree with a superior's ideas or proposals.

Task Commitment

Regardless of how the group task is determined, whether it is assigned to the group or chosen by the group members, all individuals must be committed to the group to achieve success. When members believe the task to be important and that what they are doing matters, they are more inclined to commit to its completion. However, those times when a task is assigned or a request is made of you to volunteer your time and energy to a task you have to decide if you want to be part of the group. Without your full commitment to the job or task, you will miss meetings and shirk your responsibilities to the group. Therefore, you would be better suited to decline membership rather than to jeopardize the group's success.

Group Rules

Rules refer to the behavioral guidelines established (or perceived to be established) for conducting group business. In some cases-organizational meetings, for instance-group rules are spelled out in a formal operating guideline such as parliamentary procedures. Sometimes group rules simply develop within the context of the meeting or may be adapted from etiquette guidelines. In either event, most group rules develop throughout the course of the project or activity, and they vary from group to group.

Group rules are another mechanism for developing cohesion in the group. Established or implied guidelines assist members in effectively relating to each other. Once the initial anxiety of meeting each other has been surmounted and some guidelines developed, group members are able to relax and focus on the task at hand.

One important caveat to remember regarding group rules is that they are culturally based. Group members' preferences or **norms** will influence the group operations. **Norms** are learned responses that define or limit appropriate behavior. In essence, what one person may consider appropriate behavior, another may find impolite. As Americans, we have a tendency to interrupt others' speeches to offer our input. Other cultures, however, consider it to be impolite to interrupt another speaking, regardless of the circumstances. Because of our tendency to be **ethnocentric** and to interpret others' behaviors from our own cultural perspective, we must take the opportunity in mixed culture group settings to discuss rules that will guide individual participation in deliberations and discussions so that each member understands what is expected and permissible and what is not.

Group Consensus

Consensus refers to total group agreement. However, consensus cannot be achieved without the democratic process where each group member interacts and contributes to the discussion and resulting decision(s). Group members ask questions and use important listening skills and techniques—such as restating in their own words what other members have previously said—to summarize or question a point. Typically, one group member will ask if other members are supportive of a decision. At that time, if all group members are in agreement, the decision is reached by consensus. If group members are not in agreement, discussions may continue until all participants have provided input and a new statement has been developed that incorporates different viewpoints. In this case, all group members must participate in the discussion so that the resulting statement represents the entirety of the group position.

In some cases, however, consensus still cannot be reached after many group discussions. In those situations, the group can take a vote of its members. For example,

You are a member of a seven-person group that is examining a change in shift schedule for your police department. The department currently works five eight-hour shifts. The Chief has requested that group members explore the possibility of changing the shift schedule to four ten-hour shifts. After lengthy discussions, the group cannot unanimously agree on a decision. Some members are entrenched in the old shift pattern and strongly oppose the new shift concept. Other members strongly favor the new shift change since it will provide them with additional off-duty time. The group, therefore, must vote. While a voice vote is immediate and allows other members of the group to know individual positions, the secret ballot is most often the preferred ballot method. Secret ballots allow group members with less individual resolve to be more candid in their opinion. Since the interests of the entire organization are based on the integrity of the group, the secret ballot is generally more reflective of an individual's true desire. Therefore, your group chooses the option of the ballot vote. When the ballots are tallied and recorded, the vote stands four to three in favor of the new shift. If the vote had been six to one or five to two, the decision would have been given an overwhelming mandate. Since the vote was four to three, questions could arise about support for the proposed change and further study may be necessary. Nevertheless, since the vote was four to three, the principle of majority rule is the only choice. The decision would be in favor of the shift change,

Preparation

As part of your involvement in a group, your responsibility is to be prepared for group meetings. Preparedness involves reading any materials given you at or delivered to you after prior meetings. A careful review of this information will make sure you and all other group members are able to participate fully in all discussions. When group members are un- or ill-prepared to interact, the whole point of the meeting is wasted.

Another means of preparing for group meetings is to review your personal experiences. In many situations, the group will be charged with responsibilities you have some familiarity with from prior experience. Your own experiences may prove valuable to the group.

Regardless of the topic being discussed, the kind of preparation required will vary. In some cases, library research, surveys, and/or interviews may be required for particular topics. In any event, adequate preparation is the key to a successful group function.

Role Requirements

Each group has two distinct types of roles that need to be filled: task roles and maintenance roles. **Task roles** are those things a group must do in order to fulfill its mission. Whereas **maintenance roles** are those necessary group behaviors that keep the group working effectively together. An additional type of role that occurs in groups is problematic and should be avoided-**negative roles. Negative roles** cause the group to suffer and the work does not get accomplished. These types of group behaviors need to be dealt with in order to minimize disruptions and to maximize meeting efficiency.

Task Roles. Individuals in groups engage in certain behaviors that assist the group in reaching decisions. Groups are typically comprised **of information or opinion givers, information seekers, analyzers, expediters,** and **recorders.**[8] **Information or opinion givers** provide content for group discussions. Individuals seek out material to review for facts and/or opinions that will make valuable contributions to the discussions. **Information seekers,** on the other hand, probe for information from other group members. For example, "Do we need this information before we can move to the next point?"

Analyzers examine the information and the reasoning involved in the discussion. They attempt to probe into statements of fact to determine if the information is true, questionable, or relevant only to certain aspects of the issue at hand. Analyzers also attempt to fathom the reasoning of other participants, asking questions such as "Sgt. Grubb, you're generalizing from only one instance. Can you give us some other examples?"

A very important role in group activities is that of the **Expediter.** These individuals try to keep the group on track in the discussion. Oftentimes group members will stray from the topic and expediters will make statements such as "I appreciate your comments, but I can't understand what they have to do with resolving the issue."

Recorders are those individuals who take careful notes to make a record of the group's procedures and decisions. They then compose and distribute these notes in the form of **minutes** to group members prior to the next meeting. The minutes will include major motions, key debates, and conclusions agreed on by the group and will stand as the public record of the group's activities.

Maintenance Roles. Maintenance roles help the group work together smoothly as a unit. **Supporters, tension relievers, harmonizers,** and **gatekeepers** are the names associated with these individuals in the group environment.[9]

Just as the name implies, **supporters** respond either verbally or nonverbally to good points made by group members-to offer them support. Smiles, nods, vigorous headshakes and comments such as "Good point, Kathy," or "That's the best idea I've heard all day, Matt" are examples of behaviors in which supporters engage.

Tension relievers are those group members who attempt to alleviate monotony or to encourage the group process to avoid losing its momentum through comments, jokes, or a well-placed digression. While these activities contribute little or nothing to the discussion, they do offer participants an opportunity for a break in the action, a chance to relax and improve their spirits.

Harmonizers "are responsible for reducing tensions and for straightening out misunderstandings, disagreements, and conflicts."[10] In any group setting, tensions are likely to occur, especially when the topic is particularly important. Harmonizers are those individuals who attempt to diffuse potentially hostile situations by making comments such as, "Hold on, everybody; we have some good ideas here and we don't want to lose them by getting into arguments and name-calling."

Gatekeepers make sure that every group member has the opportunity to participate in discussions and that no one individual dominates the group. In addition, they often recognize cultural differences and attempt to ensure that each group member understands terms, stories, or other information.

Negative Roles. The types of behaviors engaged in by individuals in groups should be supportive of the environment; however, occasionally members play certain negative roles. **Aggressors, jokers, withdrawers,** and **monopolizers** are examples of these roles.[11]

Aggressors (or Critics) are individuals who denigrate others, criticizing almost everything others do or say. They tend to blame other group members when things go awry. Critics also derive a great deal of satisfaction from belittling the suggestions and comments of others and go to great lengths to make their disapproval known. The best way to control this type of behavior is to confront Aggressors. Ask them if they are aware of their behavior and the impact it has on group functions. Strongly stated positive expectations should be given to Aggressors to clarify their desired role behavior.

Jokers tend to be group members who like to be the center of attention either by joking, mimicking, or clowning. The best way to handle jokers is to ignore them when serious work is needed, or allow them to interject when a situation needs to be diffused or lethargy infiltrates the group.

Withdrawers (or Tight Lips) do not like to participate in the group. Sometimes these individuals are too shy to contribute or they lack confidence to speak up. On other occasions, Withdrawers may be exhibiting indifference to the group or simply backing away from a hot topic. Withdrawers can be used constructively in the group environment by delegating specific responsibilities to them. Giving them specific tasks helps them to get involved. Also, Withdrawers respond well to compliments. In group discussions, Withdrawers should be asked questions in a further attempt to draw them out.

Monopolizers (or Blabbermouths) have an opinion on every topic and are long-winded in discussions. They like to dominate meetings, regardless of the subject. For some individuals, this behavior is a source of ego gratification, but for others, it is a power play. Other group members should be discouraged from reinforcing Monopolizers. However, they should be encouraged if comments are useful to the group.

Leadership Functions

As we discussed on the foregoing pages, task and maintenance roles are vital to the operation of an effective group. Likewise, a group must have a leader or facilitator. You might think the responsibilities of a leader can be filled by individuals comprising task and maintenance roles. However, a group leader has jobs that include things such as planning meeting agendas, overseeing group interaction, and summarizing discussions.

Agendas

An agenda lists the topics that need to be covered at your meeting. Leaders must prepare the agenda in advance of each meeting and ensure that each group member receives an advance copy so that everyone may be prepared for discussions. Group meetings do occasionally deviate from the printed agenda, but members should recognize that all agenda issues will need to be handled before the project is complete. An agenda helps the group remain focused on the task at hand.

Group Interaction

Leaders oversee meetings in order to ensure that all group members have an opportunity to express opinions or to offer input to the discussion. Additionally, leaders monitor behavior in group meetings so that no individual feels threatened or harassed by other members.

Most individuals bring a wealth of knowledge, skills, and motivation to group meetings. The problem, though, is that without help from a leader, they do not always operate at peak efficiency. To help the group function effectively, leaders must ask appropriate questions to initiate discussion, to focus discussion, to probe for information, or to deal with interpersonal problems. Every group, therefore, needs a leader-not just an individual who has better communication skills than others or who is more sociable or motivated. The group leader is either task-oriented (authoritarian) or person-oriented (democratic) in leadership style. Task-oriented leaders focus on the problem at hand, identifying what needs to be done and how to accomplish it. They tend to exercise control over the group by outlining specific tasks for each group member and by suggesting roles for them as well. Person-oriented leaders, on the other hand, focus on the interpersonal relationships of the group members. They encourage discussions among group members and foster an atmosphere where all individuals feel comfortable in making suggestions. Under a person-oriented leadership style, the group itself ultimately determines what the group does.

Ultimately, leadership means "exerting influence" and "reaching a goal."[12] In examining leadership styles, research[13] has shown that more work is accomplished under a task-oriented leader. However, motivation and originality are greater under a person-oriented leader. Perhaps the best approach to leadership has been suggested by Fred Fiedler: "Whether a particular leadership style is successful depends on the situation: (1) how good the leader's interpersonal relations are with the group, (2) how clearly defined the goals and tasks of the group are, and (3) to what degree the group accepts the leader as having legitimate authority to lead."[14]

Limitations and Strengths of Small Groups

Group interaction has both strengths and limitations. As evidenced by the roles discussed in the previous section, disadvantages will appear which influence the group's ability to resolve issues. However, the two most prominent disadvantages of group discussion are time and "groupthink."

Limitations

Time

Decision-making is a time consuming process for a group. When we function as individuals, we have the opportunity to think through ideas and choose the one best suited for our purposes. In a group, however, discussions must ensue that allow all members to voice opinions and to respond to those of other group members. Describing ideas, clarifying misunderstandings, and responding to questions take substantial time. Additionally, deliberations concerning alternate proposals require time. However, when you desire creativity and thoroughness, a group is the best setting for achieving your goal. In this case, the advantages of group interaction outweigh the disadvantage of time.

Groupthink

Groupthink is an internal group control phenomenon that results when groups are extremely cohesive. In this situation, group members have become increasingly close, less critical of each other's ideas, and less willing to engage in analysis and arguments that are necessary to develop the best outcomes.[15] In essence, they have come to believe that their group is invincible and incapable of making incorrect decisions. As a consequence, group members are less careful in screening and evaluating ideas generated in the group. The result is inferior group outcomes. Symptoms of groupthink include the following:

- "Group invulnerability
- Unquestioned morality
- Rationalization of mistakes
- Vilification of opposing groups
- Self-censorship
- False consensus
- Forced conformity
- Blockage of outside information."[16]

Prominent examples of groupthink" have occurred at the highest level of government in this country from the 1940s to the 1970s: Pearl Harbor, the Marshall Plan, North Korea, the Bay of Pigs, the Cuban missile crisis, Vietnam, and Watergate.[17] Two of the symptoms for groupthink in these cases involved (1) the group's stereotyping of enemy leaders as stupid and evil, and (2) the group's absolute belief in its own morality.

In addition, specialized crime units, such as SWAT, and narcotics units can also generate these two symptoms because of the nature of their work and the nature of the criminals they seek to capture. These groups vilify their adversaries so that "they" [the criminals] ultimately become dehumanized. You need only review daily newspapers to read reports of police tactical units who have violated the civil rights of Americans because of their overzealous pursuit of the enemy. Again, an example of groupthink in the extreme[18]

Recommendations for avoiding groupthink include the following:

- "encourage ideational conflict;
- assist in the development of the central negative role;
- guard against leader domination of ideas;
- keep consciousness-raising within limits;
- examine the advantages and disadvantages of a proposal; and
- use a problem-solving agenda system."[19]

Strengths

Groups do possess greater strengths than individuals, one of which is the number of available resources. In addition, groups also are typically more creative and possess a greater commitment to decisions than individuals.

Resources

Because of its sheer number of members, groups exceed individuals in the number of ideas, perspectives, experience, and expertise brought to the table. In addressing a problem, group members' differing resources are a key to effectiveness. An example of these resources would be the different backgrounds of the group members (i.e., culture, education, training, and military service).

Thoroughness

Groups tend to create a system of "checks and balances" for each other. When one member does not understand a particular segment of the issue, another member does; when a member becomes bored, another is interested; when a proposal is developed and one member sees no gaps or problem areas, another member does. However, discussion and interaction between group members is what makes a group thorough, not just the sheer number of members.

Creativity

Another important factor in group work involves creativity. When group members interact with each other and communicate effectively, they tend to generate ideas. An individual, on the other hand, eventually runs out of ideas. "As group members talk, they build on each other's ideas, refine proposals, see new possibilities in each other's comments, and so forth. The result is often a greater number of overall ideas and more creative final solutions."[20]

Commitment

Group members have an enlarged commitment to decisions because of two sources: (1) participation in the decision-making process, and (2) greater resource allocations. When group members participate in decision-making, they are more committed to a decision, an important fact if group members will also be active in implementing the decision. The other factor, resource allocations, is important because group decisions are more likely to include points of view of individuals involved in the implementation of their suggestions or recommendations.

Time constraints and groupthink are limitations of group processes. However, the advantages of increased creativity, thoroughness, resources, and commitment outweigh any group shortcomings. As long as individuals balance time commitments and refrain from conformity, they will be able to see the value of groups.

Cultures and Groups

For group communication to be effective, it must consider the implications of cultural differences from a verbal and nonverbal perspective. Groups are typically comprised of varying individuals from a gender standpoint as well from a cultural perspective. An important consideration for group interaction is that of understanding individual differences such as those outlined below.

Individualism

As Americans, we tend to favor **individualism.** We believe that each person is unique and important. Contrast this belief with that of other countries such as Japan, Colombia, or Pakistan, and you will see a greater emphasis on **collectivism** in those societies. These countries consider everything contributed to be part of the group rather than spotlighting an individual within the group for his/her personal activities—an important element of individualism.

Individual Assertiveness

Individualism also serves as a building block for **assertiveness.** Again, Americans expect people to speak up, assert their ideas, and stand up for their rights. Assertiveness has many focuses: describing feelings, giving valid reasons for beliefs, suggesting a behavior or attitude we think is fair. While this characteristic is important in the western world, other cultures (Japan, Thailand, Philippines) view this type of behavior as offensive.

Equality

Another Western value is that of **equality.** In group activities, this value influences communication because each individual is considered to have an equal right to speak and no member is considered to be better than the others. In other cultures, however, hierarchies often exist which define people according to a set of criteria. Male members may speak more, be given more deference, and their comments given greater respect than female counterparts.

Progress/Change

Progress and change are of importance to Westerners. In fact, Westerners do not see progress as a mere belief or activity; it is a basic mind-set by which they operate. Since progress and change are so important, Westerners tend to focus on the future and to believe they can impact or control everything. No group would feel it had accomplished its mission if the group failed to recommend changes, even if no changes were actually necessary. Societies such as Japan and China revere their history and believe in preserving their traditions. In that setting, group decisions are made relative to sustaining traditions.

Uncertainty and Risk

The United States, Finland, Sweden, and Ireland are countries where citizens accept uncertainty with relative ease. Because Westerners are focused on progress and change, they also are more tolerant of risk. "To embark on new paths, try bold innovations, and experiment with untested ideas require daring and willingness to take risks."[21] Countries such as Peru, Japan, Greece, and Germany, however, do not easily accept risk or uncertainty.

Informality

Americans and other Westerners tend to be very informal. They greet each other directly and in a relaxed manner. After initial introductions, Americans usually ignore titles and formal rituals in favor of relaxed, casual interaction. Cultures such as those in Japan, Egypt, Turkey, and Germany do not support such informality.

Acknowledging and understanding cultural differences are important to effective group processes. In this age of diversity, we must become cognizant of how our behaviors impact other individuals* behaviors. We should not assume that all group members are the same and everyone follows the same set of cultural norms. Successful communication in your group results from knowing each individual member, valuing each member's contributions and questions, and respecting each person's culture.

Summary

In summary, small group and team communication is vital to the success of an organization. Effective small group characteristics encompass a good work environment, an optimum number of members, cohesiveness, commitment to task, group rules and consensus, adequate preparation, and appropriate role assignments. Groups, however, possess both strengths and limitations. One limiting phenomenon that occurs as a result of extreme group cohesiveness is that of groupthink." Prominent examples of groupthink" have occurred at the highest levels of government in this country from the 1940s to 1970s. Groups, however, do possess greater strengths than individuals. Groups are typically more creative and possess a greater commitment to decisions than individuals. In addition, groups have a greater number of available resources. These advantages of increased creativity, thoroughness, resources, and commitment, however, far outweigh the group shortcomings of time constraints and "groupthink."

Key Terms

Solidarity	Group	Team	Cohesion
Team-building	Rules	Norms	Ethnocentric
Consensus	Task roles	Maintenance Roles	Negative roles
Information/opinion givers	Information seekers	Analyzers	Expediters
Recorders	Supporters	Tension relievers	Harmonizers
Gatekeepers	Aggressors	Jokers	Withdrawers
Monopolizers	Agenda	Groupthink	Individualism
Collectivism	Assertiveness	Equality	

Discussion Questions

1. Differentiate between the terms "group" and "team".
2. List five (5) effective small group characteristics.
3. Discuss the responsibilities of a group leader/facilitator.
4. Do "jokers" serve any value within the group setting?
5. Are harmonizers important to an effective small group?
6. What are the limitations of small groups?
7. List five (5) symptoms of "groupthink". In your opinion, which symptom is the worst? Why?
8. List five (5) recommendations for avoiding "groupthink."
9. What are the strengths of effective small groups?
10. List groups of which you are a member. Discuss your role(s) in each group.
11. **Ethical Issue:** The Chief and the Command Staff have studied an issue that is not

popular with the line personnel, but their support is necessary for successful implementation of the project. Would it be inappropriate for the Chief to select those individuals who support his project as members of a group to study the issue and make a recommendation? Why or why not?

12. **Ethical Issue:** Would it be inappropriate for members of a group who favor four ten-hour work shirks to band together secretly in an effort to thwart the suggestions or recommendations of other group members who favor five eight-hour work shifts, especially if the first group (the four ten-hour work shifts) knew their suggestions or recommendations were superior?

13. **Ethical Issue:** Should group members of higher rank (lieutenant, captain, major) or status (field training officer, senior officer, detective) be allowed to sway or heavily influence group suggestions or recommendations because of their position? If your answer is no, why, since they hold supervisory or senior positions?

Topics for Further Consideration

Directions: Complete each of the following items in an individual capacity and then in a group capacity. Compare your personal responses to the group solutions.

1. The organization is considering removing seniority as an element for consideration in shift assignments or transfers. Individually: What is your opinion? What elements do you think should be discussed considering this change? Would you support this change? Why or why not?

2. The organization is considering eliminating the use of tobacco as a condition of employment. In an effort to reduce the amount of sick time, the organization is planning to make this requirement mandatory for all members. Is this fair to the members of the organization who are tobacco users and who were hired prior to this mandate? Would you support this change? Why or why not?

3. The organization is considering changing the assignment of time off (routine days off, vacations, etc.) from a seniority basis to one that accommodates married members with children (Christmas, New Year's Eve, Thanksgiving). Would this be an equitable solution? Would you support or oppose this change? Why or why not? .

Notes

1. Barbian, J., "A New Line of Defense." *Training, 39(9),* September 2002, pp. 39-47.
2. Durkheim, E., *The Sociological Tradition,* trans. R. A. Nisbet. NY: Basic Books, 1966, pp. 47-48.
3. Palmiotto, M. J., *Community Policing: A Policing Strategy for the 21st Century.* Gaithersburg, MD: Aspen Publishers, 2000, p. 42.
4. Wood, J. T., *Communication in Our Lives.* Belmont, CA: Wadsworth Publishing, 1997, pp. 265-66.
5. Ibid, p.265.
6. Verderber, R. F., *Communicate!* Belmont, CA: Wadsworth Publishing, 1999.
7. Wood, Ibid.
8. Verderber, p. 265.
9. Ibid.
10. Ibid, p. 237.
11. Ibid.
12. Ibid, p. 248.
13. Ralph White and Ronald Lippitt as cited by Verderber, Ibid.
14. Verderber, p. 250, as above.
15. Wood.

16. Cragan, J. F., and Wright, D. W., *Communication in Small Groups: Theory, Process, Skills.* Belmont, CA: Wadsworth Publishing, 1999, p. 220.
17. Ibid.
18. Ibid.
19. Cragan.
20. Wood, p. 270.
21. Wood, p. 279.

CHAPTER 12

CONFLICT RESOLUTION AND OTHER SPECIAL FORMS OF COMMUNICATION

Learning Objectives:

1. To identify and diagram the continuum of various conflict resolution approaches.

2. To compare and contrast the advantages and disadvantages of the various approaches.

3. To identify and explain the twelve stages of conflict resolution.

4. To identify the four types of individuals who take hostages.

5. To identify the four options utilized by police and corrections officials.

6. To identify the criteria for an event to be classified as negotiable.

7. To identify personal traits of a negotiator.

8. To identify the equipment necessary for negotiators.

9. To identify the effects of stress on negotiators.

*In the popular new police drama on NBC, Third Watch,
veteran officer, Sullivan, is explaining the essence of police work
to his rookie partner, Davis. "We are problem-solvers; our job is
to solve people's problems."*

Third Watch, NBC Television (2001).

A more truthful and accurate description regarding the criminal justice system has never been uttered than what you read in the quote introducing this chapter. Not only do criminal justice professionals resolve problems, but they do so under the most adverse conditions. Furthermore, they become involved in very complex situations since the problems usually involve individuals who are less than skillful communicators and who allow emotions to control their reasoning and decision making. Since emotions are frequently involved in the types of problems in which criminal justice professionals find themselves, **conflict resolution** is an appropriate term to describe the process used to solve these problems.

What problems do criminal justice professionals encounter? On a daily basis, law enforcement officers deal with domestic disorders, neighbor disputes, and traffic. Parole officers are involved with their clients who have difficulty with their employers, their landlords, and their families. Corrections officers are constantly trying to maintain order in a less than ideal communal living arrangement as well as trying to resolve interpersonal conflicts between inmates. Most of these situations have some elements in common.

Unfortunately, a large number of people who become involved with the criminal justice process are either uneducated or undereducated. These individuals were either socially promoted past their level of competence or withdrew from high school after becoming disenchanted. In either event they failed to acquire the educational skills necessary to compete in a fiercely competitive environment. Skills generally associated with a sound education are good communication skills (the ability to read, write, calculate and comprehend at a functional level) and good reasoning skills (critical thinking and delayed gratification). A majority of individuals who become involved in the criminal justice process are deficient in these skill areas. They are unwilling or incapable of attempting to exercise those skills described above and, therefore, either willingly or unwillingly become dependant upon others to resolve matters for them. However, some individuals do not fit into the preceding profile. These people are well educated and more than capable of competing in society but for whatever reason are also unwilling or unable to resolve certain problems and, therefore, involve criminal justice personnel at some level.

Conflict Resolution

Conflict resolution, also referred to as dispute resolution, is a term used to describe a process whereby the parties involved may achieve some measure of success without leaving either party devoid of dignity or respect. Optimally conflict resolution attempts to create a win/win situation by allowing both parties to gain something in return for giving some consideration to the other party. Remember, this is the ideal situation and achieving this goal may be very difficult. Disputes may be handled formally or informally, with the latter being more frequently utilized.

Depending upon the severity of the dispute and the means available to the disputants, a continuum or sliding scale may be used. At the most informal end of the scale would be the **avoidance of conflict** where the individuals or parties simply avoid situations that place them in contact with each other. On the opposite end of the spectrum is the **extralegal approach**, which involves a great deal of persuasion or coercion and is outside of generally accepted legal standards. Examples of this type of approach are demonstrations and boycotts. The most extreme form of the extralegal approach may be the threat or use of physical force. Between these two endpoints are the more moderate means of resolution. Informal discussion and problem solving is one method by which two reasonable parties may come to some agreement and is the venue most frequently used. Both parties generally make concessions and the dispute is settled; however, the matter may also be dropped for lack of interest or the lack of power to force a solution. Two other means of resolving conflict are **negotiation** and **mediation**.

Negotiation and Mediation

Negotiation involves engaging the opposing parties in a temporary relationship whereby both voluntarily agree to examine the issues and position of the other to bring about a clearer understanding and perhaps a solution to the impasse. **Mediation** is a progression of the negotiation method. Mediation utilizes a neutral and mutually agreed upon third party to aid in bringing the parties together to resolve their differences or resolve "sticking points" in which neither side will concede. These third parties usually have limited or no decision-making authority. Relying instead upon their ability to bring light and reason to the disputants, mediators are involved when the parties can no longer rely upon each other to calmly and objectively review the issues and reach a conclusion. Third parties may be involved in other ways. For instance, an individual who is not necessarily impartial, but is not actively involved as one of the disputing parties, may serve as a mediator in the administrative dispute resolution approach. In this situation the mediator is attempting to balance the needs of the organization and the needs of the disputants. Governors, County Executives, City Managers, and Mayors may all serve in this capacity in the public sector while Chief Executive Officers (CEO) and Board of Directors Chairpersons fulfill this role in the private sector.

Arbitration

Arbitration is a further example of a volunteer third party enlisted to aid factions in resolving disputes. Arbitration generally differs from mediation in that more than one intervening individual may be involved, typically a board or panel. Furthermore, this board or panel is not involved nor has any direct relationship to the parties engaged in the dispute. More importantly, this board or panel may have the authority to bind parties to an agreement, which significantly differs from previously mentioned options. This judicial approach typically involves attorneys and a judge and/or jury, who are bound to resolve the dispute within the confines of the appropriate federal or state statutes. Clearly this approach is a classic example of a win/lose scenario; however, it does have the benefit of being legally binding and legally enforceable.

While disputants do yield control of their destiny to another party, they enjoy the control wielded by the authority of the Court in a successful outcome.

While the Court has the authority to enforce a decision concerning a dispute between or among parties, the Legislatures (state or federal) have the authority to create and enact bills, which may force one of the parties to cease action or initiate action in the public's interest. An example would be the elimination of a monopoly, such as AT&T in the 1970's or forcing automobile makers to install passive restraint systems (airbags) in new vehicles in the 1990's. Even corporate giants such as Microsoft fear this type of intervention because of the staggering cost involved and the distinct possibility of an unfavorable outcome. To better illustrate the multiple approaches to conflict or dispute resolution Christopher Moore[1] created the following chart. With the inclusion of third parties the likelihood of a win/lose scenario becomes more evident and the use of coercion or force increases.

Table 12-1. <u>Continuum of Conflict Management and Resolution Approaches</u>

Decision-making by Involved Parties	Decision-making by Involving Third Parties	Legal Decision-making by Involving Third Parties	Extralegal Decision-making
Avoid Conflict, Informal discussion & Problem-solving, Negotiation, Mediation	Administrative, Arbitration	Judicial, Legislative	Nonviolent, Violent

Mediation

As mentioned previously, **mediation** is the introduction of a third party who is acceptable to the parties involved and has limited or no decision-making authority in an attempt to bring about a voluntary settlement of the conflict. Mediation is not a new concept; it has an established history in a majority of the world's cultures. Many religions employed the concept of mediation in their respective teachings or doctrines. A contemporary interest in mediation may have occurred as a result of frustration by labor over management practices or the increasing amount of litigation and the staggering costs associated with lengthy court battles. In any event the use of mediation has grown dramatically in the United States over the last two decades. Mediation is currently experiencing a surge of popularity and implementation. According to Moore, mediation first begins by building and testing a hypothesis. This process is accomplished by a series of six steps which encompasses the following:

1. Collect data about the dispute
2. Develop hypothesis about critical situations (faced by parties) and cause of conflict

3. Search for theories that explain conflict and suggest interventions
4. Select and develop a theory and possible intervention(s) and what the intervention should accomplish
5. Test the hypothesis
6. Accept or reject the hypothesis

This series of six steps leads to the twelve stages initiated by the mediator in an attempt to resolve the conflict. Of these twelve steps proposed by Moore, five occur prior to the beginning of formal mediation and seven occur during the decision-making process. These twelve stages set the foundation for a methodical and successful approach to conflict resolution.

1. Establish a relationship with the disputing parties
2. Select a strategy to guide mediation
3. Collect and analyze background information
4. Design a detailed plan for mediation
5. Build trust and cooperation
6. Begin mediation
7. Define issues and set an agenda
8. Uncover hidden interests of the disputing parties
9. Generate options for settlement
10. Assess options for settlement
11. Final bargaining
12. Achieve a formal settlement

Having established this list, certain elements should be examined in detail.

The Twelve Stages of Conflict Resolution

Foremost among the twelve stages is establishing a relationship. This stage is critical because it is the foundation upon which trust is built. Trust engenders credibility and optimism in finding a common understanding. Collecting and analyzing background information is imperative in determining the mind-set of the opposing parties. Gender, age, race, education and other socioeconomic factors are essential in profiling or sketching the major participants. Once this profile is established, then it becomes possible to determine how to deal with the presence of strong emotions, inappropriate stereotyping, misperceptions, and clarifying communication. Once trust and cooperation are present, the initial fear associated with a combative or defensive mind-set is reduced or eliminated. An opportunity is created to define the issues and set an agenda. This stage is extremely important since it brings the opposing parties together by having them come to a mutual decision–the first step toward resolving the conflict between them. Building upon this initial success the mediator calls for the parties to generate options for settlement. At this point the parties may choose to return to their original positions and offer modest options or minor concessions. However, a skilled mediator will remind them of the need for multiple options and that an earnest effort will benefit both sides in an equitable resolution. The final bargaining stage calls for both parties to reach a settlement either through small accommodations, major concessions, or formalizing a process by which a substantive agreement may be achieved.

Mediators may be called into action by either of the disputing parties, by referral from concerned parties other than the disputants, or by governmental mandate. According to recent studies the rejection of mediators and the mediation process have been as high as fifty percent. Why this enormous refusal? Perhaps the mediation process is not well known or not fully understood. Or possibly disputants have an over-reliance upon litigation as a means of resolving difficult issues. In any event, the likelihood of rejecting mediation remains extremely high.

The criminal justice system, taking its lead from industry and government, has taken advantage of the benefits provided by the mediation approach. Court officials have implemented mediators in the process of resolving family disputes such as divorce proceedings and child custody battles. Corrections officials have utilized mediators to bring an end to lawsuits initiated by inmates rather than endure the negative public relations fallout and costs associated with a protracted court battle. However, from both a law enforcement and corrections perspective, most mediators are summoned as the result of an imminent threat to life or property such as hostage or barricade situations. These (mediators) crisis negotiators are required to make contact with individuals, determine their demands, resolve tense and hostile standoffs, and preserve life. Individuals involved in these situations fall into four groups: individuals taken by surprise during the commission of a crime, professionals, mentally unstable persons, and terrorists/religious zealots.

Most hostage situations arise from a rapid response by law enforcement officers to either a robbery in progress call or an alarm call. In either event the result is the same, innocent clerk and/or bystanders held captive by the shocked and frequently unsophisticated perpetrator. The suspect is agitated and unpredictable and the hostage(s) is usually in the same mental state, which places everyone involved at great risk. Not a typical conflict situation faced by most mediators, but one that is all too common for criminal justice practitioners.

Professionals become involved in these situations also by accident or as a means to broker a deal for a more lenient sentence by the court. However, these individuals are calmer and more predictable but more astute in their dealings with law enforcement officers than the previous group.

Mentally unstable individuals frequently take hostages or barricade themselves in an attempt to commit suicide but use officers to complete the act. Referred to by law enforcement professionals as "suicide by cop," this method allows the individual to accomplish the goal without personally pulling the trigger. While not as agitated as the robber taken by surprise, the mentally unstable perpetrator is still unpredictable and presents a threat to hostages.

The greatest threat to hostage safety is posed by the fourth group, the terrorist/religious zealot. A member of this group is committed to a political cause or a religious ideal. As a result of this commitment, this person is not only not afraid to die, but expects to die and earn salvation as a reward for having made a glorious political or religious statement. Most dramatically illustrated on September 11, 2001, by the attack on the World Trade Center in New York City, this type of individual is almost impossible to stop. Fortunately this type of individual is rarely encountered.

Since most mediators are not faced with the type of situations discussed above, law enforcement and correction officials need to designate certain members of their organizations to handle these events. Training is the essential element in establishing a sound foundation for crisis negotiation by criminal justice practitioners. Untrained or poorly prepared personnel, no matter how well intentioned, may irreparably damage the negotiation process.

Hostage and Non-Hostage Situations

Well-trained personnel are to distinguish between hostage and non-hostage situations. This is vitally important since hostage situations are less likely to involve injury or death. Hostages are viewed as collateral or as leverage for acquiring a desired outcome. This desired outcome might be as global as the release of political prisoners or the promotion of a cause. Or the outcome may be something as simple as financial gain. In any event, the demands are usually reasonable and have a desired outcome in mind.

Non-hostage situations are more dangerous to the individuals being held since they may be driven by strong emotions on the part of the perpetrator. The desired outcome is not clear and may involve demands that are meaningful only to the hostage taker. Rather than being viewed as an asset in the bargaining process, the hostages are viewed as the agents of some past wrongdoing or misdeed.

Only once the situation has been determined as hostage or non-hostage is negotiation an option. The FBI has listed the following criteria for an event to be classified as negotiable.

1. A need to live on the part of the hostage taker.
2. A threat of force on the part of the authorities.
3. Demands by the hostage taker.
4. Negotiator must be seen by the hostage taker as a person who can hurt the hostage taker but is willing to help.
5. Time to negotiate must be available.
6. A reliable channel of communication between hostage taker and negotiator must be available.
7. The location and communication between hostage taker and negotiator must be secure.
8. Negotiator must be prepared for the hostage taker to make decisions.

Since officers respond to hostage and non-hostage situations, options to deal with these events are essential. Four options are generally open to law enforcement or corrections officials. These four options are (1) assault the location, (2) utilize a sniper, (3) utilize chemical agents, and (4) negotiation.

Assaulting the location is highly dangerous and frequently ends in individuals being critically or mortally wounded. Utilizing the sniper is also hazardous since the perpetrator my not be killed immediately or the wrong person may be identified as the perpetrator and killed. Chemical agents may pose health risks to both the suspect and the hostages. Negotiation is both time and labor intensive, but has the advantages of promoting good public relations and serving as mitigation in any future civil liability suits.[2]

The Negotiation Team

Essential to any successful negotiation is the formulation of a team. While the team may vary in size depending upon the size of the agency and the complexity of the situation, the general rule is that the team be comprised of as few members as necessary to competently handle the situation; and these members should possess complementary skills. Smaller teams usually insure better communication and, therefore, are more coordinated in their efforts. In general, small well-trained teams are more successful in accomplishing positive results.

If at all possible, the FBI recommends that the crisis negotiation team should consist of three members: the primary negotiator, the secondary negotiator, and the intelligence/liaison negotiator. Each member has a specific role to play and is crucial in a successful outcome. The primary negotiator actually communicates with the suspect and experiences a great deal of physical and emotional stress. This stress is a direct result of constantly evaluating and re-evaluating the suspect's mental and environmental position. How agitated is the suspect? Is the suspect becoming more agitated or calmer with the passage of time? How is the suspect relating to the hostage(s)? Do they present a threat to the suspect's safety or are they being docile and compliant? Has anyone been injured or killed at this point in the event? Have containment and control been established? Have an inner and outer perimeter been created?

The secondary negotiator is responsible for monitoring the primary negotiator as well as keeping notes and offering advice. The intelligence/liaison negotiator interviews people associated with the suspect and gathers other pertinent information. Furthermore, this individual acts as a liaison with the command staff, serving as a conduit for information from both parties. This position is essential since the crisis negotiators are best served by occupying a location away from the command staff.

The intelligence/liaison negotiator role may be expanded or extended to other individuals, which enlarges the size of the team but may facilitate communication with local political leaders and the omnipresent press. If the immediate team needs to be expanded imperative is the need to include only essential previously trained individuals. The Mayor, City Manager, or other political leaders may desire to be involved in order to control information released to the press or secure resources necessary for an extended situation. The profile of the situation and the location of the incident may heighten the desire of political executives to become involved. However, some appointed or elected officials may desire to distance themselves from the situation in an effort to minimize any possible negative outcome.

In either event, imperative is the need to have one individual responsible for providing accurate information. This information may come as a briefing to supplemental team members or a news briefing to the press. The intelligence/liaison negotiator may desire to delegate this responsibility to another team member. If at all possible, team membership should be restricted to sworn personnel with the possible exception of the previously mentioned political leaders and perhaps a mental health consultant. Tactical and traffic considerations may also expand team size.

On occasion, it may become necessary for the primary negotiator to either position the suspect so that the event may come to a swift conclusion or distract the suspect so that the SWAT (Special Weapons and Tactics) team may make an entry. Because of these possibilities, only law enforcement personnel should negotiate with the suspect. Non-law enforcement personnel may be reluctant to perform either of these tasks and are, therefore, unsuitable. Furthermore, one of these well-intentioned individuals (spouse, lover, parent, friend, etc.) may exacerbate the situation.

Since restricting communication to the crisis negotiator is of paramount importance, controlling the telephone line(s) is essential. By denying origination (telephone company removes the ability to dial out and restricts access to police only) two objectives are accomplished. The suspect is denied an audience, most frequently the press, and communication is limited to the police negotiator. In some situations a throw phone or bag phone is delivered to the suspect and conventional telephone service to the location is suspended.

Utilities (such as power and water) to the location may also be interrupted for a variety of reasons. Power may be interrupted to prevent the suspect from monitoring the event via television or to cover the entry of a SWAT team. Water may be removed in an attempt to gain surrender from the suspect by creating discomfort or to be restored at a later time as a reward for a concession made by the suspect. In any event, the restoration of services makes an effective bargaining tool.

Tools like these are used to delay or avoid deadlines. Frequently suspects make deadlines in an attempt to force negotiators into a weakened position. As a general rule these deadlines are empty threats and relatively few hostages are harmed as a result of a missed deadline. However, negotiators take these deadlines seriously and seek every opportunity to circumvent them or use them to their advantage. These mental or psychological tactics are part and parcel of the crisis negotiator's toolbox. While physical tactics are part of the process, they are more appropriately employed by the command staff in concert with the SWAT team. Even in the best of situations, well-trained professionals may forget or overlook some step or procedure that may prove to be detrimental at a later time. Therefore, establishing a checklist is essential in order to ensure that procedures are followed and in the proper order.

Correctional Facilities and Hostage Situations

Correctional facilities are not immune to hostage situations and, in fact, have created some of the most startling headlines over the last thirty years. Attica, Oakdale, and Camp Hill all represent examples of prison riots in which many individuals were killed or injured and millions of dollars in damage to the institution were sustained. Corrections officials, like their police counterparts, utilize essentially the same team concepts and structured approach. Negotiators in prison settings have some advantages. Generally all the participants are inmates or corrections officers. The situation is confined to the institution and intelligence negotiators usually have access to extensive records on the participants (health, psychological, disciplinary, etc.). Since the hostages may be correctional officers, this may place added stress upon team members for a successful outcome. Primary and secondary negotiators may experience extreme emotional pressure to insure their comrades' safety and gain their freedom.

While the situation may be contained within the confines of the institution, other problems may occur. The assault option may not be employed without a more likely possibility of the loss of staff personnel and a tremendous number of non-involved individuals. Furthermore, the deployment of snipers and/or chemical agents may exacerbate rather than ameliorate the potential for loss of life since most prison situations generally involve more than the one or two perpetrators present in a police event. In the negotiation option, the team structure is essentially the same except that higher-ranking government officials will assuredly be involved. Prison riots or correctional situations always garner press coverage and individual careers are launched or destroyed depending upon the outcome. Therefore, the state Commissioner of Corrections, the Governor, or their federal counterparts are always involved, which may make the negotiation process much more complicated and difficult to control.

Hostage Negotiation Equipment

In order to successfully approach any hostage situation the proper equipment is essential. The most basic and yet the most important piece of equipment is the negotiator. What characteristics define a competent negotiator? Obviously the ability to communicate well is vital, but there are several other characteristics that successful negotiators possess. McMains [citing Fuselier (1986)] lists the following personality traits.

1. Emotional maturity
2. Good listening skills
3. Straightforward and credible
4. Ability to persuade and use logical arguments
5. Practical intelligence "street-wise"
6. Ability to cope with uncertainty
7. Ability to be flexible
8. Ability to accept responsibility–sometimes without having the authority
9. Ability to maintain team identity and remain cognizant of the larger issues
10. Total commitment to the negotiation approach and a belief in that philosophy

Formal interviews and a thorough screening process are vital to the selection of these individuals as they are clearly the most valuable piece of negotiating equipment. In addition to well-trained personnel, routine office supplies are needed. Pens, pencils, paper, notebooks are all useful items and need to be readily available. Tape recorders with spare batteries are also helpful. Additional equipment should include pagers, cell phones, and personal digital assistants (PDAs) since these aid in the communication process and keep vital information flowing into and away from the scene. If possible, the team should have a laptop computer with Internet access since this allows for a great deal of research to be conducted in a very short amount of time. Some experienced negotiators pack bags with items of personal comfort such as inclement weather/foul weather gear, extra clothing, medicine (aspirin, antacid, eye drops, etc.), and some staple food items (trail mix, jerky etc.). These bags permit them to maintain the mental and physical energy necessary for any type of extended negotiation. Stress makes enormous mental and physical demands upon the negotiator's body and these demands need to be addressed as soon as possible to keep the negotiator fresh and focused.

Stress for the negotiator comes from a variety of sources. Certainly conversations with the hostage taker produce stress, but so too do the expectations of political leaders, command personnel, news media, and officers directly involved in the incident. In order to deal with this enormous amount of stress, negotiators will employ several techniques to maintain their emotional and physical well being. Breathing exercises are effective and so too are relaxation techniques. If possible, the negotiator should stand and stretch or engage in light exercise as this will increase the circulation provide better flow to the brain. The increased blood flow allows for better cognition and fights the effects of fatigue.

Food and liquid intake are also important in fighting the effects of stress. Caffeine and nicotine should be limited, as well as fatty foods. These substances rob the body of energy and promote the deleterious effects of stress. Water intake should be encouraged since the body becomes dehydrated when under stress and meals should be light and frequent. The most important element in reducing stress is to acknowledge its presence and to accept that it can negatively affect individual performance. Even Superman was vulnerable to kryptonite.

Once a situation has concluded, a Post Incident Briefing is essential to not only critiquing performance but to helping alleviate the stress incurred by the negotiator. These briefings should allow the negotiator to vent any feelings, positive or negative, concerning the situation. The negotiator should be meticulous in describing the physical layout of the scene, the emotions associated with the incident, any physical effects from the incident, suggestions for future operations, and any unfinished business associated with the incident.

Summary

The first part of this chapter deals with the fundamentals of conflict resolution and the approaches to negotiation. In most settings, the art of negotiation is a matter of time, compromise, and posturing. The worst outcome is a loss of personal pride or financial status. Options available to non-criminal justice events usually include avoidance, negotiation, mediation, and arbitration. However, when conflict resolution is applied in the criminal justice setting, the stakes are much higher. The likelihood of serious injury and death are omnipresent. The four options available to criminal justice personnel are (1) assault the location, (2) utilize a sniper, (3) utilize chemical agents, and (4) negotiation.

Hostage negotiation takes a heavy toll on the individual, both emotionally and physically. Hostage negotiators are unique individuals imbued with special personality characteristics. Even in the best situations, every individual involved suffers emotional and physical distress.

Key Terms

conflict resolution	conflict avoidance
negotiation	mediation
arbitration	"Suicide by Cop"
negotiable incident	primary negotiator
secondary negotiator	intelligence/liaison negotiator

Discussion Questions

1. What is the significance of the continuum of conflict management and resolution approaches?
2. What are examples of nonviolent and violent approaches listed under the heading "Extralegal Decision-Making"?

3.   What are the six steps to building and testing a hypothesis?
4.   What are the twelve stages for a methodical and successful approach to conflict resolution?
5.   What are the eight criteria used to classify an incident as negotiable?
6.   How do correctional facility hostage incidents differ from law enforcement hostage incidents?
7.   What are the ten personality traits associated with a hostage negotiator?
8.   **Ethical Issue:** Given that some negotiations have a power imbalance, would it be inappropriate for the negotiator to provide the weaker party with additional assistance in the negotiation process? Would limiting assistance to the dominant party be appropriate?
9.   **Ethical Issue:** When officers are confronted with a hostage situation, why negotiate? If negotiation is in progress, why not have the negotiator position the suspect so that a SWAT sniper could end the standoff quickly and save hostages from possible harm?
10.   **Ethical Issue:** Would it be inappropriate for the commanding officer at the hostage scene to supervise both the SWAT team and the hostage negotiator?

Notes

1. Moore, C. W., *The Mediation Process: Practical Strategies for Resolving Conflict* (2nd ed). San Francisco: Jossey-Bass, 1996.
2. McMains, M. J., and Mullins, W. C., *Crisis Negotiations: Managing Critical Incidents and Hostage Situations in Law Enforcement and Corrections*. Cincinnati, OH: Anderson Publishing Co., 2001.